DEDICATION

This was the easiest part.

I dedicate this book to:

My best friend and beautiful wife Ger.

To my two wonderful daughters, Sarah-Anne and Lynn,

who thankfully get their beauty and intellect from their mother.

To our fantastic beautiful granddaughter, Eva 'Bubbles',

who always brings a smile to our faces.

&

To the divers of the Naval Service Diving Section:

To those who have passed,

To those who are with us,

To those who are yet to come,

And to Gerry Diskin, who made the ultimate sacrifice.

First published in 2015 by Eva Books Ireland
38 Belmont Place, Cobh, Co. Cork

© Martin J. Buckley

ISBN: 978-0-9934110-0-7

CONTENTS

ABBREVIATIONS

A/Mech	Able Mechanician		DF	Defence Forces
A/Sea	Able Seaman		DFHQ	Defence Forces Headquarters
A/Sig	Able Signaller		DGPS	Digital Global Positioning System
A/Steward	Able Steward		DMO	Diving Medical Officer
A/Tel	Able Telegraphist		DO	Diving Officer
AAIU	Air Accident Investigation Unit		DS	Directing Staff
ABLJ	adjustable buoyancy life jacket		DSM	Distinguished Service Medal
AMC	Army Medical Corps		DTG	date time group
ARW	Army Ranger Unit		DV	demand valve
AUV	autonomous underwater vehicle		EA	electrical artificer
BASAR	breathing apparatus search and rescue		EDA	European Defence Agency
			EEC	European Economic Community
BFW	Board of Works		EMA	early morning activity
BIB	built-in breathing system		EOD	Explosive Ordnance Disposal
BIM	Board Iascaigh Mhara		EOR	Explosive Ordnance Reconnaissance
BR	book of reference			
BRNC	Britannia Royal Naval College		EPIRB	Emergency Position Indicating Radio Beacon
CCRS	Cliff and Coastal Rescue Service			
CD	clearance diver		ERA	Engine Room Artificer
CDBA	clearance diver breathing apparatus		EXO	exoskeleton
			FDR	Flight Deck Recorder
CDO	clearance diving officer		FOCNS	Flag Officer Commanding Naval Service
CFO	commander fleet operations			
CFR	commission from (the) ranks		GS	Garda Síochána
CG	Coast Guard		GWU	Garda Water Unit
CM	coastal minesweeper		HMS	Her Majesty's Ship
CMS	coastal minesweepers		HP	high pressure
CO	Commanding Officer		HSA	Health and Safety Authority
COH	Commanding Officer Haulbowline		HSE	Health and Safety Executive
			IED	improvised explosive device
CONS	Commanding Officer Naval Service		ILMCDO	International Long Minewarfare Clearance Diving Officer
COS	chief of staff		ILV	Irish Lights Vessel
CP	control panel		IMES	Irish Marine Emergency Service
CPO	Chief Petty Officer		INS	Irish Naval Service
CPU	Control Panel Unit		IRA	Irish Republican Army
CT	computed tomography (scan)		JTF	Joint Task Force
CUH	Cork University Hospital		KMB	Kirby Morgan BandMask
CWS	Coastal Watch Service		L/Mech	Leading Mechanician
D/CoS	Deputy Chief of Staff		L/Sea	Leading Seaman
D/Trg	Director/Training		L/Shipwright	Leading Shipwright (carpenter)
DCI	decompression illness		L/Signalman	Leading Signalman

L/Stoker	Leading Stoker (boilers)	PE	physical education
LÉ	Long Éireannach	PO	Petty Officer
LMCDO	Long Minewarfare Clearance Diving Officer	PT	physical training
		PTI	physical training instructor
LP	low pressure	R/Adm	Rear Admiral
MCDO	Minewarfare Clearance Diving Officer	RAF	Royal Air Force
		RAS	replenishment at sea
MCWS	Marine and Coast Watching Service	RCC	recompression chamber
		RCN	Royal Canadian Navy
ML	motor launch	RHIB	rigid hull inflatable boat
MO	Medical Officer	RIB	rigid inflatable boat
MRCC	Marine Rescue Co-ordinating Centre	RN	Royal Navy
		RNAS	Royal Naval Air Station
MTB	motor torpedo boat	RNLI	Royal National Lifeboat Institute
MV	motor vessel	ROV	remote operated vehicle
NCO	non-commissioned officer	RTU	return to unit
NEGAT	negative	RV	rendezvous
NHQ	Naval Headquarters	S/Lt	Sub Lieutenant
NS	Naval Service	SA	Supply Assistant
NSDS	Naval Service Diving Section	SABA	swimmer's air breathing apparatus
NUI	National University of Ireland	SAR	search and rescue
O/Mech	Ordinary Mechanician	SCUBA	self-contained underwater breathing apparatus
O/Seaman	Ordinary Seaman		
OC	Officer Commanding	SD	Ship's Diver
OCNBAD	Officer Commanding Naval Base and Depot	SDDE	Surface Demand Diving Equipment
		SDO	Ship's Diving Officer
OCND	Officer Commanding Naval Depot	SHB	Southern Health Board
		SO	Staff Officer
OCNOC	Officer Commanding Naval Operations Command	SOP	standard operating procedure
		SPO	Senior Supply Assistant
OIC	Officer in Charge	SS	steamship
ONUC	Opération des Nations Unies au Congo (UN Operation in the Congo)	SSS	side-scan sonar
		TAS	torpedo anti-submarine
		USAF	United States Airforce
OPS	operations	USN	United States Navy
OSC	On-scene Commander	WO	Warrant Officer
PADI	Professional Association of Diving Instructors	XO	Executive Officer

ACKNOWLEDGEMENTS

Some men see things as they are and ask why. Others dream things that never were and ask why not.

George Bernard Shaw

When I started out to record this account of the Naval Service Diving Section, I had a great vision of what I wanted to achieve in writing a history. However, reality kicked in. I admitted very early on that my imagination and ambition ranged much further beyond what I was actually able to achieve in any practical way. This was due entirely to a remarkably vivid and fertile imagination and my own shortcomings. But whatever about my considerable inabilities, they were certainly overawed by the enthusiastic receptions, assistance and courtesy that I received from everybody that I encountered on my travels. I don't know how this book is going to read or fare in the 'league tables of historical books', but I can only hope that I did justice to all those people who helped me.

The majority of the content of this book is taken from interviews with naval divers past and present, so to them I owe a huge debt of gratitude both for their time, courtesy, patience and of course their interviews. I am grateful to the Defence Forces Press Office for its kind permission and approval for my conducting the interviews with those serving personnel without whose input the book would be greatly diminished. I extend thanks also to Commodore Hugh Tully FOCNS, similarly without whose permission and approval my travels to the naval base would simply not have happened. A debt of gratitude is without doubt owed to my very good friend, ex-work colleague and former 'boss' (now) Lieutenant Commander Tony O'Regan CDO, who though on occasions would remark, especially when I phoned him, 'I'm actually fucking busy here, Mart, but what is it?', nevertheless was endlessly patient and provided great assistance.

Special acknowledgment must go to Mr Bernie Diskin and family for allowing me to acknowledge Gerry's passing and for it be recounted here. Gerry's death was a traumatic event for everybody, not least his family. I believe it is only right and proper that he be remembered. I hope that I have recorded it appropriately. Thanks also to retired Garda Sergeant Tommy 'Tosh' Lavery for his help, particularly in recalling the *Betelgeuse* operation and for general discussions about previous ops. I extend thanks to Rear Admiral Mark Mellett D/CoS Support, Irish Defence Forces, for proofreading this book and for his foreword. Mention must also be made of John Borgonovo for steering me along the right track and for his most encouraging words. To Messrs M., S. & J., way out west, thank you for allowing me to operate, and thank you for your implicit trust. Enjoy the read.

And finally to my family, always there and always ready to help me, especially when I cornered them. Even though you'd often throw your eyes to Heaven, sigh deeply and drag your feet, I always took that as a sign of your enthusiasm and affection.

FOREWORD BY REAR ADMIRAL
MARK MELLETT, D/COS SUPPORT

It is 05:10 on Tuesday 13 July 1993. While most citizens sleep, off the west coast of Ireland the LÉ *Orla* is steaming at full speed to close and support her deployed boarding party several miles ahead. The boarding party's 5.4-metre rigid inflatable boat is operating in marginal conditions and has just nearly been rammed by a twenty-tonne smuggler's yacht. Dawn is breaking. It is imperative the boarding party overpower the smugglers before they have time to react further, as the yacht will be scuttled, vital intelligence lost, its cargo of two tonnes of narcotics scattered on to the sea floor, and prosecution of this, the largest interception of narcotics in Irish territorial waters up to this time, will be jeopardised. For the command team on the LÉ *Orla* it is white-knuckle time. The doctrine of a 'stand-off' boarding is new to the Irish Naval Service; for this type of operation there are few other options but to keep the warship covert over the horizon while sending the boarding team forward. The risks are high but so are the rewards. One way to mitigate the risks is to send your best team forward. One way to get the best team is to pack it with naval divers.

So it was that one of the most successful narcotic operations was brought to a conclusion. Key divers on that operation were Lt Declan Fleming, L/Sea Fergy Cunningham and Petty Officer Martin Buckley. I have known Martin Buckley for over thirty years. He is an extraordinary seaman and an extraordinary diver. He is a maritime warrior who has dedicated most of his working life as a member of Óglaigh na hÉireann, serving his government and the citizens of Ireland. He is one of just over a hundred men who have earned the right to be called an Irish naval diver, one of the most elite units of the Irish Defence Forces.

Ireland is an island state with one of the largest sea-to-land ratios in Europe. With a jurisdiction of almost a million square kilometres, it is almost three times the size of Germany. The citizens of Ireland enjoy sovereign rights over the seabed and sub-seabed resources. These sovereign rights translate into property rights of the Irish generation of today and future generations. Our jurisdiction encompasses trillions of euros of yet-to-be-found hydrocarbon and mineral resources. We have one of the richest fisheries as well as the richest renewable energy resource in the world. It is a jurisdiction with a spectacular land–sea interface and some of the most beautiful scenery in the world. It also encompasses what is statistically some of the most hostile seas in the world, with the largest wave ever noted by scientific instruments recorded of the north-west coast of Mayo. Upholding sovereignty and underpinning sovereign rights is a function of our Defence Forces. Since the Second World War, the Irish Naval Service, as the maritime element of Óglaigh na hÉireann, has been the principal seagoing agency of the Irish state operating in these seas.

For over fifty years Irish naval divers have been at the centre of almost every major maritime incident involving the Irish Naval Service. They have rescued lives, recovered bodies, disposed of mines, and located and lifted sunken vessels. They have recompressed and decompressed diving casualties. They have played a key role in the recovery operations associated with the Whiddy disaster, the Air India search-and-recovery operation, and the clearing of ships sunk by the IRA, the *Nellie M* and the *St Bedan*. They are a band of brothers who day in, day out are prepared to put themselves in harm's way in the service of the state, just like their sisters and brothers throughout Óglaigh na hÉireann. It is a privilege to be associated with this book.

PREFACE

It's an ability to put your body through an awful lot of distress and not think twice about it. It's a discipline to be able to maintain the focus, to keep on going where most people would actually say 'sod this' – a navy diver has the tenacity to stay focused, to stay at the task and to get through, even if they are really uncomfortable and even if the conditions are really miserable. It's an ability to set yourself as second, to the priority of getting the job done.[1]

Rear Admiral Mark Mellett, 2014

'Undoubtedly the fact that the early divers were established as an elite group from the very beginning with a huge failure rate on aptitude and training courses, favoured the sound development of the diving capability … Dedication to diving was the norm and extraordinary efforts over and above the call of duty were common.[2]

Commodore Frank Lynch (retd), 2013

Having enlisted in November 1950 and being commissioned eighteen months later, on 7 April 1952, a young, newly married Irish naval officer, Lt Joseph Deasy, was in 1964 tasked by naval Command in Haulbowline naval base, Cobh, County Cork to attend a torpedo and anti-submarine (TAS) course with the Royal Navy (RN) in the UK in early May. The first module of the course involved diving, but having no particular interest or desire to be a diver, Lt Deasy simply shrugged his shoulders, said yes and then went home. Having explained to his wife exactly what had happened, they made plans accordingly:

I didn't know I was going on a diving course … I just did not know! … a signal arrived from Dublin [NHQ] to COH [commanding officer, Haulbowline] telling them that I was booked on the diving anti-subma-rine course, that was the first I heard of diving … and that was about the weekend before we left … you see, they wanted to fly me over, my wife wanted to go with me and there was a liner leaving Cobh on the Friday for Southampton – the *Maasdam* … anyway she went out on the liner, I flew and I met her in Southampton, as she arrived the next day … Would you believe the fare on the liner at that time was £10 [old Irish currency] and it was cheaper than the air fare![3]

For his first dive as a trainee, they dressed him in a Siebe Gorman standard diving suit and helmet. The lieutenant descended down the quay-wall ladder, got to the bottom rung, paused … and stepped off. He didn't stop until he reached the seabed that lay 9 metres below the surface of the Royal Navy diver-training establishment of HMS *Drake*. Thus the lieutenant, by his simple step forward off that ladder, set in motion a slow but inexorable series of steps and events that would culminate into what we now call the Naval Service Diving Section.

Since that first step off the ladder by Lt Deasy, many naval personnel have tried and failed to be naval divers. As a best guesstimate over the fifty years since 1964, some three thousand personnel would have applied to undergo the initial aptitude training and selection process, and approximately five to six hundred probably would have been selected to move forward to commence formal training either with the Royal Navy or the Irish Naval Service. To date, only 166 personnel have qualified. Failure rates on the courses were very high and still are.

The Naval Service of 1964 was a whole world apart from what it is today. The service of that time consisted of three corvettes, the LÉ *Clíona*, the LÉ *Maeve* and the LÉ *Macha*, and an establishment of approximately four hundred personnel, all ranks. The naval base was, to say the least, a bit run down and short of what could be termed proper facilities. Diving didn't exist then and it arrived somewhat by accident. Suffice to say the lieutenant survived his experience and qualified in July 1964, four weeks after first being introduced to diving. His subsequent qualification as a TAS ship's diving officer earned him a qualification singularly unique in the Naval Service at that time, and it would remain so until 1969.

The early 1970s saw the departure of the corvettes and the arrival of the three minesweepers, the LÉ *Gráinne*, LÉ *Banba* and LÉ *Fóla*. Relatively speaking, overnight the Naval Service had changed from steam power to diesel power. The minesweepers' hull-maintenance package required that the hulls be surveyed at least once a month, checking the sacrificial planking integrity along with propeller-shaft clearances on the *A* brackets and any other job that might have been required. This led to the Naval Service sending over a group of selected personnel consisting of an officer and four NCOs and men, and during the 1970s more personnel were sent to the UK for training with the Royal Navy. Equally as important as the continuing training of personnel were the numbers of diving operations growing both internally and externally. However, an unfortunate consequence of the times was beginning to show itself. While men were being trained and operations increased, the necessary equipment and facilities that should have been keeping pace with them failed to do so. However, undimmed and undaunted, training was maintained in the UK, and another milestone was reached in September 1978 when a young naval officer from Buttevant, County Cork, S/Lt Gerry O'Donoghue, departed the naval base and underwent a dedicated professional diving course run by the Royal Navy, an international long minewarfare clearance diving officers course (ILMCDO), which was nine months long and about as difficult as the RN could make it for a student. This course and this officer were about to change the world of the Naval Service and, more importantly, the Naval Service Diving Section, but that was still a couple of years down the line.

Diving Store, early 1980s (ex-Seamanship Bay). Note the RCC at the rear of the store. The long, wooden box on the left was a torpedo-storage box. The black line on the deck was the painted outline of the boat used for seamanship classes.

The events of 8 January 1979 were arguably another defining moment in the development on the Diving Section. The massive explosion of the French-owned Gulf Oil tanker *Betelgeuse* while conducting unloading operations alongside the jetty at Whiddy Island oil refinery in Bantry Bay, County Cork resulted in the loss of fifty-one lives. The weeks and months ahead would see the largest marine salvage operation ever conducted in this country before or since. The subsequent diving operations conducted by naval divers in conjunction with the Garda sub-aqua-unit divers would be the most operationally difficult the naval divers had heretofore encountered. The issue of kit, or lack of it, would raise its ugly head, and would for one naval diver nearly cost him his life. Things would have to change and change quickly.

March 1979 saw the return of S/Lt G. O'Donoghue (aka GOD) to the naval base, and with his newly acquired qualification the Naval Service could think seriously about training its own personnel. Of all the requirements for this, the most important were a minewarfare clearance diving officer (MCDO), a recompression camber (RCC), permission from Command, and the necessary instructing staff. The instructing staff would be the least of the problems. With permission granted (however reluctantly), a rented RCC and the necessary extra diving kit purchased, the first Naval Service diving course commenced in October 1982. The significance of this course cannot be underestimated as it underpinned the severance of ship's divers training from the Royal Navy and confirmed the Naval Service as the author of its own destiny (by November 2014 twenty-eight diving courses were completed by the Diving Section). Further specialist training would commence a year later in 1983 with the first Army Ranger Wing diving course commencing, and November 1983 would see the arrival of the much anticipated naval RCC. The way was now open for many more specialist diving courses to follow. Subsequent years would see a growing number of divers qualifying, and this would bring its own problems.

Staffing levels in the Diving Section would now pose even greater problems for both the Diving Section itself and for Command. With the growing numbers of divers came more equipment, more training requirements and an expansion in operational capacity. The Diving Section clearly required more staff, but the problem lay in the fact that not only were these personnel now qualified navy divers but they also still belonged to their relevant departments. Naval personnel were organised into four branches, or divisions as they were called: seamen, mechanics, communications and supplies. The diving qualification was open to all servicemen from any branch. Diving was and still is an 'ad-qual' (additional qualification, a speciality). The issue would only be resolved by expanding the clearly insignificant manning allocation for diving at that time. The staffing level for the Diving Store fell under the control of the Training Establishment. This was essentially a list of staff-vacancy slots for all ranks that were to be filled by relevant qualified personnel. The Diving Section establishment was thus four in total: one chief petty officer, one leading seaman and two able ratings.

So the Naval Service Diving Section was beginning to expand in more ways than one. It was more by accident than by any great design that during the 1980s the Diving Section was staffed by dedicated personnel who, through their own interest, professionalism and outlook, drove and steered naval diving. Operationally the Diving Section was becoming very proficient and was mastering the art of air diving on scuba sets. Operations to air depths of 35 metres posed no problems, but past that depth any problems were due in no small part to the lack of suitable equipment – particularly surface-demand diving equipment – and to the demands of the diving regulations. Throughout the remainder of the 1980s and into the early 1990s diving operations external to the naval base were becoming more frequent, deeper, technically more awkward and for longer operational durations than ever before. All these factors would lead to difficulties for the Diving Section in other areas, as it was fast developing into a medium-sized business. Budgets, manpower requirements, equipment requirements, subsistence and diving allowances, clothing and transport – vehicle and boat – were all now becoming important issues and in some cases demanded an urgent response. Furthermore, three more minewarfare officers would be trained by the RN: Lt Chris Reynolds MCDO, S/Lt Eddie Mulligan CDO and S/Lt Darragh Kirwan CDO. According to Gerry O'Donoghue:

> … once we hit critical mass, and everything in life has a critical mass … I mean the thing about it now is everybody claims they founded the diving in the navy, 'cos it's a great team of professionals, it looks the part. Every minister and politician is dragged down to see the diving team … once we had gotten to Chris Reynolds' stage, we had two CDOs and heading for a third. We had the professional body of NCO supervisors there … I was never fit enough to keep going after forty, and I didn't want the old-fart syndrome to set in. So basically I handed over to Chris Reynolds and Eddie Mulligan – people like that. They were excellent, they were awesome. So I

had no fear that we weren't going to become a major fucking unit within the navy after that … we hit critical mass around the late Eighties, early Nineties, where we had done a few jobs, we were in the public eye, we had the RCC and we'd been in the papers a few times. Wally was gone and Joe Deasy had come in … once we got Joe, which was great, we were established'.[4]

The mid-1990s saw the Diving Section conducting more searches for missing or sunken trawlers than ever before, and that particular tasking continued through the 2000s and to the present day. But in the mid-1990s searches such as those for the fishing vessels *Carrickatine* (1995) and the *Jenalisa* (1996) brought to a head the need for the Naval Service to move ahead in sub-surface-search technology. With the freeing up of monies and the critical issues raised and argued, the arrival of excellent surface-demand diving equipment (SDDE) and the much needed sub-surface search equipment in the forms of a side-scan sonar, magnetometer (both acquired in 1999) and a remote-operated vehicle (2000) brought the Naval Service Diving Section to a new level.

The acquisition of this type of equipment had led directly to increased levels of training by outside agencies and to specialist-type training courses. The ethos of the Naval Service Diving Section to then had been one of near self-sufficiency when and where possible, but slowly and surely this was becoming more and more unrealistic. The equipment was becoming more technical and sophisticated than ever before, and no matter how hard they tried, the Diving Section could not be all things to all people. The time for external assistance from the technical departments of the Naval Service had arrived.

Since 2000 another three CDOs have been trained, two by the Royal Navy – S/Lt Anthony O'Regan and S/Lt Conor Kirwan, younger brother to Darragh – and latterly S/Lt Shane Mulcahy by the Royal Canadian Navy (RCN); this officer was to spend one year in training with the RCN. Allied to this was the expansion in the programme of external training with outside agencies. More and more courses were being undertaken by service divers with commercial diving centres in Scotland and southern England, qualifying naval divers to UK HSE part 1 commercial-diver status. Diver medical-technician courses would also be undertaken in the UK, thus further enhancing the ability of the Diving Section to operate remotely and for extended periods. A dramatic increase in the availability of vehicle transport and, indeed, specifically designed diving boats brought about more changes. As all these developments, capabilities and tasking were happening at an accelerated pace (for the Naval Service, that is), what was failing to keep pace was the allotment of dedicated manpower to staff the Diving Section fully. The cost of equipment and facilities contained within the Diving Section was now in the millions, and required the manpower to maintain it. It also meant that non-diving personnel would for the first time be placed into the Diving Section to run the various technical accounts and to provide various technical supports.

As mentioned earlier, there has always been a somewhat difficult relationship between the Diving Section and Command over manpower and staffing levels. The diving officer now had a real struggle to keep staffing levels at a level whereby the Diving Section would be ready to meet all its commitments. Whether it was a diving operation, training commitment, RCC treatment, maintenance schedule or running a new-entry diver-training course, all these required manpower.

This book is not a definitive history by any stretch of the imagination, but offers, I believe, a good and accurate account, particularly in the three main areas described herein – namely External Operations, Diver Training and the Naval Service Recompression Chamber and its use. The number of diving jobs completed over the years run into the thousands, the amount of man hours dived or spent on operations into the hundreds of thousands, and the number of miles travelled more than enough to have completely worn out one diving truck, two Nissan patrols, two trailers and the several wheels that came adrift from them. I couldn't even contemplate accounting for all that. Nevertheless, I fervently hope the book reflects on how the Naval Service Diving Section developed over the years from 1964 to 2014, particularly its personnel and the advances in diving gear, specialist sub-surface search equipment and specialist training. In researching this book I have recorded over a hundred hours of interviews with divers young and old, current and retired. The more I listened to those recordings while transcribing their interviews, the more I realised that this was turning out to be their story as told through their interviews, and supplemented by a multitude of reports and numerous newspaper articles. It is hoped, then, that this book may in some way record for posterity an account of what is undoubtedly a most unique unit both within the Irish Defence Forces and the Irish state, manned by an equally unique group of men, both in the past and at present.

In writing any account of the Naval Service Diving Section and recalling the men who took part in the various operations and training over the fifty-year period, we must not forget those we have lost along the way. Of the 166 qualified naval divers, four are deceased: Paddy Lynch, Tommy Johnson, John Harrington and Dermot Halpin. Irrespective of the time that each may have spent as a diver, their service to the Diving Section, the Naval Service and to the state must not be forgotten. Their time and efforts contributed to making the Naval Service Diving Section a better place. They gave of themselves, and though they have gone they will live on in the history of the Naval Service Diving Section.

> The one thing I will say is we certainly didn't do it for the money … 'cos there was none … You never knew when the phone was going to ring for a diving job. When the phone rang you didn't think anything of it, you just left … and the wife would say, 'Where are you going?' 'Don't know!' … or 'When will you be back? 'Don't know!' … or 'When do you have to go?' 'Right now' … and the minibus would pull up outside and you'd just go out and get into it …'
>
> Declan Fleming (Lt; retd)

INTRODUCTION

THE NAVAL SERVICE:
A PATROL THROUGH ITS HISTORY

I am tomorrow, or some future day, what I establish today.

I am today what I established yesterday or some previous day

James Joyce

By way of an introduction to this account of the history of the Naval Service Diving Section, I was advised to at least detail in general terms where the Naval Service began. Special mention must be made here of Pádhraic Ó Confhaola, whose excellent doctoral thesis 'The Naval Forces of the Irish State, 1922–1977' (NUI Maynooth, 2009) was a much-used resource in this introduction.

It could be argued that the history of the Naval Service had its roots in the civil war. When British Crown Forces departed Ireland in 1921 they left behind a network of coastal lookout stations that stretched around the coast of Ireland, in addition to a naval base in Haulbowline – including a dockyard – two armed trawlers, *Inishsheer* and the *John S Somers*, and the armed yacht *Helga*, of Easter Rising infamy and which was subsequently renamed *Muirchu*. These were under the control of the Free State army and during the civil war were put to some use. Indeed, the combined army/maritime operations in 1922 – such as the operations in Westport, Fenit and, most importantly, the landing in Cork in August of the year – would be the first of their kind for the General Command of the Irish Free State army and proved in the main very successful. For the Westport operation – whose landing force was under the command of Colonel O'Malley – the *Minerva* was used, while for the Fenit operation, commanded by Brigadier General O'Daly, the *Lady Wicklow* was employed. In County Cork, for what was arguably the most important naval landing of the civil war, the vessels *Arvonia* and *Lady Wicklow* were used. This time, however, the Free State force – under the command of Major General Dalton – didn't quite have it all its own way. The irregular forces in command of Cork and its environs had essentially blockaded the passage up to Cork by half scuttling two vessels, the *Owenacurra* and the *Owenabue*, at what were considered to be strategic points on the river.

In 1922 the Free State government managed to procure four small motor launches (ML) for use by the National Army, designated ML1, ML2, ML3 and ML4.[1] Like all small boats, even though they looked pretty and on a good day had a good turn of speed, at sea they proved essentially unfit for purpose. However, they did add to the already growing list of naval assets that the National Army could call upon. During the period 1922–23 the list of vessels in constant use or being called upon (or commandeered) by the National Army grew. In March 1923 the Royal Navy officially handed over the dockyard in Haulbowline to the state, and with it a deep-sea tug called the *Dainty*; she was to become the flagship of the ever-growing 'fleet'. The government and the National Army Command found – no doubt through their collective growing experience – that the only real vessels of any worth that they had the finances for were trawlers. In essence trawlers would have been relatively cheap and by their build reasonably good sea boats. A major shortcoming was that they were not built for armed conflict – having wooden decks – and certainly were not built for crew comfort, but they were no doubt cheap and that suited perfectly. Six such 'armed' trawlers, of the Mersey class, were purchased in 1923: the *John Dunn, John Dutton, William Honner, Christopher Dixon, Thomas Murray* and the *Thomas Thresher*.[2] The government went on to buy six 'armed' trawlers of the Canadian Castle class: these were designated TR24, TR25, TR27, TR29, TR30 and TR31.

In May 1923, just as the civil war was ending, the government established the Coastal and Marine Service (CMS) under the command of Major General Joseph Vize and with its headquarters in Portobello Barracks. The year 1924 would see the largest ever number of vessels under the command and control of the state: twenty-six vessels of assorted shapes, sizes and classes. However, instead of kicking on from there and formalising the CMS structure – its organisation, manpower and command and control – the government had other things in mind. With the cessation of hostilities, the requirement for such a 'large' fleet and the cost of maintaining the vessels – together with associated wages and the purchase of fuel – were called into question by the department that mattered (and still does), the Department of Finance:

The Department of Finance was vehemently opposed to any attempt to found an Irish navy and by avoiding the use of naval insignia and ranks, it might have been hoped to divert any suspicions that might have arisen. Finance was horrified by the cost of refitting and maintaining the fleet, and the fact that unforeseen expenses continually arose no doubt deepened their hostility towards the service.[3]

The department would shape the future and it couldn't wait:

Finance estimates for 1922–23 show defence spending at 7.5 million pounds, about 27.8% of Government spending, and 1923–24, 10 million pounds or 29.9% of spending.[4]

Clearly, Finance couldn't countenance this type of spending, and subsequently measures were effected to considerably reduce this spending. Of course, in light of the situation that led to the setting up of the 'fleet', and given the state of the economy and public finances, it only made sense to reduce both spending and the size or collection of vessels, but the department didn't seem to want to stop. The situation was not aided by a most pertinent article in the Anglo-Irish Treaty of 1921, Article 6, which the Department of Finance possibly used as its bedrock argument or justification for all the spending cuts:

Until an arrangement has been made between the British and Irish Governments whereby the Irish Free State undertakes her own coastal defence, the defence by sea of Great Britain and Ireland shall be undertaken by His Majesty's Imperial Forces, but this shall not prevent the construction or maintenance by the Government of the Irish Free State of such vessels as are necessary for the protection of the Revenue or the Fisheries.'[5]

So without much further ado, the CMS was disbanded in 1924, along with its various sister departments, such as the Coastal Infantry, the Marine Investigation Department and the Coastal Patrol. In all they had lasted just eleven months. Though efforts were made to keep a much-slimmed-down force, it was not to be. Given the demobilisation following the civil war and the dismantlement of the 'fleet' and other cost-cutting measures, defence spending by 1932–33 had reached a low of just over a million pounds. With a sense of historical irony given all that had passed in the years since 1916, there remained only one vessel, the *Muirchu* (formerly the *Helga*), which was handed over to the Department of Agriculture and Fisheries. She had survived the Rising, the War of Independence, the civil war and the shredding of the Coastal and Marine Service, and was still working as a fisheries-protection vessel, though in this regard she had her work cut out.

The next occasion on which the government would be put to the pin of its collective collar and be forced again to react to the situation was the Emergency almost fifteen years later. However, two events in the intervening years are worthy of mention: the granting of the powers of arrest to the *Muirchu* and the handing over of the three Treaty ports: Cobh, Berehaven and Lough Swilly. In 1933, with the passing of the Fisheries Act, the *Muirchu* became the only vessel in the state with the powers of arrest for fisheries offences. In 1938 the return of the Treaty ports was negotiated. On 11 July 1938 Cork Harbour and Spike Island were handed over, Berehaven was returned on 30 September, while Lough Swilly was returned on 3 October. The handing over of the Treaty ports was one thing, but the absence of any sort of naval force following the departure of the Royal Navy was another. The army, in order to offset this, attempted to replace the now departed RN with vessels of its own. A plan was submitted to government for a fleet including patrol boats and armed trawlers, but as was the norm this plan never got anywhere though in May 1938 two motor torpedo boats (MTBs) were eventually ordered from Thornycroft in the UK. These were designated M1 and M2.

February 1939 would see the establishment of the new Coast Watching Service (CWS), with headquarters in Portobello Barracks. There must have been a palpable sense of déjà vu running through the relevant government departments at the time. In September the government reconstituted the fledgling CWS into the Marine and Coast Watching Service (MCWS). The government then tried to procure additional vessels to augment the MTBs, and though the British government didn't allow the further sale of trawlers to Ireland, it sanctioned the sale of another two MTBs. The Marine Service was created and was subsumed into the Marine and Coast Watching Service in September that year. The Marine and Coast Watching Service was divided into six different services, each service being independent while mutually supporting it sister services. Those services were:

- Coast Watching Service
- Patrol Service
- Coastal Defence Artillery

- Port Control and Examination Service
- Maritime Inscription
- Mining (Sea Mines) Service.

Irish Shipping was formally established on 21 March 1941. However, in the context of the history of the Naval Service the Patrol Service was very important. In November 1939 the *Fort Rannoch* was handed over to the MCWS by the Department of Agriculture and Fisheries, while a month later the *Muirchu* also found its way back into the hands of the MCWS. In January of the following year – 1940 – both ships were recommissioned as 'public armed ships'. The year 1940 would also see the commissioning of four MTBs designated M1, M2, M3 and M4. M1 was commissioned in January, M2 in June, M3 in July and M4 in December. On 7 June 1940 the government declared a state of emergency, and by year's end two patrol vessels and four MTBs were in operation. It wasn't that there were large numbers of vessels floating around, but a home or a base was required, and while a couple of places had been proposed, the logical place and one that was ready-made to become the home base for the flotilla was the ex-Royal Navy base at Haulbowline in Cobh, County Cork. So on 7 July 1940 the ex-RN naval base officially became the naval base for the Patrol Service. The first officer commanding the naval base and dockyard was Comdt N. Harrington. In January and February 1941 two more MTBs arrived: M5 and M6.

With the ending of the Second World War in May 1945, many of the services attached to the Marine and Coast Watching Services were also terminated. History was repeating itself yet again as the government began disbanding the MCWS. The first to go was the Port Control and Examination Service. Then the Coast Watching Service went, but the Maritime Inscription was retained and would the following year – 1946 – become the Naval Reserve, An Slua Muirí. March 1946 saw the Marine Service become a permanent part of the Defence Forces. The post-war government now realised that things could not revert to what they had been prior to 1940, and began in earnest to create and maintain a fit-for-purpose Naval Service. Its wartime and peacetime requirements and duties were outlined, and the government began a search for suitable vessels to meet those criteria. Clearly there were restricting factors regarding certain types of vessels no matter how desirable they might be, but as with every purchase decision made regarding any type of vessel since the civil war, cost was the ultimate deciding factor. Invariably the cheapest was sought, and consequently the corvette was decided upon for the Naval Service. Three ex-Royal Navy Flower class corvettes were purchased in 1946: HMS *Oxlip*, HMS *Bellworth* and HMS *Borage*, all three of which had seen service during the war. In November 1946 the *Oxlip* was commissioned as the LÉ *Macha* 01, the *Bellworth* was commissioned in December as the LÉ *Maeve* 02, while the *Borage* was commissioned as the LÉ *Clíona* 03 in February 1947. The names Banba, Fóla and Gráinne were earmarked for the next three corvettes, but the ships were never purchased;[6] those names, however, would be used over twenty years later. Now that the Naval Service had three 'new' corvettes, the two existing patrol vessels, the *Fort Rannoch* and the *Muirchu* were to be decommissioned, returned to their previous owners or disposed of – no doubt whichever was the cheapest option.

Those chosen to head up this new service were men who had served during the war with foreign navies – primarily the Royal Navy – and had organisational experience. The first head of the new service was a Royal Navy commander, Henry Seville Jerome, who served for the first five years as captain and director of the service. The next senior appointments were Lieutenant Commander Cheb Forde, who was promoted to commander in charge of engineering, and the Irishman Acting Lieutenant T. McKenna, who on promotion to Lieutenant Commander was in charge of the Marine Depot in Haulbowline. The 1947 Defence Forces (Temporary Provisions) Act formally altered the name of the Marine Service to the Naval Service, and thus the Naval Service of today (2014) was officially born. The 1947 Act also brought about the reorganisation of the three branches of the Defence Forces, and henceforth the Naval Service and the Air Corps would become separate commands within the Defence Forces.

During the early 1950s there was some uncertainty about the actual use and future of the Naval Service. What was the best course of action regarding future vessels, equipment and infrastructure? Allied to this, and more importantly from an operational perspective, was the situation regarding the actual state of the vessels and their maintenance, or lack thereof. The lack of manpower in general and in the engineering departments in particular was another major issue, and an inability to crew the three corvettes together at any one time made life very difficult for all concerned. Indeed, a further order for three corvettes was apparently cancelled due to severe manpower shortages. In December 1956 Commander McKenna was promoted to captain and took over the appointment of director of the Naval Service. In 1957 the LÉ *Macha* underwent a major refit and refurbishment, as did the LÉ *Clíona* in 1958. The LÉ *Maeve* was out of commission, but to bring her back on line she would have hers in 1960. The shortage of manpower, serviceable ships and spare parts, together with a lack of maintenance and money, clearly placed the Naval Service under huge strain. Just when things couldn't get worse, the United Nations Convention on the Law of the Sea (UNCLOS) made a determination whereby the national territorial limit of three nautical miles was to be extended to twelve. The nautical footprint had just increased by three hundred per cent.

By 1967 the effective lifespan of the Corvettes had been reached. Efforts were made to extend by a couple of the years their usefulness, particularly given that the twelve-mile limit was in place, but in reality it was a stopgap, and it couldn't go on for much longer. It didn't, and the inevitable finally arrived. The LÉ *Macha* was decommissioned in December 1968, the LÉ *Clíona* in July 1969, and the LÉ *Maeve* in January 1970. So there it was – finally, no more naval vessels. Well, not exactly, for the state owned a fisheries-research vessel, the *Cú Feasa*. Clearly this situation couldn't be countenanced even by the government, and moving with a speed that must have shocked even them, the Naval Service managed to source and purchase three Coniston class minesweepers from the Admiralty: HMS *Oulston*, HMS *Blaxton* and HMS *Alverton*. In February 1971 the LÉ *Gráinne* CM10 (ex-*Oulston*) was commissioned, and in March the LÉ *Fóla* CM12 (ex-*Blaxton*) and LÉ *Banba* CM11 (ex-*Alverton*) were commissioned. The arrival of the minesweepers to the Naval Service beckoned another new dawn regarding vessel type and on-board equipment, but they also brought with them the need for a ship's hull-maintenance programme. The hulls were aluminium with teak planking forming the outer layers. This and other new hull-fitting requirements demanded the services of divers. The Naval Service at this precise moment in time had but one naval diver, a naval officer, Lieutenant Joseph Deasy. Matters now demanded that the Naval Service required more divers. Thus, naval diving commenced in earnest.

The LÉ *Deirdre* – commissioned in May 1972 – was the original of the species in more ways than one. She was born out of an urgent need by the state to fill the slots left vacant by the corvettes. In a rare move, the government of the day signed, sealed and delivered (launched) a brand-new patrol-class vessel built in an Irish shipbuilding dockyard in Cork by Irish workers and launched all in the one year, 1971! (The ship went on to serve the state for more than thirty years and with honour.) It was a remarkable feat indeed, and all the more noteworthy when taking into account the paltry resources and finance previously extended to the service by the state. (Sometime in the early 1990s the ships companies throughout the fleet began to 'christen' their ships after cartoon characters or similar, and secured onto the ships' funnels large, round, painted motifs with the relevant character. The crew of the LÉ *Deirdre* christened her *The Original of the Species*, and her motif was an image of a large, hairy mammoth.) Thus, the arrival of the LÉ *Deirdre* marked the start of an era of purpose-built, home-designed-and-produced class of vessel built in Verolme Cork Dockyard – an era that would last until 1984 with the last ship built, the LÉ *Eithne*.

In June 1973 Capt. T. McKenna retired, and succeeding him was newly promoted Capt. Peter Kavanagh. Capt. Kavanagh served with distinction during the Second World War on all the merchant vessels he sailed on. He was ship-wrecked twice in his career, and received numerous awards and citations from foreign governments. The year 1973 also was when Ireland joined the European Economic Community (EEC). In 1976, in line with UNCLOS recommendations and an EEC fisheries agreement, Ireland claimed an exclusive 200-nautical-mile economic zone. The Naval Service was placed under immense pressure by this agreement as it had only the one vessel capable of patrolling to this limit. But it's an ill wind that doesn't blow somebody some good. In light of this, further ships would now have to be ordered and built. This wasn't going to happen overnight, but while waiting for orders to be filled, other available ships were sourced to fill the gaps, and in two cases were acquired. The ex-Commissioner of Irish Lights tender *Isolda* was purchased in 1976 and commissioned as the LÉ *Setanta* A15, while in 1977 the ex-Danish Stern trawler Helen Basse was leased for a year and commissioned as LÉ *Ferdia* A16.

The order for another Deirdre-class vessel was placed in 1975; this was to be the LÉ *Emer* P21. Her hull was laid down in Verolme in February 1977, she was launched in September, and entered service on being commissioned on 16 January 1978. Although the LÉ *Deirdre* was by no means the best vessel ever built in Verolme, she was the first of her kind and represented a new departure for the Naval Service, which had learnt a lot from her: future ships of her class were built and fitted out much better. In July 1978 the keel of the LÉ *Aoife* P22 was laid down, and she was launched a year later, in April 1979, and commissioned in September. Following her in short order was the LÉ *Aisling* P23, laid down in January 1979, launched in October and commissioned in May 1980. She was the last of her class to be built, and the next vessel would by far and away outstrip any of the P20 class.

In 1980 Commodore P. Kavanagh retired after seven years in the appointment, with Commodore Liam Maloney succeeded him to flag officer. The Naval Service had by now gotten the bit firmly between its teeth, and with it also finance. The next class of vessel would be a completely new departure for the Naval Service, and in some ways it was an expensive experiment in both ship design (P30 class) and capability: the LÉ *Eithne* P31 was a helicopter-carrying patrol vessel complete with flight deck. In so many ways this challenged the Naval Service. There was so much new gear, equipment, design and so much training involved. A state-of-the-art vessel, she carried a helicopter for aerial maritime patrolling that was owned, crewed and run by the Air Corps. She came equipped with a Dauphin SA365 helicopter. She was laid down in December 1982, launched in December 1983, and finally commissioned on 7 December 1984. She was supposedly the first of four in her class, but ultimately finance dictated otherwise, and somewhat ironically not only was the LÉ *Eithne* the first and last of her class, she was in fact the last ship to be built in Verolme as the dockyard went into receivership on the very day the LÉ *Eithne* was being moved back to Haulbowline to be finished off.

In 1986 Commodore Liam Brett succeed Commodore Maloney as flag officer when Commodore Maloney moved to fill the appointment of deputy chief of staff support at Defence Forces headquarters in Dublin. In 1988 saw the arrival of another two ships and of a different class altogether. The two vessels were ex-Peacock class of the Royal Navy, Hong Kong Squadron. Designed and built to operate in the Far East, each vessel came armed with an OTO Melara 76mm naval cannon and gyro stabilised; some said that the Royal Navy built the ship around the cannons. So in May 1988 the two ex-RN vessels HMS *Swallow* P242 and HMS *Swift* P243 became upon commissioning the LÉ *Orla* P41 and LÉ *Ciara* P42 respectively. In the 1990s a replacement programme for the four P20 Deirdre-class offshore patrol vessels was planned.

In 1990 another change of flag officer occurred, with Commodore Brett retiring after five years in that position (having served forty-four years in the Naval Service) and Commodore Joe Deasy assuming the office. Commodore Deasy didn't spend too long as flag officer, and retired in 1993, being succeeded by Commodore John Kavanagh.

In 1996 the Naval Service celebrated its fiftieth anniversary – an event that culminated with a fleet review in Cork Harbour of not only the Irish naval vessels but numerous naval vessels from invited countries around Europe. The review was taken by the commander in chief of the Irish Defence Forces, An tUachtaráin Mary Robinson, and by the flag officer.

The first vessel of class to be decommissioned was the original LÉ *Deirdre*, in

2001, with the LÉ *Emer* being decommissioned in September 2013. The Naval Service, seeking to replace them, looked at future-proofing the next generation of ships for operations in the North Atlantic over a nominal lifespan of thirty years. Future-weather models, sea-state trends and wave heights in light of global warming were all given consideration. Other issues to be taken into account included the structure of vessels, retro fitting, crew comfort, greater automation in certain systems, larger boarding RHIBs and their launch/recovery systems. Built by Appledore Shipbuilders in Devon, the LÉ *Róisín* P51 class was commissioned into the Irish Naval Service fleet on 15 December 1999, just in time for Christmas. Her sister ship, the LÉ *Niamh* P52, was commissioned on 18 September 2001.

Another change of flag officer occurred in 1992, with Commodore John Kavanagh retiring and Commodore Frank Lynch assuming command. In 2010

Rear Admiral Mark Mellet

Commodore Lynch retired and Commodore Mark Mellett assumed command. In 2013 Commodore Mellett was promoted to Rear Admiral, having assumed the appointment within the Defence Forces as deputy chief of staff support, while Commodore Hugh Tully succeeded him as flag officer of the Naval Service.

Another series of vessel-replacement contracts were signed with Babcock Marine operating out of Appledore Devon UK. Three vessels were ordered and a new generation of naval vessel was inaugurated. Though the new vessels were to be built to the same design as the P50 class, they would be some 10 metres longer and 400 tonnes heavier. Any improvements recommended from *Niamh* and *Róisín* were incorporated into the P60 design. The Naval Service took delivery and commissioned the latest generation of naval patrol vessel the LÉ *Samuel Beckett* in May 2014. The second-of-class ship the LÉ *James Joyce* is currently under construction at Babcock Marine, with delivery expected in 2015. A third-of-class vessel remains unnamed, has just had the metal cut for its keel, and will probably be delivered either late in 2015 or early 2016.

With a comprehensive ship-replacement programme in place and with what appears to be a good government policy of providing the necessary finance for such a programme, the Naval Service is in a far better place now that it has ever been in its relatively short but very interesting history.

1

DIVER TRAINING, 1964–81

From a staff officer operations' and later commander Fleet Operations' point of
view, the diving unit over the years developed into the most professional unit
we had in the navy. From a dangerous-job perspective, training, equipment and
the constant on-call situation that we had, they were always a very, very good
arm of the navy. For me they were the most professional outfit we had, and they
had to be, because if they weren't and they made a mistake, they were dead!

Former commander Fleet Operations, Commander Eugene Ryan (retd), 2013[1]

Siebe Gorman standard diving gear was the order of the day for Royal Navy
divers back in 1964, and it would be the same for Lt Joe Deasy on his first
introduction to diving. This ubiquitous diving suit has stood the test of time. It
was by no means light – in fact everything about it was heavy, but it was designed
for diving and not for sprinting. Lt Deasy's first dive, like the manner in which
he was informed of the course, was nothing if not direct:

> … the course started almost immediately, the diving course that is … first
> of all everyone had to wear a hard hat and suit and they dumped you in the
> camber, and they had laid things out round for you to pick up.[2]

At no stage in his youth or as a young naval officer had the lieutenant shown any
interest in diving or even entertained any thoughts about becoming a diver, so
when asked if he had done any diving up to this point, his reply was an emphatic
'No'. So what were things like for him, and what did he recall of his first day there?

> Well, I'll go back a bit… when I went across first to the Diving Section,
> they said 'Where's your medical.' I said 'Medical, what medical?' You see,

the people here [Irish Naval Service] didn't know a fecking thing, not a thing … so they sent me over to the doctor and he tapped me here, he tapped me there, and do you know what he did? There was a stairs, double stairs, and he made me run up and down three or four times and then he tested me … and he said 'You're OK' … but anyway, the hard hat was next … we did a lot of work, classroom work beforehand, setting things up, and getting equipment, and the structure of the course, etc., taking notes … immediately after that month I went down to Portland … but at that time in the navy [Irish] people couldn't separate diving from anti-submarine … it was all underwater …'[3]

Lt Deasy went on to finish his diving course and the long TAS course, arriving back to Ireland in November 1964. For the next six years nothing in the way of diving took place. The lieutenant wrote letter after letter, stressing the need for more divers in the service. According to the diving regulations, he required at least another diver, a supervisor and attendants if he alone was to keep his qualification up to date.

I liked to try and persuade people you know … the way I approached it was in the manual. The diving manual required that you can't dive without all these people in attendance. And if we were to be serious about a diving branch, we've got to train people first … to keep standards I was not going to get into a suit and get into the water on my own … I wanted to set a standard and thank God it happened …[4]

But most importantly, he stressed that a Diving Section would be of great benefit both to the service and, by extension, to the state. It was a long wait, but it took the arrival of the three minesweepers in 1971 to finally really kick-start diving in the Naval Service. In the meantime, while the minesweepers and official diver training with the Royal Navy were both another year away, a young naval cadet was rising to the challenge of naval diving. The man to accept that challenge was a young Naval Service cadet by the name of Frank Lynch. Frank was attending Britannia Royal Naval College (BRNC), Dartmouth for cadet training. The year was 1969.

I did the first dedicated ship's diving officer course by a member of the

Naval Service while I was undertaking cadet training with the Royal Navy in 1969. I managed to do well in the Britannia Royal Naval College swimming team, and the officer in charge of the team fixed me up on the course during summer leave in August 1969. I gather the Irish state was not charged for the course.

The course was tough, with a high dropout rate. The fact that it was warm made the drysuits particularly uncomfortable. I can vividly remember a mile-plus mud run over very soft mud. The small guys were able to stand and actually run. In my case, being a hefty young lad, I had to crawl the whole way. One of my fellow student divers, Berny Bruen, went on to become a commander diver and he was in charge of the RN divers during the Falklands/Malvinas War off the coast of Argentina in 1982.[5]

In 1970 Lt Peadar McElhinney from Strabane, County Tyrone took up his

Diving class and instructors, SDO course, HMS Vernon, *Portsmouth May 1964*
(centre, back row): Lt Joseph Deasy NS

place on a ship's diving officer course. The difference this time was that this was the first advertised diving course as such in the Naval Service, and was not a part of cadet training in the UK, and it came on the back of the arrival of the new minesweepers:

> The case was made but the department [Department of Defence], the problem with the civil service unless they are convinced something is required they won't buy it, they won't invest in it … and this is where the diving really started, we got the minesweepers [and] because the mine-sweepers had nylon sheeting covering the mahogany planking there was a requirement to inspect them every month or more frequently if there was heavy weather … so the main reason why there was a change in policy by the civil servants was that they really didn't have a choice … so the navy said OK, but we have to get ship's divers … So I said OK, whose around, and there weren't that many officers around at the time, the navy was very small … five hundred or so … short of navigators … shortage all round, so there wasn't that many officers to pick from. Anyway I said I'll have a go at this, it looks exciting, interesting and something else to do, it's another thing to get involved in, so that's what I did, I volunteered and went for it.[6]

Lt McElhinney was followed over shortly afterwards in early October 1970 when the first four NCOs from the Naval Service were selected and sent over to HMS *Drake*, Plymouth to undergo the first ship's divers course. They were L/Sea George Jefferies, L/Stoker Eamon Butler, L/Signalman Pierce Power and L/Signalman Paddy Lynch. In interviewing George for this book, he told me that he was originally in the army, which he joined in January 1961 at the ripe old age of fifteen years and four months: 'I was a big boy.'[7] He served in the Congo with the 37th Infantry Battalion ONUC, and in August 1962 spent his seventeenth birthday in Elizabethville, Congo. On his return he joined the tentage section with the Ordnance Corps, qualifying as a tent maker in Clancy Barracks, Dublin. He subsequently left the army in December 1963 to go fishing on trawlers. George then decided to re-enlist, but this time in the Naval Service, in late 1964, and he passed out in March 1965 having completed another full sixteen weeks of training. It was a real case of the army's loss and the navy's gain. George mentioned that the selection process of the four guys to go on the course was essentially based on their swimming prowess and on their overall general fitness. The diving course

PO George Jefferies (left), Lt Peadar McElhinney

was originally posted in routine orders, requesting applications for a forthcoming diving course in HMS *Drake*. The course lasted a month, with all four personnel finishing on 13 November 1970. According to entries taken from L/Sea Jefferies' diving logbook, the students reached a maximum depth of 120 feet and accumulated over 1,350 minutes of diving time. The air equipment used during the course was SABA (swimmer's air breathing apparatus – what the Royal Navy called its inverted twinset but built to its specifications) and SDDE (surface-demand diving equipment). The diving suit was a Dunlop rubberised suit complete with a neck seal and clamp, and the demand-valve regulator was a Siebe Gorman Mk VI twin hose with a full face mask and nose clip. George goes on to describe their first day:

> We arrived over there on the Sunday morning … we got our joining cards and we went to the dusty and we got our bedding and he took us over to where we were staying and then over to the mess and signed into the ratings mess – you had to sign in everything in the Royal Navy, you had a card to sign in everything and it had to be stamped by everyone … it was a great system.[8]

George describes how the following morning, after being introduced to the officer in charge of the course while wearing their service dress no. 1s (full dress uniform), they were introduced to the kit and to the Royal Navy's diving methodology of positive, affirmative instructional techniques, which would stand him in good stead in the years to come:

> They brought us into the Diving Store, issued us all our gear, issued your suit, issued with diving bottle, your knife, your fins, and they were the most useless fins I had ever seen, terrible fucking yokes … We were shown how to get dressed, how to turn on the gear, and how to get into the water … and I remember, Eamon Butler was my buddy and he was tending me, and I remember been given by Maggy Lockwood, PO Lockwood … he was the PO in charge of the course. We had 50lbs shots [weights] down at 10 metres; I was given a length of chain and I was given a hammer and chisel, and you had to go down and cut that chain underneath the water; other fellas were given lengths of chain with hacksaws … I remember coming up after about twenty minutes, proud as punch, when the chain broke, I got the belt of an oar on top of the head – 'Get back down and cut another one and don't come up till two equalisations [50 bar]' … that was our instructions, middle of winter, freezing cold and I mean freezing cold … and that was the way they trained you, which was a grand way I thought.[9]

George took on board that particular lesson very well, for there have been more than a few navy divers who would swear both to his accuracy and efficiency with the oar during training. They passed the course and the newly appointed divers would return home to Ireland and to the naval base, the first ever Royal Navy-trained ship's divers. However, they wouldn't dive again for almost a year as there was no gear available.

In January 1972 the next group of would-be divers followed in their rating colleagues' footsteps towards HMS *Drake*. A/Tel Anthony Sheridan, A/Mech Johnny O'Neill and A/Steward Gerry Dwyer would all complete their course, too. Anthony and Johnny both fell into diving by accident, and not for the first time was Lt Peadar McElhinney talent spotting. Their recollections of their aptitude tests were informative as they were the first such aptitude tests to be undertaken. Johnny O'Neill recalled:

> I remember when we did the aptitude test, I can't remember who brought me down, it was purely out of the excitement and challenge of something different … never having been underwater … they brought us down to the

Basin [dockyard area] and we jumped off the wall, that was a bit of *craic*. I'll always remember that, the fucking cold, I think it would have been November, December, very cold, then they brought us down a shot line ... they put a Dunlop suit on you, brought us down the shot line with a blackout face mask and with most of the fellas everybody wanted to be a bleeding diver then, the thoughts of getting into the water with a blacked-out face mask, fellas were just packing it in there and then.[10]

And in the interview with Anthony Sheridan, Tony had this to say:

I'll tell you exactly what happened, I was on the *Banba* at the time and we were down in the Basin and we were swimming, a whole crowd of us, lovely summer's day, and I love swimming and McElhinney, he was the captain ... he was there, 'cos I was such a good swimmer he recommended me for the course ... to me I know how Comms [Communications branch] were and I knew I wouldn't be allowed to go on the course ... and I passed the medical and I went then [UK] ... and there was murder over it ... phone calls between Comms and the CO ... and that was it really!'[11]

Their recollections of their training are interesting and some of the situations they found themselves enlightening. John:

We went over in January, it was snowing, it was winter and it was freezing ... I think there was forty or fifty on the course and fellas were bailing out every day just from the cold, it was really bad, it was something we had never done before ... fuckers screaming at you ... I was determined to come back with the gold badge no matter what ... I stood on the bottom and you had sort of weighted boot on us, it was just to see how long we would last, and we had these full face masks. I was actually crying into the face mask it was so fucking cold ... I was just shaking on the bottom ... the suit had filled up with water, and that was the reason why I was shaking ... I had hypothermia, I was fucking frozen solid, but I was determined not to come up, because I wanted to get that badge. I didn't want to fail.[12]

Anthony:

You know for me you see that's a really important question you asked initially; did I have ambition to become a diver? I didn't … I just fell into it, you know … it's just this officer saw me and I said I'll give it a go, never thinking I'd get it … it was a great experience, but for me the main thing on the course, the big thing … that I wouldn't fail it, I was absolutely clear and determined that no matter what they threw at me I would take it and that I would not fail.[13]

They didn't, but more importantly, the interviews record not only their resilience but also their determination to succeed no matter what was presented to them. So the solid groundwork and firm foundations necessary to build the Diving Section were being laid. But more was required and more was to come.

In 1973 the next batch of personnel to head to HMS *Drake* for their ship's divers course were L/Sea Paddy Carolan, A/Sea Noel Garrett, L/Sea Tommy Johnson and L/Signalman Denis Sheridan. Not for the first time Lt McElhinney was out talent spotting, and he had noticed and influenced directly another young seaman to go down the road of diving. Paddy Carolan recalled:

Anthony Sheridan (left), Paddy Carolan

I was after doing PTI courses, unarmed-combat courses, gymnastic courses, and I was on the LÉ *Fóla* [note similarity with Anthony Sheridan] and McElhinney was there and he says to me one day, 'Are you interested in going on a diving course?', and I said 'I never had thought about it' ... 'Well, come on,' he says ... I got into a suit and I jumped off the wing of the bridge and swam around the Basin and came back up and was told 'Yeah ... you're on the diving course' ... and that was it ... they were picking people that were fit and active.[14]

George Jefferies had travelled to the UK with the divers as a liaison NCO. When George wasn't liaising, he was diving with the course while they were doing their evolutions.

L/Sea Tommy Johnson

On 1 May 1978 L/Sea Tommy Johnson died from a severe form of leukaemia. One Monday morning he was walking to work with George, and while George noticed that Tommy was limping, Tommy just passed it off as a kick he received playing football on the ship up in Rathmullen (County Donegal) the previous week. Tommy was on the LÉ *Fóla* at the time, and the ship sailed that Monday 24 April, on patrol. On the Thursday, Tommy was removed from the ship, having been seen by a local doctor in Kinsale. On Friday morning he was removed to St Vincent's Hospital in Dublin, where he died on the Monday. George recalled Tommy's passing:

> The day he died, Mother of God, there really was a pall of sadness descended over the island, there really was. When word came back that Tommy had gone, I don't know what happened ... the island everyone was completely, totally and utterly shocked.[15]

Tommy was your typical Kerryman: from Ballydavid, Irish his first language, a great sense of humour, hard as nails, and an excellent sportsman. He was extremely well liked throughout the service and was an excellent diver. Ironically for a diver, while Tommy had a great many attributes apparently swimming wasn't one of them. George was the liaison NCO for Tommy's course in the UK, and part of the UK course structure required constant student assessments, both verbal and practical. George recalled that on this particular day, both he and the RN chief in charge of the course were conducting verbal assessments:

(back, l–r): J.J. Dunbar (non-diver) George, Peadar, John O'Brien; (front, l–r): Denis Sheridan, Tommy J., Noel G.

It was Tommy's turn and the RN chief beside me began by asking him questions about technical stuff on the diving sets and other various bits 'n' pieces regarding the equipment. You know, how much endurance from a SABA set – all that stuff.

Tommy answered them satisfactorily. Then the RN chief in his lovely British accent continues: 'Now Mr Johnson, I want to ask you a couple of questions regarding rules and regulations about diving. Now what is the regulation regarding food and diving?'

You can only eat a light meal two hours before you go diving, Chief'.

'That's correct Mr Johnson, and what would you consider a light meal then?'

'Ahh sure, about eight or nine spuds Chief, eight or nine would be good enough.'[16]

The year 1974 saw another officer heading over to complete his ship's diving officer course. This time it was Lt Dan O'Neill, and he would be the first engineering officer to do so. However, Lt O'Neill didn't get to commence, never mind finish, the first course:

> I came back … I qualified in May 1974, I did it twice because I went over and got the flu … I went down to the course the first morning, and I was feeling very sick and your man said 'You've a temperature – get over to the sick bay' … spent two weeks in [HMS] *Vernon* … a stay in the hospital in [HMS base] *Haslar* … I was sent home, lost a stone … the money had already been paid, the Brits always wanted the money up front … so I was sent back in May I think … it was great, I went away in winter and did the course in May … not too hot, not too cold, not too messy. [17]

In 1975 the Naval Service was short of officers, particularly navigating officers. As a short-term solution, the service opened up its doors to foreign-naval and merchant-marine-trained officers with the necessary navigational qualifications and skills. So it was that Liam Donaldson, a Dubliner from Mount Merrion, Dublin, was commissioned into the Naval Service in 1975 as a lieutenant, having previously served as a lieutenant in the Royal Navy on a ten-year short-term commission. Liam joined the RN as a cadet in 1965, and it was here during his cadetship in BRNC Dartmouth that Liam first became involved in diving:

> When I was a cadet in 1965 with the RN, I was never a great sports-man … at the end of my cadets' training [term], instead of going on leave for a month, I went to the diving school in HMS *Drake* … all of the

sub-aqua-club guys went down, and we only had to do a three-week course because of the fact that we had done so much with the CDs in Dartmouth … so I went to sea as a cadet, as a ship's diving officer …[18]

I asked Liam how things compared between the RN and the Naval Service at the time:

When I came to Ireland the gear was just – you know – was just, uugh … the monthly checks, Jesus, you know, take your breath of air … poor! … but it got very good, and I think really it didn't get really completely professional until Gerry [O'Donoghue] went in there, and Gerry sort of took it over … we were just doing, you know, you'd get a call to go down and do a job on a ship. You'd gather up Chief Carolan or somebody or anybody you could to go down and do that dive, and then you'd head back to your own job again. I mean we really were flying on fumes, really, running on empty and it really was only when Gerry took over and he got dedicated staff to run it …'[19]

Liam entered the general list in the navy and was soon despatched to the LÉ *Deirdre* as navigating officer.

In 1975 a young man from Buttevant, County Cork – while still a cadet in Dartmouth College – became at the age of eighteen the youngest ship's diving officer in the Irish navy both then or since. Gerry O'Donoghue went on to become a living legend within the Naval Service – well, at least within the Naval Service Diving Section:

In 1975 … I was a cadet. I was a fucking cadet, Jesus spare me. I guess I always had an interest in scuba and snorkelling – I had never done any diving before but in England when you're a cadet during your junior year – which for me was the summer of '75 – you were given an opportunity to do a summer-vacation activity, and a ship's diving officer course was one of those. So I applied for the ship's diving officer course and I got it, because I had been a member of the sub-aqua club in the naval college at the time … the MCDO there recommended me, the navy [RN] didn't object, and I was let do it … so I was a qualified ship's diving officer in 1975 at eighteen … of course, I was a cadet, which meant that when I returned home from training back to the naval base, once I'd even dared talk to Jefferies, Duffy,

Garrett and the lads, I think I pushed them over the edge, they just went fucking stupid … I remember George just went red, he just went red in the face when I said I was a cadet, and then when I said I was a diving officer, then he simply snapped, he just went completely fucking purple … and I walked into the store like I owned the place, how they didn't fucking kill me I'll never know.[20]

Funnily enough, those same ex-NCOs are still wondering the same thing today. However, Gerry would go on to complete the ILMCDO course, but that was a little bit later. Once armed with this qualification, he became a man on a mission. That was still three years away; in the meantime he also had his watchkeeping exams to pass.

Martin Carroll (standing); the diver in the water is A/Sea Tony Moore

Horsea Island: Royal Navy Diving Training Facility

Horsea Island (pronounced Hawsey) was not a purpose-built diving area but an old Royal Navy torpedo-proving ground or range. Initially established by the Royal Navy's Fleet Torpedo Department around the mid-1870s, the department required a specified range of 800 yards in a secluded, non-tidal area. Horsea Torpedo Range, as it was called then, officially opened in March 1899. The range itself was 800 yards long, 20 yards wide at the firing end, and 80 yards at the other, but importantly for future divers it was only 30 feet at its deepest. It would later prove absolutely ideal for diver training, though that wasn't the plan just then. However, advances in torpedo design at that time – particularly with regard to their motors – meant that 800 yards wasn't sufficient, and so an extension to the range was completed in 1905 – the length was now 1,115 yards. Further torpedo development and advances through the First World War saw torpedo development being transferred elsewhere but with Horsea receiving a makeover to allow it to be used for motor-torpedo boat and submarine development before and during the Second World War. Interestingly, it was also used as a Marconi wireless station, and continued to be used by the RN up until 1960. Around 1960 Horsea Island was again reinvented, with the Royal Navy developing it as a centre for diver training, fire-fighting and amphibious tank trials.

In July and August 1976 the next group of volunteers headed to the UK: L/Sea John Walsh, A/Sea Martin Carroll, A/Sea Tony Behan and A/Sea Mick Colfer. There was a change of venue, with the divers now being trained at the newly designated diver-training school at HMS *Vernon*, Portsmouth, with the diving being conducted at Horsea Island. Martin Carroll recalled the days leading up to his diving course:

> 'Twas amazing, like – we went up to Cork, myself and Mick and somebody else on the Saturday, and we were flying out on the Sunday. So Mick, he'd these big shoes on, platforms, they were the in-thing at the time. Mick was 6 foot fucking 3 inches and he was wearing a pair of platforms ... he was looking out to see if there was a bus coming, we were outside some shoe store on Patrick's Street [Cork] ... didn't the mirror of a fucking bus hit him and knocked him over ... three fucking stitches later ... Mick Colfer and oul' platforms, like, and the fucking mirror of that bus was fairly high.
>
> In '75 we were supposed to be going away in September or October, there was savage bombings in London at the time, forced the course off.

We finally went away in '76 on the course and would you believe we weren't on the course a day when the British ambassador to fucking Ireland was blown up in Meath … Ahhh Mother of Mercy … the first fucking day.[21]

John Walsh:

> I did my diving course in 1976, because believe it or not it was my second attempt at it. I tried it one time, we were coming in the harbour after doing the four-to-eight watch, and there was a signal came on board that I had an aptitude test … I just told them I was resting off and heading home … so I skipped that one and then a few months later I did an aptitude in the Basin. It was something I always wanted to do, I suppose … seen the other guys, George, Eamon, Anto, Paddy Lynch, Johnny O'Neill, they did theirs in [HMS] *Drake* in Plymouth, we did our one in [HMS] *Vernon* in Portsmouth.[22]

George travelled again to HMS *Vernon*, and this time managed to obtain a place on a ship's diver supervisor's course, and duly succeeded in passing.

In 1976 two qualified ship's divers returned to HMS *Vernon* to attend a clearance divers 2 (CD2) course. It would be the first time for such a course, and it would unfortunately also be last time. John Walsh described how he and Noel Garrett went onto become CD2 divers. A CD is a clearance diver, and the 2 denotes a leading hand/petty officer rank. This course was the only one of its kind in which Naval Service divers attended in the UK. It involved swimming with oxygen re-breathers for attack swimming, and mixed-gas sets for deep-diving stealth operations and mine warfare. It was as intense a course as the two of them could get. They lacked diving experience and a certain amount of specialist knowledge, stuff that would have made their lives an awful lot easier if they had had it, but they didn't. So with a lot of effort and some burning of the midnight oil, the longer they stayed on the course and held it together the easier it became. John recalls:

> It was August 1976 when I completed my ship's divers course … a misfortune happened an A/B at the time in so far as … he broke an ankle or something and he couldn't make the CD course that was scheduled for October of that year, and on the rebound I was only coming back of my

SD course and I got that instead of Tommy [Johnson] because Tommy couldn't go … myself and Noel went over to England for six months … three months before and three months after Christmas and then came back.[23]

In 1977 two more cadets would qualify as ship's diving officers: Mark Mellett and Brendan O'Halloran would undergo and complete the course in HMS *Vernon*. Mark Mellett recalled his experience:

There was a lot of RN on the course and a lot of internationals; it was a fantastic course, great *esprit de corps*. I remember I was able to master the art of mud running quite handy. I was light enough on my feet to be able to nearly float along on the mud … so when we used to go mud running I was generally ahead of most guys. So when I came back it was only a matter of becoming familiar with Naval Service diving and how we operated here.[24]

If 1964 and 1970 were defining years in the blossoming short history of the Naval Service Diving Section, then 1978 would also be regarded as another such year, for not only did 1978 see another four more NCOs and ratings heading over to HMS *Vernon*: L/Mech Gerry Duffy, A/Sea Muiris Mahon, L/Sea Reggie Lloyd and A/Sig Frank Moody. Perhaps more importantly, in that same year S/Lt Gerry O'Donoghue travelled to HMS *Vernon* to participate in a minewarfare diving officers course. This would be Gerry Duffy's third attempt to get onto the UK course as his previous attempts ended with him heading to sea instead. However, this time Gerry proved successful and would go on to be one of the navy's finest ever divers:

Like I said, 1974 was my first introduction to diving. I had dived a good bit with Paddy Carolan, Tommy Johnson and George, and then I passed the course [aptitude test] to go to England and for one reason or another I was sent to sea … then the next time I did it, I had an argument over an incident in Lough Hyne west Cork – Noel [Garrett] was pulling me down, and Liam Donaldson was pulling me up, I could only go one way … I was sent back to the base … and then after that Danno just came to me and said 'It's about time you did this' – I was an NCO at the time so I had a good insight into getting away so … finally completed the RN course.[25]

(left) Joseph Deasy as captain naval base, signing logs and certs for diving course;
(right) a young Lieutenant Frank Lynch

Another diver with Gerry on that course was Mossy Mahon:

> Tommy Johnson was the instructor and Liam Donaldson was the diving
> officer. I passed the aptitude test in the Basin … did a few swims, did a dive
> in blacked-out face mask … maybe a twenty-minute dive … I think there
> may have been four or five of us on that day but I passed … we did more
> minutes prior to going over there than we actually got on the course. In
> July/August of that year, we went, myself, Reggie Lloyd, Gerry Duffs and
> Frankie Moody, and Noel Garrett came with us [as liaison NCO] … we
> were well prepared, we were better than the RN guys.[26]

In October 1978 an international long minewarfare clearance diver's course
commenced in HMS *Vernon*, with eight students from eight navies from around
the world. Representing the Irish Naval Service was Gerry O'Donoghue. This
course was very tough, very demanding and – like the two CDs, Noel Garrett
and John Walsh who travelled over to the UK before him – Gerry was neither
prepared physically or had sufficient diving time and experience to fully appreciate
the demands of the course. However in true Irish and naval fashion, it was a case
of head down, say nothing, plough on and hope for the best. I asked Gerry via an
email for his recollections about the course and how he got on:

Serendipity, fortunate happenstance, plays a greater part in our lives that most of us are prepared to admit. After my ship's diving course, which in itself was a casual 'leave activity' provided by the Royal Navy to prevent cadets wasting their four weeks annual holiday, I had always expressed an interest in becoming a specialised minewarfare and clearance diving officer. I had even my RN course officer recommend me for one. Around that time someone, I presume Joe Deasy, Frank Lynch or Danny O'Neill, must have been putting in for this course in the annual training estimates. Naturally, every year it was deleted. This was an expensive course and as the Naval Service took up a huge portion of the Defence Forces overseas-training budget, it was an easy target.

As a newly minted S/Lt I was not the chosen candidate for this course, I'm pretty sure that Frank (Lynch) was. As luck would have it, Frank was getting more senior and was not available and I was volunteered instead. What little I knew about the actual LMCDO course included the fact that I was not fit enough and did not have enough diving minutes to complete it successfully. I did manage to get a few dives in and a few mud runs but these only confirmed my suspicions. Of the eight students on the course I had the least amount of diving minutes. All my fellow students were the top diving officers from their respective navies. This was an error I made sure we did not repeat when we sent a candidate to subsequent courses.

The first two weeks of endurance diving were not fun and I was lucky to survive being cut. After surviving those weeks and the Horsea Lake 'live in week', the rest of the course was a breeze. How else would a group who did their deep diving in Scotland in January actually volunteer to go back for two extra weeks in February? Naturally, I passed out as top student, but this is the minimum expected standard and seldom commented on in the Diving Unit.[27]

Gerry was determined that things would change and change they did. When he returned home with his MCDO qualification in hand he was now the foremost expert in military diving not only in the Naval Service but within the Defence Forces in general.

In 1979 three more ratings departed the naval base bound for HMS *Vernon* for their diving course: A/Sea Philip Gray, A/Sea Chris McMahon and A/SA Dermot O'Sullivan, who was the first supply assistant in the navy to undergo diver

training. The three commenced training in HMS *Vernon* in January 1979 and qualified on 22 February. Chris McMahon was no stranger to diving or to dive sites, having an older brother, Derry, who had established the Athlone sub-aqua club, so Chris, when spotting the relevant routine order while serving on the LÉ *Setanta*, duly applied for the aptitude test:

> Just the three of us were picked with Noel [Garrett] going as well … we were diving for nearly three months. It started in September and we were up and down the harbour all the time – we had clocked up mountains of minutes before hand. When we went to do the course, twenty-five students started and only four finished – the three of us and one Iranian. We used wetsuits here, and in England we used Avon drysuits, neck entry and the upside-down sets, and a full face mask.[28]

What Philip had to say about his aptitude test showed the sometimes funny positions that students found themselves in and the

(l–r): Eamon Butler, Gerry Duffy, Anthony Sheridan and Johnny O'Neill Note the Avon (rubberised) dry suits with neck ring and clamp, and the suit-inflation bottles that rarely provided sufficient inflation. Gerry is modelling what was probably Paddy Carolan's shark-skin-effect wetsuit.

decision-making process that they had to make in seconds and which ultimately would lead them to either pass or fail an aptitude:

> I remember my very, very first dive, and Noel Garrett was the supervisor and we put on this drysuit and lead boots and we were fecked into the tide, down by the dockyard. We had absolutely, at that stage, no training, so it was a case of let's see who panics first and let's see who doesn't, so … I remember going in and dropping like a stone, obviously you couldn't see. I landed on my arse. I felt this squiggle underneath me and then a pretty vicious nip. I had no idea, but it was a flipping conger I had sat on and it had bit me. I'm in a drysuit, it holed it and I started to fill up pretty quick. The only thing I had been told if you're coming up was to give one pull and four pulls. So anyway I gave the pulls and came up to the surface and I met with Noel's face and he scared the shit out of me, and all I got was 'What the fuck are you doing on the surface, get the fuck back down!' … I tried to talk to him with the full face mask on and the nose clip had fallen off, and I was spluttering and all that. Now I was *not* feeling very comfortable at all, but I'm not joking you, I was actually more scared of him than going back down again. So of course I went back down and stayed there for twenty minutes, filling up and becoming like the Michelin Man. Next thing I'm told to come up, and it took four guys to pull me up, I being so big and of course I got more grief from Noel: 'Why the fuck didn't you tell me!' So that was my first introduction.[29]

In 1980 another two officers and four ratings become Naval Service divers. John F.M. Leech and Chris Reynolds were cadets at this time, and like many of their colleagues before them they availed of the opportunity to attempt the ship's diving officer course while on term break during cadet training with the Royal Navy. While Chris went on to complete his course, John (who would qualify in 1985) was nursing a sore ear:

> I did my first course in HMS *Vernon* with Chris [Reynolds], because we did our course together. On the third week I got an abscess in my ear and the fuckers took me off the course so I couldn't finish that course. What happened was, I just got to the weekend of the third week, and unfortunately I just got an abscess in my ear on Monday morning … I kept my

mouth shut obviously. I tried to get through it and by Monday afternoon there was blood coming out of my fucking ear. So the instructor pulled me aside and politely told me to 'get the *fuck*' off his course … so I wasn't able to complete the course, which was a shame – but that's life.[30]

John went on to make a full recovery and became a ship's diving officer after successfully completing the third ship's divers course in 1985. Chris had this to say about how he got started on his diving course with the Royal Navy:

I was in Dartmouth as a cadet-midshipman, and during the leave period they don't let you home – you have to do a leave activity, and so I signed up for a Scooby Doo exped in Cyprus. This officer came back to me and said, 'Listen, that's all booked up, but I've got two options for you, one is doing tour guide on the HMS *Victory* …' – 'No thanks' – and the second is some

(l–r): Danno O'Neill, Martin Carroll, Gerry O'Donoghue, Tony Behan. A rare photograph, for it actually provides photographic evidence that Gerry O'Donoghue actually did do a mud run.

John F.M. Leech on his first diving course doing the infamous mud run, 1980

diving on the south coast. I swear to God, some diving on the south coast, so I went 'I'll take the diving on the south coast ... next thing I know, I'm running around the mud flats of Horsea Island with a great fucking telegraph pole on my shoulders wondering what the fuck is going on here! I really fell into it by accident. I didn't know what a ship's diving officer was, I just signed up for some diving activity on the south coast of England. Eight started and three finished: me, a Pakistani and a guy from Bermuda.[31]

I asked Chris was it a big shock to him when he got home and saw how things were run here instead.

It was ... and especially when George [Jefferies] was my first coxwain. I came back ... I had qualified as a ship's diving officer but I was a cadet. So I came on board the LÉ *Aisling* and George was the coxwain and Pat McNulty was the exec, and I introduced myself to the XO, explained who I was ... Cadet Reynolds just back from Dartmouth College blaa blaa blaa, and by the way I'm a ship's diving officer. So there was no ship's diving officer on the *Aisling* and George was the senior supervisor obviously. When he heard that a cadet was an SDO I was called into the coxwain's office and the door was closed. A couple of minutes later I duly had my arse handed back to me when George told me in no uncertain terms that 'under *no fucking circumstances* was I a ship's diving officer, and that I was to go and get a bucket and deck scrubber and scrub out the liberty boat and boarding boat today and every other fucking day for the rest of my fucking life while he was the coxwain on board' ... that brought back a bit of reality to me.[32]

George clearly had an aversion to cadets thinking they were diving officers. The second officer to successfully complete his diving course in HMS *Vernon* that year was the young S/Lt Shane Anderson, who had a slightly different entry into diving. He was essentially directed to undergo the training in HMS *Vernon* on the back of showing some aptitude for diving in a very impromptu and loosely labelled aptitude test conducted in the naval base. In interviewing Shane, he spoke about becoming a diving officer, and how, in trying to do so as a cadet in England, he became an unwitting submariner instead:

I ended up on a submarine. I looked for the diving course but it was full.

Gerry [O'Donoghue] got the place, and then I was told that there was a submarine course I could do if I wanted to, so I did that instead ... so it was myself and Joe Deasy as the navy's only submariners ... I did a month on a submarine up out of Holy Loch, Scotland, an Oberon-class submarine out of Holy Loch ... we did a three week patrol on it and sat in on part of the 'perishers' course, which is the RN's submarine commanders course. We did a week in the Naval Base in Faslane and then spent three weeks on the sub patrolling around the north coast of Scotland. HMS *Oberon* was her name, she was diesel electric, a 1950s vintage, absolutely brilliant – I would have loved them as a career but we didn't have them [lucky enough!]. It was very enjoyable and the captain was a man from Limerick ... it was very interesting and it was one of the more enjoyable periods of my career.[33]

I was surprised to hear how Shane had arrived at his diving course, even though I had served with Shane. So I asked him how it was that he hadn't travelled the usual route to diving at that time:

... 1980 in HMS *Vernon*. I did my aptitude test in Haulbowline, and then I was nominated and told that the course was there and you're going. I wasn't given a choice, you are going, so off I went ... It wasn't a structured aptitude test, it was very much a case of get in the water and let's see what you can do ... I was put into the Basin and then into the police chamber. GOD [Gerry O'Donoghue] was in charge and he said, 'Yep, I think you're up for it, away you go' ... I was always comfortable in the water, so it was very much a case of get on with it and do it.[34]

Also that year – 1980 – A/ERA Ollie McMurrow, A/ERA Declan Kelly, A/Sea Billy Lahive and A/Sea Martin Diggins departed for HMS *Vernon*. All four successfully completed their diving course.

The last of the Royal Navy-trained divers for the Naval Service completed their training in 1981, for a new beginning was on the horizon both for the Naval Service and for the Diving Section. First, a young lieutenant working in naval headquarters in Dublin, Tom Meehan, commenced and successfully completed his ship's diving officer training in HMS *Vernon* in June.[35] Then, Cadet Ron Long and S/Lt Paul Logan commenced the diving course in July during their term break from their respective courses, and subsequently qualified as ship's diving officers.

Ron describes his initial foray into diving:

I remember one guy, whose name escapes me now, but they dressed him up and put a pair of lead boots on him and made him march down the steps into the tide, and your man didn't know how to swim or anything. I remember looking into his face mask and seeing this absolute blind panic as he was fucking disappearing under the surface … so yeah that wasn't very successful for him!! … but I actually liked it … it was only a kinda of an exercise for an afternoon for two hours, but yeah I thought I could do this.

So I went to the Naval College in Dartmouth. There was a clearance diver there in my division, a sub lieutenant, they called

(l–r): John Walsh, Martin Carroll, at RN School

The Four Horsemen
of the Apocalypse
(l–r): Gerry Duffy,
George Jeffs, Johnny
Walsh and Noel
Garrett

him an Upper Yards man, he came through the ranks … he was a real brilliant guy … so I spoke to him about the aptitude tests in Dartmouth … so he said to me, 'Right', he said, 'you have to accept that there's going to be water in your mask, it's going to be around your eyes and up your nose, OK, but none of that counts, right … you're going to have to get used to that and down there in the river, well, that's a pretty grim spot, but it's just a question of adapting to it – you'll get through it.'[36]

Paul Logan had this to say:

I underwent the ship's divers course with Ronan Long, now in NUI Galway, in 1981. Both of us were in the UK, Ron on his cadet training and myself on the international sub-lieutenants course with the RN [eight months in various RN establishments including BRNC Dartmouth]. We did some diving while we were on the course there with the college diving-training unit … so I applied to do the ship's divers course as part of an adventure activity in July 1981 with the RN. I reported to the RN school at HMS *Dryad* [shore establishment] in Portsmouth with some RN officers to undergo the course. [37]

The final three enlisted personnel would commence their separate courses within two weeks of each other, in June and July. L/Sea Martin Buckley and A/Tel John Lynch departed the naval base in May and commenced their training on SDR 161 (ship's diver course number), while A/SA Paulus Forde arrived over into HMS *Vernon* two weeks later, and commenced his training on SDR 162:

Author's RN diving course, SDR 161, June 1981, HMS Vernon: Martin Buckley (front, right), John Lynch (back, second from right)

> I had never even been inside the store … Gerry Duffs is inside and sets about explaining to me what's going to happen on the aptitude test and he's pointing at some stuff on the ground and he's sort of you know, like, looking at me like I've two

The diving cert presented to the first Naval Service diver, Lt J.A. Deasy, Éire Navy, ship's diver officer, awarded at HMS Vernon, 26 June 1964

heads and saying 'Come on, Bucks – we don't have time to be acting the bollix, get dressed, come on, two minutes, let's go' … the next three days were just a blur; up and down from Dublin getting a diving medical … I got a tooth pulled on the Friday morning. Then it was up to Dublin on the Saturday afternoon and flying out to London on the Sunday afternoon flight followed by a train down to Portsmouth and HMS *Vernon*. Jesus what was I thinking?[38]

So concluded the final Royal Navy ship's diving courses for officers and men. It had been seventeen years – 1964 – since the first officer, Lt Joe Deasy, had entered the waters on his TAS diving course, and it finished with A/SA Paulus Forde on his ship's diver course in May 1981. In between those years some thirty-nine officers, NCOs and men trained there. Some of our very finest divers were trained by the Royal Navy, and while it was the end of an era, certainly all ties with the Royal Navy diving school wouldn't be broken. The clearance diving officers would maintain the link.

Naval diving such as it was then was facing a most critical point in its potential to develop into a formal, regulated and professionally run section. In interviewing Gerry for this book, he commented on the parlous state of diving in the service around this time. While it may have appeared to have been functioning correctly, it was in essence like the proverbial duck: 'all calm and serene on the surface but paddling like a fucker underneath', and only operating on the back of the interest that the divers themselves were showing. Gerry added:

Basically I kinda set myself up at that stage that I thought we could get an MCDO and I applied for the MCDO course when I came back [from the UK and then having been commissioned]. So I did the MCDO course in '78– '79 – basically I was twenty-one or twenty-two years old then, and getting the course was a fluke because they wanted Frank [Lynch] to do it. They didn't want a pup like me, obviously, they wanted Frank, but thankfully Frank was destined for better things ... I actually wrote a paper as part of my MCDO course, the aim was to found a diving unit. It was so easy ... a donkey with a ship up its arse would have seen that the navy needed an established diving unit. It's no great credit to me, basically coz I had Danno [O'Neill] who supported me. Danno was awesome, he backed me, and in fairness to the other guys, Frank and Peadar, they were very busy doing other things but helped when and where they could.

When I came back from the UK, I took one look at what was there, and the team [and] I decided on the spot that I had to stop it ... I wrote the first letter to Wally [Commodore Liam Maloney] cancelling diving. So I cancelled Donaldson's log, I cancelled Frank's log and even cancelled Peadar's log, I went down to the store ... all the logs were cancelled, and I basically wrote a letter to Wally saying that all diving had to cease in the navy, you can imagine how well that was received.

Then I was given my famous bollicking by Wally in his office. Standing to attention for the best part of forty minutes, with [Capt.] M.R. Murphy and Wally, he just completely reamed me ... and then he said, 'What do you want to get diving full-time in the navy?' I said I needed sixteen men full-time and that was the start of it, that was the magic number ... a full-time diving team, that became the mantra forever. After that it was great because people came on board ... they let me do a refresher course for people and I started rescreening guys. I got rid of some guys and I got new guys going ... That was when you guys came in ... it was certainly getting better at that stage.

The other thing I did then that I was pleased with was to make a bunch of you guys supervisors. Remember that it was a big progression, because the thing was I was putting an ensign in charge of a diving team … for fuck sake, an ensign – give me a break. You guys were going to eat him alive for a start, and God help him if you didn't like the poor fucker, and of course I had chiefs and petty officers … yourself, Mossy, Welshy, Duffs, Garrett, Jeffs, et al., you had to be aggressive enough to do the job. You had to be able to ream out lieutenant commanders before you could do that job, because you had to be able to say 'No, I'm not doing that job' … yeah, that was a big move.[39]

It was time now for the Naval Service and the Naval Service Diving Section to develop, to move forward and to commence what it was always striving for: to train its own divers. Well, at least that was the fervent wish of Joe Deasy and others previously mentioned. There were now qualified personnel of the highest calibre available for instructing. While the actual diving equipment and facilities were not what they should or could have been, it was most critical that the break be made from the Royal Navy and that the training of our own divers begin.

Divers prepabing to jump from the Irish Steel bridge … good luck!

2

A NEW BEGINNING: DOING IT OUR WAY, 1982–2014 AND BEYOND

The mentality of a navy diver is, 'I will go out and dive today, and I will get cold and my suit leaks and its all par for the course. Am I having a good time, *no I'm bloody well not, it is just a excruciating misery*, but you get on and you do it. And when it's done and afterwards when you're reflecting in the afterglow of whatever it is you've done, it is that sense of achievement and warmth that actually compensates you to a huge degree. We've all gone through those pains, but you get over it and you get on with it. We've all had the cuts, the abrasions, the wounds that won't heal, and the open sores for weeks, but you just get on with it.

When you look back, it makes you a stronger person. So when you are actually caught in that real serious event whereby there is nobody else around except yourself, you will have that strength of character to just knuckle down and pull it all together because you know that you've been there loads of times before.

There is nothing like reflecting on the fact that practice makes perfect, so if you can motivate yourself to do it and get through this stuff when there is no actual strategic requirement to do it, then it's a piece of piss to do it when there is.

Rear Admiral Mark Mellett, 2014

Thirty-nine Irish Naval Service personnel of all ranks had been trained by the Royal Navy since 1964, and as the numbers grew so did the ambitions of some of those personnel that someday the Naval Service would train its own. Clearly, that was the vision of Joe Deasy, but like all ambitions and aspirations when working in any organisation, it's very hard for one person to make

the necessary progress. It invariably needs more like-minded people. Hence, when the likes of Peadar McElhinney, Frank Lynch, Dan O'Neill, George Jefferies, Eamon Butler and others joined the ranks of divers, it was never going to be too far over the horizon. Sending personnel to the UK was all very well, but it was not cost-effective, and all that was really happening was that the Naval Service was dodging the real issue – when would it start training its own divers? It was reaching its tipping point, it just needed that extra element to kick-start the entire operation, that *X* factor. The departure to the UK of the young S/Lt Gerry O'Donoghue on his minewarfare clearance diving course in October 1978 would finally join up all the dots. The opportunity didn't exactly happen overnight, but when it presented itself, the necessary personnel, skill sets, equipment and willingness needed to be in position.

What were the essential requirements needed to commence diver training within the Naval Service? A mine warfare officer as training officer, qualified diving instructors and qualified divers. It required an office, store and classrooms. It required diver-training areas suitable for training in both day and night, and it required a syllabus of training, all of which were available. There was just one other thing missing and it could have stopped the entire project dead in the water: diver training required the on-site presence of a recompression chamber (RCC). The Naval Service didn't have one, and though plans were afoot to procure one, it didn't look like it would be getting one any time soon. Instead, the navy would hire from a diving company. Thus, all the necessary elements had been put in place – it now required the formal notification to all personnel within the Naval Service that the first Naval Service ship's divers course would be run in November 1982.

The first naval divers course, November 1982

The first ever Naval Service diver's course was originally scheduled to commence sometime in October 1982. The original letter of request has been lost to time, but in a letter dated 1 November and addressed to FOCNS by the diving officer, Lt Gerry O'Donoghue, a new commencement date of 8 November was proposed, with a finish date of 10 December. A simple course overview was offered and a nominal roll of students was annexed:

> It is intended that each student should achieve 1,500 mins of diving time. The course will include instruction in Ships Bottom Searches, Seabed Searches and basic underwater work. All diving will be carried out as per BR. 2806.[1]

As the commencement date approached, the diving officer was still putting the finishing touches to his course syllabus and still playing hardball with Command. This centred on the question of the RCC availability. It was the one thing that would stop the course from going ahead. The diving officer, well versed in the internal workings and politics of the Naval Service, knew that if he was to get the necessary piece of equipment and get it when he needed it, he would have to show Command that, firstly, there was money to be saved, secondly, that it wouldn't mean tying up a naval vessel for longer than was absolutely necessary, and, thirdly, that if they didn't do it, it would simply delay things considerably and ultimately cost more in the end. It was very neatly summed up thus:

> It is pointed out that an expenditure of £500 at this stage will result in a net saving of £16,000 if this course had to be carried out abroad.[2]

Money talks, and so the diving officer would win the day. Knowing that the service would take the cheaper option, he didn't care, he was getting his chamber. The request for an RCC was acceded to, and the commencement date for the course would be met. The fight for the Diving Section's own RCC would continue on behind the scenes.

An overview of the course

The naval diving course was designed very much along the lines of the Royal Navy's ship's divers course – there was no need to reinvent the wheel. At that time – in 1982 – the thinking behind the Naval Service course was that we could match the RN with diver training in everything except manpower, facilities and time. The Naval Service wasn't going to train students just to an RN ship's diver standard – it was going to the next level: it was going to train the students to at least a clearance diver 3 (CD 3) level. This was serious stuff. It's stating the obvious, but the Naval Service was very small in comparison to the RN in every way. There were fewer men to choose from and less equipment to work with. The only way the Naval Service could overcome these differences was to ensure that the divers were trained better, trained harder, learned more and dived longer in the time allotted for the course.

So early starts were the norm for the students and more often than not they'd be dragging themselves out of their bunks at 06:30 hrs. Everything had to be prepared by the students prior to the diving staff arriving, and the diving programme started every day at 08:00 hrs. Night dives were conducted twice a week. Trainee divers could expect not to finish any earlier that 19:00 hrs each day, except on night dives, when it would be later. All students would develop a very high standard of personal hygiene and personal admin.

They also needed to be lucky, for luck plays an important part in any diver's training – luck in the sense that the diver needed to stay clear of injury, strains and colds – anything that could affect his training. The student was only allowed a maximum of seventy-two hours sick time for the entire course. The student diver's biggest enemies – and there were a few – would be ear infections, diarrhoea, cuts and bruises. A student to give himself the best possible fighting chance of successfully completing the course had at least to stay clear of these. The instructors had only so much time to offer and it was up to the student to stay in the game. There would be night dives every Tuesday and Thursday. Students had to ensure

that they kept themselves warm and dry when out of the water. The students had a lot to keep themselves occupied with, but the most important thing for all student divers – and this would be driven home by the instructors – was that every time he was finished his dive he had to be ready and prepared for his next dive. He had to have ready at all times, day or night, everything he needed to conduct a dive. There was no latitude in this for the student – there couldn't be and, indeed, there wouldn't be.

Finally, the student divers would be introduced to a time-honoured word taken from the Royal Navy. That word was 'AWKWARD' – a word that was and still is synonymous with all navy-trained divers. It is the only word that when spoken demands immediate response, attention and concentration from the divers. It is the command word for action. On the command 'AWKWARD', all trainee divers must immediately stop whatever they are doing and get dressed into their suits and be standing by their gear within three minutes, awaiting more instructions or a diving brief from the supervisor. Operation 'AWKWARD' would ring out many times over the first and subsequent weeks, and the student divers would get used to it very quickly.

Course layout

The course itself was six weeks long, with a module per week. The following is a breakdown of each week:

Week 1: Lifelines and signals

Typically, this week being the first week would have seen the students getting to grips with their diving gear. The diver would learn approximately forty different types of lifeline signals – both communication and working signals. A lifeline is secured around a diver's waist, and by this means signals are passed either to the diver or to the surface. To this day, they are still thought of as a primary means of communication between both the surface and the diver. The divers would learn to become comfortable in the water, to regulate their breathing and to learn how to move and be directed underwater.

Week 2: Jackstay diving

This week would see the divers beginning to dive in pairs marked with a float line to the surface while swimming along a jackstay line that lay along the seabed. This line is used as a search technique – however, when used in training it keeps the divers on a controlled line moving back and forth over several hundred metres.

Week 3: Compass swimming

This week would see the divers swimming together in buddy pairs, and using a compass swim board for direction. This would also introduce the divers to mid-water swimming. A more than difficult type of diving/swimming to do, especially when working as a buddy pair in a tideway or in poor visibility, which is why the first two weeks are really important for the divers as they get to know their equipment, their drills and each other.

Week 4: Ship's-bottom searches

This week would see the divers learning the bread-and-butter skills as a ship's diver. Here they would learn the skills and techniques involved in clearing or sweeping a ship's hull as part of a team of divers. They would be challenged because now they would be against the clock and would have to find simulated explosive charges placed on the ship's hull.

Week 5: Tool work and deep-diving work-ups

Hammer and chisel when not doing the deep-dive work-ups, normally in the 18–25-metre range in the mornings, then below 9 metres for the tool training in the afternoon.

Week 6: Deep diving and qualification dives

This week would be taken up with the qualifying deep dives, normally done from a ship anchored in a sufficient depth of water. Normal qualifying depth would be 32 metres or so. The presentation of diving logs and badges in the commanding officer's office on a Friday morning normally concludes the diving course.

In amongst all the diving training were lectures on diving principles and laws, diving disorders and illnesses, therapeutic treatments, and instruction on some technical aspects of the diving gear, compressor operation, charging of sets, boat handling and outboard engines. They were full weeks.

On 8 November 1982 eight students commenced the first ever ship's divers course as run by the Naval Service Diving Section. The course officer was Lt Gerry O'Donoghue, the senior instructor was CPO George Jefferies, the two directing staff (DSs) were PO Gerry Duffy and PO Muiris Mahon. Various other divers would assist the staff in diver training and stand-by diver duties. Though eight students commenced the course, only four would finish. I asked Damien Power why he became a diver:

> The advertisement [routine order] had gone up ... Chris McMahon had trained me in recruits; he was already a leading hand and a diver. Phil Gray had trained us on our gunnery course and he was a diver, then Billy Lahive ... all of them divers and this diving course coming up, probably gonna be the first in Ireland ... and you know, the way that I was always told it, that seventy-two people did the induction [aptitude test] and only eight passed it ...'[3]
>
> ...
>
> So the one thing you were told when we started the course, you could be kicked off it at any time, you were constantly under that pressure, you could fail it at any time ...[4]

Asked how he felt at the end of the course, Damian replied:

> Fantastic ... I felt proud about it, like, so many guys have tried it ... you were under constant pressure the whole time that it could just be taken away from you – you could fail ... an injury ... you had to keep going, couldn't just stop and take a rest, you couldn't, it just wasn't acceptable, you had just to keep going.[5]

Did he ever get any words of encouragement?

> I was on the *Emer* at the time, and Noel [Garrett] was the Coxn. Now, I was told that I was heading straight back to there, back to the *Emer* after the course, and Noel simply said to me before I left the ship, 'Don't fucking

fail the course if you're planning on coming back here, it's as simple as this. If you fail or get fucked off, I'm telling you, you won't be coming back here … now good luck.'[6]

The course ended on 17 December 1982, and four successfully completed: A/Sea Ciaran Monks, O/Sea Damien Power, O/Mech Brendan Cotter and A/Mech Jimmy O'Keeffe. Of the four students that failed to finish, three were removed due to medical reasons, so luck or lack of it played a part. Two of the successful students, O/Sea Damien Power and A/Sea Ciaran Monks, would in 1985 be sent to RNAS *Culdrose* to complete the Diving Section's first and only search-and-rescue course.

In the post-course report, the course officer had the following to say in relation to the course:

> … The quality of these divers is considered to be above average. Each achieved an average of 1,400 minutes on the course. This is approx. 50% more diving time than achieved on the RN run course.
>
> …
>
> … This course has resulted in a large improvement in the professionalism and morale among all NS divers, many of whom volunteered their spare time to assist.[7]

So the first ever Naval Service diving course was completed. Four students had passed, an RCC had been hired, and the diving staff had safely and professionally conducted their first course. It certainly did improve morale amongst the divers throughout the service, for not only did we run our own course but we actually did it better that the RN. The navy had turned a corner and another milestone had been achieved. Not only that, two qualified divers had also successfully completed their supervisor training and had received their qualifications:

> This indeed was a major achievement insofar as the Naval Diving School is now capable, at relatively little cost, to train its own divers to a standard even better than that achieved by our own divers during their training in England. Great credit must be given to Lt O'Donoghue and the instructor staff for providing the high standards of efficiency and instructional techniques necessary to achieve such good results.[8]

Commodore Maloney, in a congratulatory letter from FOCNS to OCNBAD for onward conveyance to the Diving Section, remarked how 'Efforts of this nature are to be admired and encouraged and can only improve the morale and self-confidence of the Service as a whole'.[9] It seemed both COs were concerned about the morale of the service, never mind that of the Diving Section. So any mystery attached to training Naval Service divers had been put to bed. Where possible, any shortcomings in instruction, equipment, facilities or staff as identified in the course critique and debrief of the students would be attended to prior to the next course.

The second naval ship's divers course, 1983

A letter of proposal to conduct the second ship's divers course was submitted to Command for approval:

> Sir,
> It is proposed to hold the a/m course at Naval Base, Haulbowline between the 9th May and the 20th June '83. The maximum number of students is six (6). It is proposed that two of the students should be Officers, possibly engineering officers.[10]

For the first time it appeared that there would be officers on the course, and should these officers be successful they would become the first navy-trained ship's diving officers. Time would tell. The syllabus of training for the course also began to show changes from the first course. There was the introduction to different types of seabed searches and the techniques used, plus a minimum requirement of two dives to 35 metres with chamber operation, and a chamber dive to 55 metres. All this meant that the course content was beginning to grow, which would add greatly to the skills that each diver would develop.

Prior to the course commencing, over forty diving aptitudes had been conducted, with six students selected. With their diving medicals completed, the course commenced on 11 May with six students, five of whom successfully completed the course, one of them an engineering officer. The successful students were Ensign Mick Boyle (engineer), L/Sea John McCarthy, A/Sea Owen Murphy, A/Mech Jim Bartley and O/Sea Paul McDonnell. The course also saw for the first time the logistics involved in placing a recompression chamber on board a naval

vessel. The LÉ *Aisling* was the ship tasked with providing support for the deep-diving phase of the course. It would prove more than capable of carrying the chamber and it ancillary equipment. Over thirty years later, when asked for his thoughts or comments about his course, former navy diver John McCarthy had this to say:

Second naval ship's divers course, 1983 (l–r): A/B Owen Murphy, A/B Jimmy Bartley, A/B John McCarthy, A/B Paul McDonnell, S/Lt Mick Boyle

> I will say that the course has remained with me all my life as a resource that I can call on when I need it as it gave me an inner strength to overcome many physical challenges over the years. I've completed road races, cycle tours, etc., which I shouldn't have completed as I didn't train enough for them, but all the time I knew deep down that if I persevered I'd do it – this I attribute in no small way to completing the diving course.[11]

In an interview with Chief Petty Officer Jim Bartley, Jim recalled his thoughts on why he became a diver, his aptitude test and the course:

… so I was kind of a water baby, anyway, and of course my father was a diver in the army and he had dived with ye [navy divers] a few times over the years, and so when I saw that then I took an interest … and they said 'Well, look do you want to try a dip and see what you think?', so I said 'Absolutely' … they brought me into the police camber – just 'in you go', straight down, and myself and Decky fluted around the bottom of the camber for about ten or fifteen minutes, then back out – 'Yeah, you're grand and thank you very much' – that sort of thing … and that was my first time ever putting diving gear on, and that was my aptitude.[12]

Regarding the diving course, Jimmy recalls:

Obviously the instructors were yourself and George … we spent a lot of time surface swimming, mud runs over in Ringaskiddy, jumping off the fecking bridge and jumping off the sides of ships … we got a lot of our endurance cleaning the underneath of the *Setanta*, cleaning the barnacles and sea squirts from the hull with triangular scrapers, and wire brushing to death the propeller blades.[13]

The post-course report, as addressed to the flag officer, stated:

The course was considered to be a complete success. The students achieved an average of 1,700 mins diving time. The Deep Diving section in particular was most successful. The LÉ *Aisling* proved to be suitable to carry an RCC and ancillary equipment without modification. The ships' officers and crew were most helpful.

It has now become established that the NS can run its own basic diving course. It is therefore requested that the attached syllabus be incorporated into the T.I.16. It is also requested that some form of Certificate … be produced.[14]

The course was also a summer course – it would be the last such summer course. The consequences of running a course in the summer were that night dives started and ended very late, and the weather was invariably better than in the winter.

The first Army Ranger Wing (ARW) diving course

In 1983 it was determined by the ARW Command that it required a capability that would enable it to operate in a maritime environment both on the surface and sub-surface. The ARW turned to the Naval Service, and after a series of phone calls, meetings and discussions, an agreement was reached that the Naval Service, and in particular the Naval Service Diving Section, would provide for ARW needs and requirements in diving instruction. There was little delay after the formal agreement had been reached before the ARW personnel arrived in Haulbowline to commence the first ARW compressed-air divers course, later to be changed to the more appropriate title of combat-divers course. But that was in the future – for the moment the ARW had to get to grips with the basics. The diving course was preceded by the students coming down to the naval base to be given instruction in basic seamanship. The Ranger personnel were soldiers from diverse units – primarily from the Army – and no doubt the maritime environment and seamanship were alien to them. So to offset this void in their military education, all the students underwent a week's training in seamanship, knot ties and splices (especially knots),

First ARW combat divers course, 1983: 'Danger – men at work'

boat handling and naval terminology. Once concluded, the way was clear for them to commence their diver training. Gerry O'Donoghue, the base MCDO and course officer at that time, commented about the lead-in to the course:

> I will certainly train them as attack swimmers as in air swimmers, and that's when we got involved in that, and that worked out pretty well … now we had a great relationship with them – I know for a fact that you did. They were very pleased with our level of commitment, and you know damn well the Rangers love working with the navy, 'cos we fucking turn up. We do what's required and we stay till the job is finished.[15]

An NCO (long since retired) who was a student on the course commented:

> There was a couple of ways of doing things, getting the guys over to the UK, or work with the Naval Service. The Naval Service were in any event RN-trained and qualified, and the second thing was there was some degree of, if they didn't have the particular level of expertise or if there was finishing off to be required, then we would look for that with the Royal Navy.[16]

On Monday 20 June 1983 the seven students commenced their diving training. The selection of the particular students to undergo the course was, to say the least, unscientific, but given the times it couldn't have been otherwise:

> … no training done whatsoever, but it was decided the people were selected on the basis of their ongoing usefulness [to the unit on their return] – essentially they all could swim, reasonably comfortable in the water, I suppose. Some of the guys had particular expertise in certain areas. Some had tactical knowledge; communications training, explosives experts and a couple of guys had endurance.[17]

The course they were undertaking was based closely on that of the ship's divers course but with more emphasis on underwater compass swimming. The objectives of the course weren't too dissimilar to that of the naval course. The primary objective was to train the students to dive safely using compressed air, and to have a firm understanding of the rules, regulations, theory and physiology that governs air diving. The remaining objectives were then how best to use this newly acquired skill of diving to further enhance the ARW requirements. Given that they were using single sets, endurance was crucial. Time in the water was of importance – every minute spent in the water was time well spent:

> But as it turned out, our analysis of the ideal guy didn't work out in practice … we hadn't realised the physics of the thing, the physiological problems caused by stress or people who couldn't control stress were such that they would end up being operationally ineffective.[18]

A senior student on that course also commented about what he considered the essence of the course was for him, and how the course was such that other than the actual physical and technical aspects of diving, it also taught a diver a lot about himself. The course was not for everyone:

> … look, it was a daunting prospect being underwater like that … I wouldn't fault anyone for it [being sent off the course for safety reasons]. It's back to the old story. The whole thing about going to the Wing [ARW], it suits certain personalities, it's not necessarily about guys being good soldiers or bad soldiers, it's about being a particular type of soldier, and the same with diving. You have to have a particular attitude and mindset for it … it's make it the first time around as we don't have time to deal with you … It taught you competency with the kit, but more importantly it taught you about diving within your limits. So as opposed to the civvy side, where they are quite happy to buddy breathe and all that sort of stuff, ours was all geared around diving within your limits, to look after yourself. And sure look, you couldn't see what you were doing in any case, the vis was just crap. It was all touchy-feely stuff. I mean the whole idea about hand signals was all very well but when you couldn't see your hand in the first place …[19]

They needed to become familiar with their kit and with each other. They needed to work quietly and at night. They needed to know ships, ships' hulls and ship fittings. They needed to be able to navigate underwater and to operate in pairs and as a dive team. As soldiers, they had an awful lot to learn:

> The course was an absolute essential, but to me it indicated the huge gap,

the huge expertise we had to develop from there … it really reinforced to me the gap in expertise. We thought that _____, being a top-level instructor in the 'Scooby Doo' [civilian] diving world, would compare reasonably well with the Naval Service diving. In fact he didn't … quite apart from anything else … just on the technical side alone … George Jefferies, his technical knowledge was so far ahead it really showed to me that it was a complicated process when you're dealing with people's lives. When you're doing the job, you need to underscore and apply those skills and logistics much more rigidly than the civilian guys do … it really was a big deal … it was very important that we learnt from that basically the knowledge of our own inadequacies. So we didn't try and get involved in something beyond our capacities … we could lose somebody as a consequence.[20]

Another student on that course recalled his first dive in the police camber in the naval base:

> Down we went for forty-five minutes, lifelines around our waists, and we were attended from the surface … no sort of pool work or anything like that, it was straight into the camber … but it was the making of us as well. We were on our hands and bleeding knees there going around and bumping into each other with thumbs up, couldn't see a fecking thing, all the shit had been disturbed … funny in a nightmarish sort of way.[21]

He also described what it meant both to himself and to the rest of his course to have completed the first diving course, which must have been very demanding for them all:

> When we got back to the Wing [ARW] we thought that it was as hard as our own selection course [the initial entry selection course for would-be personnel into the ARW]. That if you got through it then you earned your diving badge. Like it wasn't fucking handed to you, you had to fucking earn it. You sweated fucking blood and tears for that badge … it was doing selection again except in water.[22]
>
> …
>
> … Like if you remember, you guys were the main men down in the Naval Service … you guys were the hardy fuckin' hoors … like I have to say

that the guys were the hardest in the Naval Service, like well respected and all that … yeah, it was fucking great, that's why we enjoyed it so much … yeah, fucking hardy hoors alright.[23]

The course was completed on 8 July 1983, with six students qualifying as combat divers. Like all first courses, a lot of things were good, some things needed to be refined; the second course would be an improvement, that was assured. However, like the ship's divers course before it, there would be no more summer courses. Training needed to be conducted in harsher weather conditions, where the challenges would be greater, and the night diving earlier. There have been many courses completed since that date, both for Ranger divers and diving supervisors, and their training continues:

> To sum up, I remember having a chat after we got back from the diving course – we were doing a debrief on lessons learned – and we were overwhelmed with the capacity … of you guys in the navy, the expertise you had.[24]

The use of the Naval Service Diving Section as a training establishment for ARW divers continues to this day.

The third naval ship's divers course 1985

The next course, in 1985, saw an increase in duration. This course would be run over an eight-week period as the divers were engaged in an expedition to a freshwater lake – Lough Cummeennapeasta – in the Magillacuddy Reeks, and the divers were to be involved in a TV show – welcome distractions no doubt for the students. The application for permission to run the course was made through the CO Base to FOCNS on 18 January 1985. The course commenced on 4 February, by which time the selection process had been completed. From a total of sixty applicants, ten students were selected to undergo training:

> A total of sixty personnel were given aptitude tests prior to the course. Fifteen candidates attained a sufficient standard to be considered suitable for the course. Ten students started the course; this included one ARW NCO, who was to be trained as a compressed-air diving supervisor.[25]

Para 3 (a) of the same letter from which the above is quoted went on to state that there were new elements in the course syllabus, including the introduction of commercial deep-diving equipment – a Kirby Morgan BandMask Mk 10 – and the aforementioned altitude diving. The section ran into the same difficulties experienced previously with the moving of the RCC from the store through the drill shed and all that it entailed. This time the ship tasked with the deep-diving responsibility was the LÉ *Deirdre*. Deep-diving operations were conducted off the Old Head of Kinsale, County Cork. John Leech was a student on that course:

> I started diving when I was a young fella; sport diving in Athlone sub-aqua club. Derry McMahon [brother of Chris McMahon] was the man who taught me how to dive as a young fella.[26]

John also was able to offer a particularly unique student insight into the naval diving course and how it was instructed and ran. He was a week short of completing his initial diving course in the UK with the

RN while a cadet when he unfortunately got an ear infection and was 'ever so politely asked to leave the course'.[27] John continued:

> The obvious difference was of course we didn't have the resources and we didn't have the equipment … we started our diving course in the old rubber drysuits and they were in utter shite at that stage … they were brutal, I mean if it happened today … but then about a week and a half into the course we actually changed over to the wetsuits … Gerry Duffs was the instructor and Jim Bartley, they were genuinely – you know the way you want to put your students under pressure and all that – I think they realised that hang on, this is getting pretty serious. What was happening was, we had guys getting into the water in the Basin, and as soon as they were hitting the water they were getting wet (inside their suits) … trying to do endurance stuff was never going to happen, we were freezing … And facilities, I mean going to HMS *Vernon* in those days,

Onboard LÉ Deirdre, third ship's divers course: getting ready for a ship's bottom search with a 'half-necklace'. (l–r): Bob Frazier, Alan Kenna, Jim Bartley (surface swimmer), John McGrath

the best of equipment, we had very high ratio of instructors to students, up to Horsea, you did your mud runs, you did your jumping …

The quality of our instructors was equally as good as the RN, I mean genuinely we just didn't have the equipment, didn't have the gear … but in fairness to the lads here, it was all carefully monitored, it never felt danger-ous, but it was very, very unpleasant because the gear was just ridiculous. I mean, the exploding suit inflation/ABLJ bottle just exposed the deficiencies we had in the section at the time. I mean, there was no investment for years; they weren't taking diving seriously for years in the navy. But it's fantastic to see it now [2014] – I mean, it is great to think that all the shit that we all went through, you included, all of us went through, has developed the section to where it is now … But it was a tough course, a very tough course, yeah. It was tougher than the RN course; the toughest part of the RN course was getting the fucking earache![28]

The post-diving report noted:

The course was completed on the 29 March, 1985. The individual aggregate diving time of each student exceeded 2,000 mins. This is far in excess of the diving time attained on RN Ships Diver Courses. Five students successfully completed the course and the ARW NCO qualified as a supervisor (annex c). The 3rd Ships Diver Course covered a broad spectrum of diving skills which ensured that all students obtained a sound basic knowledge of service diving and the high level of professionalism which it entails.[29]

The successful students were S/Lt John Leech, PO/ERA Bob Frazier, A/Sea Alan Kenna, O/Sea Tony Moore and L/Sea John McGrath (who later that year would be awarded the Defence Forces Distinguished Service Medal for his part in the Air India operation). There had been a steady climb in the total minutes that each student was getting as each course was being completed: it started out at 1,300 minutes for the first course and reached 2,000 minutes on the completion of the third, and it wouldn't be stopping there either.

The first (and only) naval search-and-rescue (SAR) course

> It was an experiment that was brilliant on paper and in practical terms it was the worst thing ever having the Air Corps coming down to the navy because the Air Corps didn't want to go to the navy – if they had wanted to they would have been sailors. They came out and they didn't want us anywhere near their helicopters, they didn't want anything to do with us – they told us that before we went on the search-and-rescue course. [30]

In 1985 the LÉ *Eithne* had been in service for a year and still some of the crew were attending specialist courses in the UK and elsewhere to build up sufficient knowledge and expertise to effectively operate a ship with a helicopter capability. It must be remembered that at the start of the 1970s the Naval Service didn't have a serviceable ship, and when it acquired second-hand ships, it had to change over from steam

SAR diver being deployed

(l–r): Mark, Damo, Ron ∴ Ciaran left early! Enroute to drop zone ... again

to diesel. Now, fourteen years later, not only had the Naval Service built another three patrol vessels of its own in Verolme dockyard but it now had a new state-of-the-art purpose-built Irish-navy-designed ship with a heli-deck and helicopter, and which had already sailed to the US and back.

The Air Corps was in the throes of deploying its new Dauphin SA365F helicopter to the LÉ *Eithne* for flight trials and ultimately for deployment for patrol duty on board. Having SAR divers was considered part of the entire package. So four of the ship's crew already qualified as ship's divers were detailed to commence SAR training at RNAS *Culdrose*: S/Lt Mark Mellett, Ens. Ron Long, L/Sea Ciaran Monks and A/Sea Damien Power. Their month-long course ran from 16 September to 18 October 1985:

> The first day we arrived there they brought us down to the swimming pool in the naval base there, air station, and then we did familiarisation drills with the BASAR [breathing-apparatus SAR] sets … they had a dry dock there [Falmouth] and it was flooded and they had aircraft steps, and they would raise them up to a certain height. We'd have to run around and run up the steps and jump off the platform.[31]

Damien went on to describe the diving and jumping from the helicopters:

> When we finished the jump training in Falmouth, then we moved onto a place called Portkerries. And that is where we did the helicopter jumps from … you might have to do tasks, they'd pick you up and you jumped, and they'd pick you back up again … the whole idea of it was they have to get you there safely, you have to hit the water safely, do what you have to do, and they'll come back …
>
> Then we went to Portsmouth, and there we did the Dunker training as well, up a big tower … we had to swim right down to the bottom and then you had to take off your set and then you had to free ascent, you had to do that first … we did the dunker then we did the helicopter crashes.[32]

The work involved by all elements to maintain a flight-operations capability was enormous for both the Air Corps and the Naval Service, and what Damien Power said at the start of this section was probably very true – *a*nyone who was there and was part of the whole Navy–Air Corps flying endeavour would concur. It

Diver away ... good jump

*First (and only) SAR course, 1985 (l–r): Ron Long, RN chief instructor,
Ciaran Monks (front), Damian Power (centre), Mark Mellett (rear),
unknown RN diver at right*

wasn't by any means a disaster, as the Air Corps and the Naval Service learned valuable lessons and experience. It was experience that you just couldn't buy. In fact in many different ways it was very beneficial to everyone. Helicopter operations from a moving platform – in this case a naval vessel – are very complex and at every stage fraught with danger. There is no room for error – a simple lapse of concentration or mistake on anyone's part – from the pilot to the flight-deck officer, the lashing numbers, the fuelling numbers – could spell disaster. History is littered with the horror stories.

When involved with these flight-deck operations while serving on board the LÉ *Eithne* in late 1986, the most impressive things about the operations were the noise levels, the vibrations and the smell of the aviation fuel. If something had to be done on deck after the helo had started its engines, everything had to be done by hand signals, with everybody focused on flight safety. But the workload on the ship and the ship's company was immense. There was no doubting it, but it stretched the crew, especially in terms of manpower: personnel were double and treble-jobbing. During flight operations the workload was huge, and if things were tight during the day, they ramped up even more during night operations. Like diving operations, during the day no problem, but turn off the lights and go into night operations and a different world happens. When all was said and done, ultimately it boiled down to this: they were the Air Corps, and they operated to an Air Corps agenda, and we were the navy and we had ours. The difference between our helicopter operations in the 1980s and the Royal Navy's was even simpler, as Damien pointed out:

> … as I said, none of them ever joined the navy, they weren't interested. They were up in Baldonnel doing whatever they do in Baldonnel, and go home in the evening, that's what they were interested in … I could see the difference between over here and over there, 'cos it was all navy over there. The pilots were navy pilots, the aircrew were all navy, a lot of them were divers … and they were used to having divers jumping in and out of helicopters, there was no big deal to them.[33]

R/Adm. Mark Mellett, a fellow course member of Damien's, had this to say:

> That course really was a great course, we came back with great skills expecting that we'd have a role with the Air Corps but they never really got

involved … likewise they never had the stomach for a naval diver in the helicopter. I think at the time there were only a few navies that used divers for deployment from helicopters – certainly the Royal Navy and I think the Americans were for a while – but for most others their winchman or winch operator did it. But with the RN it was the time factor: you could fly to a scene, deploy the diver, he'd hit the water and using his speed of entry to get down to depth.[34]

The SAR divers course conducted in 1985 was the first and last of its kind undertaken by the Naval Service.

The first MCDO, 1979: Gerry O'Donoghue (GOD)

Sub Lieutenant Gerry O'Donoghue departed Irish shores for HMS *Vernon* in the UK in October 1978 to commence the international long minewarfare clearance diving officers course, or, to shorten the title to a manageable level, an MCDO course. This course was critical in the evolution of the Naval Service Diving

Section as it would lead directly to the next step, which was to train our own divers. But first the sub lieutenant was going to have to undergo the course, to survive it and to qualify as an MCDO. If there was any knowledge at that time about the MCDO course as instructed by the RN, it was a well-kept secret. But undaunted, the sub lieutenant prepared himself as best he could and ploughed on:

After my ship's diving course, which in itself was a casual 'leave activity' provided by the Royal Navy to prevent cadets wasting their four weeks annual holiday, I had always expressed an interest in becoming a specialised minewarfare and clearance diving officer. I had even my RN course officer recommend me for one. Around that time, someone – I presume Joe Deasy, Frank Lynch or Danny O'Neill – must have been putting in for this course in the annual training estimates. Naturally, every year it was deleted. This was an expensive course and as the Naval Service took up a huge portion of the Defence Forces overseas-training budget, it was an easy target.

As a newly minted sub lieutenant I was not the chosen candidate for this course. I'm pretty sure that Frank Lynch was. As luck would have it, Frank was getting more senior and was not available and I was pulled out of the proverbial hat. What little I knew about the actual LMCDO course included the fact that I was not fit enough and did not have enough diving minutes to complete it successfully. I did manage to get a few dives in and a few mud runs but these only confirmed my suspicions. Of the eight students on the course I had the least amount of diving minutes. All my fellow students were the top diving officers from their respective navies. This was an error I made sure we did not repeat when we sent a candidate on subsequent courses.

The first two weeks of endurance diving were not fun and I was lucky to survive being cut. After surviving those weeks and the Horsea Lake 'live-in week', the rest of the course was a breeze. How else would a group who did their deep diving in Scotland in January actually volunteer to go back for two extra weeks in February. Naturally, I passed out as top student but this is the minimum-expected standard and seldom commented on in the Diving Unit.[35]

So Gerry not only started the course, but he survived to tell the tale and qualified as an MCDO. Gerry's legacy to the Naval Service Command and to the Diving Section – other than the commencement of diver training and the procuring of the naval RCC – was that he would put order into the chaos that was naval diving at the time.

The second MCDO, 1986: Chris Reynolds

In 1985 S/Lt Chris Reynolds journeyed to HMS *Vernon* to commence his MCDO course. The course ran from October 1985 to March 1986. When in 1978–79 S/Lt Gerry O'Donoghue MCDO had been trained, that officer had only shortly before completed his ship's diving-officer course as a cadet, ensuring that he had little or no diving experience. However, this time it would be very different. S/Lt Reynolds was joining the course with a good amount of dive time and operational experience, along with his natural academic flair. The sub lieutenant was a high achiever, particularly academically, and was a highly competent and strong-willed diver. He was ideally suited for the MCDO course. He was also

lucky in that the diving officer in the base at the time, Gerry O'Donoghue, was conscious of the shortfalls in the sub lieutenant's experience (probably because they reflected his own when he was tasked with undergoing the same course), and where possible addressed them:

It is also requested that due to the large cost involved a minimum of two months should be given to allow the student to be worked up, medically examined, etc., prior to the start of the course. This should take the form of a structured pre-course and be attended by the student and a substitute student. Then in the event of an injury in the early stages of the course it may be possible to substitute the student with his replacement.[36]

Gerry also knew how to hedge his bets. A couple of letters later from the OCNBAD, Capt. Brett, ended up with the flag officer directing that the sub lieutenant be rotated back ashore to avail of the training:

Because the course is a strenuous one, S/Lt Reynolds should be rotated from a sea-going to a shore appointment as early as possible so that he may complete various medical examinations, undertake more diving training and generally get as fit as possible before the course.[37]

So S/Lt Reynolds was eventually taken ashore, and over the next several weeks proceeded to sharpen up his diving skills and maths prior to leaving for the course. On 7 October 1985 Chris commenced training on his MCDO course, and over the next six months would meet many new challenges in his training. On his return he submitted a very detailed post-course report, which included the following:

> Course report Chris Reynolds … ILMCDO …30 April 86.
> … Course Officer – Lt S.N.C. Fields RN
> Course Officer – Lt R. Jermigan USN
> Course Chief – CPO (D) R. Ramsey
> … The original course should have consisted of seven officers. However one Kenyan and one Singaporean officer failed to report. During week [2], two Iraqi officers left the course, leaving it with three students …[38]

The course was based in several locations around the UK depending on the various elements of the course. It operated out of HMS *Vernon*, Portland, HMS *Cochrane* in Rosyth, Scotland, then Oban in Scotland, back to HMS *Vernon*, over to Chattenden Barracks in Kent, and, finally, back to HMS *Vernon*. The course was quite intensive, as was to be expected, and consisted of five modules: minewarfare, basic diving (introduction and operating oxygen re-breathers, etc.), tool training (cutting, welding and underwater engineering), deep diving, and finally explosive odnance disposal (EOD) work. S/Lt Chris Reynold's report also comments on two aspects of the training: firstly, he notes in relation to the re-breather dive training in Horsea:

> this period culminates in 'Live In Week' where the students live at the dive site, deprived of sleep and continually dived or put under stress, day and night. This tests the students' stamina and allows the Instructors see how the course reacts under arduous conditions.[39]

In relation to his deep-diving phase, he recalled an incident:

> It was during deep diving that the only serious diving incident occurred. Whilst 'Buddy diving' with a qualified diver on mixture gas, he suffered a serious case of nitrogen narcosis, at a depth of 54mtrs. The diver conducted an immediate uncontrolled emergency ascent, which endangered the lives of both divers.[40]

S/Lt Reynolds successfully completed his MCDO course on 22 March 1986, and in the process of graduating also topped the course with an overall cumulative grade of 91.3 per cent. Not only was it the highest score for the course, it also turned out to be the highest graded average of all the international courses run that year by the RN diving school, thus S/Lt Chris Reynolds' Irish Naval Service was awarded the international LMCDO trophy for that year, 1986.

On his return, the newly qualified MCDO, like his predecessor Gerry O'Donoghue, would make a serious impact on issues such as the procurement of equipment, the improvement of facilities and, of great importance to all the divers, diving allowance and subsistence monies, for as Gerry O'Donoghue said,

> My thing always was the MCDO's job was to get equipment – that was his only fucking function; he was to get the hardware into the store 'cos without it we are muppets.[41]

The third MCDO, 1995: Edward Mulligan

In 1995 the young sub lieutenant, Eddie Mulligan, made his way to the UK to undergo his MCDO course. S/Lt Mulligan would be the first home-trained Naval Service ship's diving officer to go over to England, and when interviewed he was very much of the mind that his training as received back in the naval base was as good if not better than that provided by the Royal Navy, particularly at ship's-diver level. S/Lt Mulligan was also somewhat unique in that he initially joined up on enlistment, in September 1987:

We were class 'Alpha' with instructors Lt Stevie Walsh, CPO Hayes, PO Mossy Bevan, PO Chris McMahon [diver] and L/Sea Paddy O'Connor. Paul McCarthy [later to become a chief diver] was also in my class and we were top and bottom bunks.[42]

On passing out of recruits he commenced his branch training as an ordinary seaman. He served at sea aboard the LÉ *Eithne* from March to October 1988. During that time Eddie had applied for the Naval Service cadet-ship competition, and was successful:

I applied for a cadetship whilst on LÉ *Eithne* with OC Cdr McNamara
… I started in the Curragh as a cadet in October/November 1988 and was
commissioned on 19 July 1990, winning the Fastnet Trophy for best cadet.[43]

In 1993 the then sub lieutenant applied for the tenth ship's divers course. He
underwent his diving aptitude test and, having passed, was selected to commence
his Naval Service ship's divers course in January 1993:

> I completed my ship's diver officer course between January and March 1993.
> The instructors were Chris Reynolds, Martin Carroll, you Martin, Spud
> Murphy, Fergie Cunningham.[44]

By the end of March 1993 he had successfully completed the tenth ship's divers
course, along with three other students: L/Shipwright Kevin Fergusson, L/ERA
Paddy O'Donnell and PO/EA Pat McDonagh. Eddie described his ship's divers
and MCDO courses in interview:

> *Why did you become a navy diver?*
> I always saw the naval diving unit as probably the most efficient organisa-
> tion within the Defence Force … insofar as they were working early, they
> were working late, very professional and I felt they were the elite of the
> Naval Service, and if I was to stay in the NS then the naval diving unit was
> where I wanted to be.
> *So you weren't disappointed as a ship's diver. Did you enjoy the course?*
> It was everything I expected and thought it would be. It was a tough
> military diving course with very, very professional levels of safety, very high
> levels of instruction and, as I said earlier, it was really what you'd expect
> from the elitist type organisation within the Naval Service'.
> *And then you went over and did your MCDO course?*
> In 1995 I did the MCDO course and again it was a nine-month course
> – May to December. With the navy [NS] I did my own course – I like
> to think I did quite well on my own ship's divers course. I enjoyed it, did
> very well … I suppose I was in the right place at the right time and had
> the right aptitude. When you go over there you feel a lot of pressure on
> you, OK, because it is a tough course and you're on a course where there's
> a fifty-per-cent failure rate … on our course there was ten students, five

Royal Navy and five rest of the world and at the end of the day there was five of us who passed out, which went in tandem to their pass rate, which was fifty per cent.

The clearance diving officers course – definitely I saw on our own SDO course the impact that the training, the previous English [RN] training had on the instructors. You know our course [ship's divers course] had a very good syllabus – I mean, when I came back and re-did the syllabus of training, I don't think there was a whole lot of amendments.

How did we compare with the Royal Navy, and on your return what amendments or changes did you identify as being in need of attention?

Yeah, compared with the Royal Navy we were right up there. One was fitness – OK, I felt where we ruled out on fitness grounds [was with]the over-forty-year-olds. I saw what Dr O'Brien did at the medical, I just felt we had to get around that and come up with a fitness scheme that would allow people progress and stay diving as long as they wanted. I think that was one of the first things we did … I think we felt our guys were better trained, trained well enough to cope with the nitrogen narcosis to be able to go on SCUBA [self-contained underwater breathing apparatus] to 35 metres, and then with the increased amount of physical training we'd have no problem carrying that. Then we looked at 35 to 50 metres being surface demand … we brought in the equipment, we improved the surface-demand aspect of diving, and not only the regulations but also our own diving-course content and practical usage … I had a good bit of experience before I went on my CDO course. I had a fairly good insight into the types of roles and jobs … the Naval Service Diving Section did.[45]

The fourth MCDO, 1999: Darragh Kirwan

The successor to Eddie Mulligan, in August 1999, was S/Lt Darragh Kirwan from Dublin. Darragh began his naval career as a cadet in 1993, his class officer being S/Lt Brian Fitzgerald. Brian himself was a diving officer and his diving badge would have an impact on the young cadet:

I joined in 1993 and my class officer was Brian Fitzgerald, who was himself a diver and obviously I would have been affected by the badge he was wearing. So it was always in the back of my mind to give it a crack. The

more I spent in the navy the more I recognised that it was the course to do if you wanted to do something more physical and mental and trust yourself. Like the ARW, they have their own course [Ranger selection course], and we have, from purely a naval perspective, the diving course ... I passed the aptitude and went off and did it ... January to March 1998. I think it was the eleven-week course, the first three weeks being PT and the next eight weeks diving. The chief instructor was you Martin, with Davy Byrne and Owen Murphy. Eddie Mull was the diving officer at the time. Yeah, it was a good course – seven of us came off that course, people like Paddy Blaa [Paddy Delaney], Trevor Murphy, Joey Manning, Gordy Cummins, Joey Morrison and Johnny McGroarty. I think that was the seven that finished the course.[46]

Ice diving familiarisation and training course, several hundred miles north of the naval base. Gordy Cummins awaiting his turn.

Less than seventeen months later, S/Lt Kirwan would find himself in the UK at the Defence Diving School commencing his clearance diving officers course, starting in August 1999 and finishing in March 2000. I asked Darragh – now a lieutenant commander (2014), some questions about his diving career and operations he was on:

How then did you find the CDO course? Did the Naval Diving course stand you in good stead and prepare you for it?

Completely. I would always contend that our standard of instruction, the type of course, the pace of the course and the intensity is equal to that anyone else could give – certainly the RN ... but certainly from my point of view I would have said that it was a carbon-copy course as the intensity, the pace of the course, the professionalism of the instructors were exactly the same. What we didn't have, we didn't have the resources or the infrastructure to run it on the level of what a CDO course would be. First of all we didn't have the equipment for a CDO course, but certainly it had a CDO feel and ethos about it, is what I found. There was nothing new that I got on that course than what I would have gotten the previous year on our own course ...[47]

But and there's always a 'but'.

Where I would have benefitted hugely from the RN course was the supervising side of it. Where you actually got the deep dives in and supervised the deep diving on a constant basis over weeks ... supervising is all about experience, and like diving it's a perishable skill![48]

The fifth MCDO, 2005: Anthony O'Regan

The next clearance diving officer to enter the ranks was a young sub lieutenant, Anthony O'Regan, from Ballybeg in Waterford city, in 2004. Like the rest of the CDOs before him, the first thing he would need to do was the diving course. Tony enlisted in the Naval Service in April 1994, and along with another twenty-nine recruits would make up recruit class Alpha. On completion of his recruit training, Tony headed to sea as a young ordinary seaman abord the LÉ *Orla*. When interviewing Tony, I asked him a few questions in relation to his decision to become a naval diver, his role as a naval diving officer and his passage to where he is today.

Why did you become a diver, Tony?

I suppose it was one of those briefs you got as a recruit. I joined in 1994 … so I thought if there was anything I would like to do, it would be a navy diver. They were held in high regard by everybody, and it seemed to be the toughest course at the time. So of course being stubborn I had it in the back of my mind. We were given a brief by the warrant officer, the 'Ranger' [WO John Murphy], so like I said, I had it in the back of my mind, but first I had to go to sea.[49]

Who were the instructors?

I was a student on the fifteenth ship's divers course in 1998. The instructors were, you, Nuggy [Noel Dunne] – it was his first course as an instructor – and Spud [Owen Murphy] … Eddie Mulligan was the course officer.

There were sixteen of us started the course and three finished: myself, John O'Regan and Dave O'Brien. You used to call the three of us the O'Regan sisters. I remember Nuggy gave me a lesson in buoyancy that I remember very fondly even to this day – he gave me the brick. I was a bit light in the water so he picked up this big brick and gave it to me to get me off the surface. He told me not to lose it and that I had better come

up with it. I carried it around with me for the next three fucking months. Everywhere I went I had to have this fucking rock with me – toilet, bed, shower, everywhere. When I had thought that you guys had forgotten about the rock, one of yas would want to know where it was. I even took the fucking thing to Bere Island with me. So on completion of the course I went back to sea then and finished my time, back on *Ciara*, and left the fucking rock in the store.[50]

In 1999 Tony's career took an interesting turn for the better. The Naval Service ran what was called a commissioning-from-the-ranks course (CFR course). This course was designed to bring forward enlisted personnel with the required educational and service qualifications, and through a selection process the successful candidates would be trained as Executive Branch officers while maintaining their current enlisted rank while under training. On successful completion of the course, the students would be signed off and re-engaged as commissioned officers with the rank of sub lieutenant. Such a course had never been run before and, indeed, none has been run since. However, such was the proposal that Tony now faced. Should he attempt to go for the CFR course or should he be drafted into the Diving Section and continue with his career as enlisted personnel. Tony applied for the CFR course and was chosen as one of the eight students to commence the training. The course was eighteen months of intensive schooling in navigation, seamanship, ship handling and watchkeeping, and having successfully completed the course Tony was commissioned in 2001:

> Yeah, so I did the CFR course, and believe it or not there were four divers on that course: myself, Damo McCormack, Adrian Hickey and Nigel McCormack. Yeah, that was nearly two years of retraining and in between that time we spent another six months at sea … CFR course was 2001–02 … I came off the *Ciara* as an able seaman and went back there as the navigation/gunnery officer … and during that time I was told to train for my CDOs course in the UK.[51]

The course took place over an extended period of approximately two years due to a series of recurring problems the Royal Navy was having with its clearance-diving sets. It took a while for the problems to be resolved but eventually Tony completed all the necessary modules of the course.

Then you did your CDOs course, Tony. How did you find that?

Between 2004 and 2006 I had to go back to the UK as they were having problems with their CDBA [clearance-diver's breathing apparatus]. So I did the deep-air phase in 2004, but then I had to go back … to do the explosives, then the underwater EOD – all that kinda stuff was done then. So during that time I spent my time in the Diving Section as I suppose the OIC diving … we then did the mixture phase in Horsea Island, and then we went up to the Kyles of Loch Ailshe for the deep-diving phase. It's up by the Isle of Skye, yeah, so we did our deep diving in the lochs of Scotland. But it was all scenario-based, like – it's typical of the Brits, it was all stopwatch management … I think you were allowed two fails on your scenario-based tests and then you were gone, you were RTU'd [returned to unit], gone … I was very nervous about going over initially at the air phase even … [but] we never gave ourselves enough credit – what we were after being taught, what I was after learning through experience and our own diving courses … I'll tell you what I learnt – that I was miles ahead of them on air [endurance], miles ahead of them on searches, laying search schemes, boat handling, even supervisor skills, conduct of diving ops. We never gave ourselves enough credit … I personally think we've taken the Irish Naval Service Diving Section to the pinnacle of air diving, we can go no further on air diving.

What about our diving course today, Tony, and our training?

Take the last course: I was the diving officer and by default course officer. They are all finishing the course now with a scuba-diving qualification from the International Diving Schools' Association, as a commercial scuba diver, as well as recognition from the HSA [Health and Safety Authority] in Ireland and the HSE [Health and Safety Executive] in the UK. So it's a big step forward, and then the surface supply is also recognised now and that's 30 metres inshore. All that we are missing now is the wet bell … the last course [twenty-eighth diving course, March 2014] was the first course in the history of the Diving Section to break 5,000 minutes for each student on the diving course … it's not that we pushed them any harder but we structured it far better, and the twenty-eighth was ran the exact same way as the twenty-seventh was.

This year [2014] we had seventeen students started the diving-course PT phase – seven of those didn't pass the divers' fitness test [a prerequisite for a student before progressing to the diving phase].We started the diving phase with ten students, three were RTU'd on safety issues, one guy didn't even bother his bollix getting in the water, and two guys didn't like it and withdrew, and four finished the course in the end.[52]

The sixth MCDO, 2007: Conor Kirwan

In 2007 the young S/Lt Conor Kirwan made his way over to the UK to undergo his clearance diving officers course. But first, in 2004, S/Lt Conor Kirwan, the younger brother of Lt Cdr Darragh Kirwan CDO, applied to undergo aptitude training for the twentieth naval divers course. Having successfully completed the aptitude test, he commenced the twentieth naval divers course in September, and along with six other students successfully completed the course in December. Subsequent to this he had successfully completed his diving supervisors course in 2006. In 2007 the requirement for another CDO was deemed necessary, and S/Lt Kirwan was nominated as the candidate. In January of 2007 he proceeded to the Defence Diving School in the UK and commenced his course. He successfully completed his course in June, and in September returned to the UK

to commence his explosive ordinance disposal course, which he completed in October 2007.

In interviewing Conor I was interested to hear what his views were on several topics directly concerning the Diving Section, such as its capabilities, its personnel and where it should be going diving-wise.

On completion of your CDO course, what were your priorities upon your return?

I would have been very clear coming back from the CDO course that I had all the qualifications, but that all the experience was within the Diving Store. So you look at the NCOs that were in the unit at the time: Nuggy [Noel Dunne], Paul Mc [Paul McCarthy], Fergy [Frank Cunningham], Paddy [Paddy Delaney],

Gordy [Gordon Cummins]. With these individuals I found myself in the position that I knew from the outset that it would take two to three years if not longer to build up the experience to deliver what I wanted to deliver. It was far easier for me to deliver the qualification and learning that I had to people with the experience than it was for me to wait until I had the experience to deliver what I wanted to. That is why we put in place the first 50-metre surface-supply course … we were being pushed to our operational limits. So therefore I decided that what I wanted to tackle should be the *Rising Sun* [see Operations] scenario come up again that we would be far better able to deal with that situation and that once that was dealt with I could then look at ROVs [remote-operating vehicles] and EOD … that when the navy are involved … that is what we bring to the scenario – technical excellence. Our equipment is maintained to the last and our people are trained to the highest standards. When you marry up perfect maintenance with excellent training and good SOPs [standard operating procedures], you reduce the element of danger to a minimum.[53]

Like all his predecessors the lieutenant worked very hard over the period of time that he was in the Diving Section as officer in charge. Over many months he and his staff worked countless hours in restructuring and revamping the necessary paperwork, course syllabi and equipment in order that the subsequent surface-demand courses would not only meet his own very high standards but, just as important, meet the RN and UK HSE standards and the Irish HSA standards. This process took a couple of years to refine to a point where on subsequent auditing and vetting by the UK HSE office, the Naval Service Diving Section received an accreditation from the UK HSE for its training in surface-supply diving.

What about accreditation and qualifications in respect of air diving?
That was what the surface-supplied course delivered, the by-product of that, and it was never the aim but the by-product of that was [that] if we were now meeting the standards of the UK RN and the HSE in the UK … why not look for the recognition and accreditation, and that is what we went and did … in 2011, I think, on one particular day I signed off on €85,000 worth of qualifications … it was something within the unit that straight away we had established ourselves as a centre of excellence for diving, industrial diving or commercial diving in Ireland.

On the military side of diving where do you see us going?

… [O]n my CDO's course it became very clear to me that we can do it as good if not better than what they do … from a military point of view, military diving is explosives ordnance disposal [EOD]. Navy diving is EOD or clearance diving. Do we have the capability to do the diving in terms of ability with the individuals within the unit to deliver that? Without a shadow of a doubt we have. Our issue is one, money, but we can access money; two is being able to support re-breather diving and what we are talking about there is … maintenance and also we are talking about training.

But the type of training that has been done to date has stood us in good stead over the years!

… [W]e are already experts on scuba and surface supplied, we can become experts in re-breather diving – it isn't an issue. The EOD training, now that's where we might have issues. But again we are dealing with the best people in the navy, who I've no doubt whatsoever would pass the EOD courses. To be an EOD operator underwater, you first need to be an EOD operator on land, which means you get to the army and you get them to deliver EOD training, to the exact same standards of the EOD officers and the EOD NCO's in the army … and once you have that EOD capability, well then you just bring it into the water and with the clearance divers who can deliver that training by taking the EOD skills from the land and making it directly transferable to the requirement in the water.[54]

The Seventh MCDO, 2013: Shane Mulcahy

The latest clearance diving officer (2014) to join that lofty club was S/Lt Shane Mulcahy from Cortland, New York, who had entered the Naval Service as a cadet of the forty-fifth cadet class in September 2005, and was commissioned as an ensign in September 2007. He underwent his deck officer watchkeeping course over the next two years or so, and couldn't apply for the diving course until such time as he had successfully qualified as a naval watchkeeper. As soon as that was achieved, he applied for an aptitude test for the twenty-fifth naval divers course. Commencing the physical fitness phase in December 2010, the course broke for the Christmas period, recommencing with the diving phase on 3 January 2011. Shane, along with four other students, successfully completed his diving course on 24 February 2011. While selected to undergo clearance diving officer training, he would not be heading over to the Royal Navy as he would become the first naval diving officer to be trained in clearance diving by the Royal Canadian Navy. He would also spend twelve months under training with the Canadians, compared to the usual nine months with the Royal Navy.

Why did you apply for the diving course?

I suppose I would have been into the diving before I was into the navy. My first experience diving would have been in 1999 – I would have done a PADI [Professional Association of Diving Instructors] discover scuba course down in Baltimore, west Cork … I would have gotten very into it at that stage as I would have been twelve. By thirteen, with my parents' support, I would have done the PADI open-water courses, the advanced open-water courses – I just became very interested. I kept the civilian diving going right up till I joined the navy in 2005. Obviously then, work took over in regards to naval training.

So how did you find the diving course then?

The three-week fitness course I would have really enjoyed. I would have entered it really quite fit … I would have kept my fitness levels quite high. I know some guys might have struggled with the three weeks, but I found it really quite good. Then the eight weeks – I suppose having done diving as a civilian, there are as many disadvantages as advantages, it's such a different world, naval diving … I really enjoyed the course in terms of physicality, the mental strain of it, yeah … I was certainly challenged.

Did the course live up to your expectations?

Indeed, it absolutely did. Indeed, in a lot of ways I would have said the physical exertion of it would have lived up to my expectations … However, in terms of the level of instruction in classroom training, it well exceeded what I would have expected [compared with] what I would have encountered in civilian training. I wouldn't have expected the level of instruction in diving illnesses and physiology that we really went into.

How did it come about that you were selected for the CDO's course?

Conor (Kirwan) was the OIC of the section when I did my course, and towards the end of the course when you get to the point where I think that I might actually pass this course, I started asking a lot of questions about CDO's and what the career progression was. I remember it was the night we passed our course that Conor came up to me with a very serious face: 'I hear that you're gunning for my job', and I just replied with a very serious face back at him, 'Well, you can't do it forever, so yeah.' From that point he kinda knew where I stood in terms of where I wanted to go. So I would have made it clear from that point I suppose.

Would you give a quick overview of where you spent time training?

Sure, I did my diving phases at the Canadian Forces Base, Esquimalt, which is based on Vancouver Island, British Columbia. Then from there we spent four weeks in a place called Gaugetown in New Brunswick. There we did an element of the explosive work, working on EOD and IEDs [improvised explosive devices], that sort of stuff. Then we spent five weeks in Quebec City on another phase, this one aimed at specifically mine warfare officers. There was lots of academic work there, lectures, theory and a very interesting last week where they run a fully simulated minewarfare exercise over the course of the week, down to the last detail.

How did your naval diving training stand to you?

The physicality of our course stood well for me. The physicality expected from you at the start of the course over there would be very similar to the physicality that you would be expected to have at the end of the course here. So if you went over there ill prepared you would certainly know about it pretty quickly. Now, their course is structured very differently … they would run preliminaries throughout the year, they would have only qualified divers on their prelims. They would have between sixty to eighty applications each year, and they would only accept eight students on their twelve-month course. Their focus would be on a very high level of training, but not necessarily pushing people off the course. It would not be unusual to finish the course with eight students, a different focus in those terms. If you were needed to be gotten rid of then, you would have been gone on the prelim. The two-week-long prelim is very intense, very physically demanding, just a different set up to us … to go over there without a basic supervisory knowledge or experience would lead you to a very steep learning curve.

What recommendations would you make for the course should it come up?

I would look at the possibility of not just sending an officer candidate but possibly sending over two candidates together. An officer and an NCO candidate … from a very basic point of view of having support with you on the course, logistically and also in terms of being able to share the knowledge and having a working relationship in coming home with someone whose had the same training as you in the same system. [55]

The twenty-eighth naval divers course

S/Lt Stephen Stack was one of the students to have successfully completed his training on the twenty-eighth naval divers course, which finished in March 2014.

How and why did you become a navy diver?
I joined up in September 2004 – the forty-fourth cadet class. You'd see people walking around with the diving badge so you'd be asking people what was involved with the diving course. You'd hear that it was an extremely tough course so that automatically would have drawn my interest to it. Just looking at the guys walking around the place, they all seemed to be fairly impressive individuals. So when I was out on the LÉ *Aisling* as a cadet, you were the coxwain and Ron Boyle was the captain, and the two of you were divers … I tried for the course in 2012 but got injured in the PT phase, actually on the second day of it … so when the applications opened up for the 2014 course, I stuck mine in again. I did the aptitude test no problems – I was a few chin-ups and dips short for the fitness test but I was happy enough with that, because I still had a couple of months to build up for that.[56]

Stephen gave a summary of what he experienced in each of the weekly phases that made up the course:

The PT phase was tough but good; we had a particularly big course starting as there were seventeen students. The way I was looking at it was that we were getting paid to train, twice or three times a day. We were like professional athletes here, so we may as well embrace these three weeks and try and enjoy it while we could.

The first week, lifelines and signals. I think by lunch hour on the

Monday we had lost four students. That week once you got into it and learnt the trick of just getting the angle of the lifeline to know where you were and the direction you were going, that sort of thing, once you got more comfortable down there it wasn't too bad. It was very cold down there … it was do-able but very tiring.

The second week, Jackstay diving. I had it built up in my mind that it would be more difficult than what it actually was. Again, the hardest thing about it was the cold, and the constant diving, trying to get the minutes up, and the cold.

The third week, ship's-bottom searches. Yeah, this was good – something completely different, it was something new. In a half-necklace together, as a group, we were doing something. Very daunting being under the water with something above your head – that took a dive or two to get used to, just being under the bottom of a ship. It would have been the most daunting thing about that particular week. Once you did a dive or two and everybody became comfortable with being on a half-necklace, coming to the surface together and all that sort of *craic*, once we got that boxed off, the rest of the week was fairly OK.

The fourth week, compass swimming. The compass attack I thought was one of the more enjoyable phases. It sort of came a bit easier for me – I was used to working with compasses and taking bearings – all that sort of stuff. You could see what you were doing, you could see your progress; you could see where you wanted to get to, and how fast you were doing it.

The fifth and sixth week: Bere Island then for the following two weeks. Very hard to describe Bere Island, it was very, very tiring both physically and

mentally. When you tell people what's involved, it doesn't sound too bad, you know, when you tell them one deep dive in the morning, a couple of shallow dives in the afternoon, then a night dive, it doesn't really sound too bad. But when you're actually down there doing it, hauling gear, do this, do that, get this, get that, up to the camp, down from the camp, it's just the constant non-stop activity, on the go constantly. It doesn't sound too bad, three or four dives a day, have a bit of lunch – your only time off is when you're asleep and even then your half expecting an 'AWKWARD' ... then you're up early for EMAs [early-morning activities] ... it's one of those things, it doesn't sound bad, but it's a lot worse than it sounds ... it was just constant pressure for nearly eighteen hours of the day, every day ... so that was Bere Island.

The seventh and eighth weeks: Then we came back and the next two weeks were introduction to surface-demand diving equipment, its systems and the tools that are in use in the section. It was a complete change of pace ... it was a completely different style of diving. The pace and tone from the instructors was a lot more relaxed, but the level and standard of instruction was still intense ... the tempo started to ease a bit, but if you let your own standards

Twenty-eighth naval divers course, 2014. These four divers are the last so far of the 166 naval divers to have qualified since 1964 (students holding logbooks) (front, l–r): CPO Noel Dunne, Lt Stephen Stack, O/Sea Diarmuid Hallahan, Lt Cdr Tony O'Regan, O/Sea Ryan Carroll, PO Gareth Smith, PO Courtney Gibbons; (back, l–r): L/S John Fenton, A/B Gary Price, A/S Keith Dempsey

drop the instructors still hammered you. The last week was using the tools, and we did some recompression-chamber stuff. Personal admin. stuff was happening and uniforms to get ready, and then we had the presentation of certs, logbooks and most importantly in my case the Silver Dolphins, and in the lad's cases their Gold Diving Helmet badge.[57]

The course officer twenty-eighth diving course was Lt Cdr Tony O'Regan MCDO, who informed me that this course was the first to achieve over five thousand minutes dive time per student over its eight-week duration. I informed Tony that my minutes achieved for my diving course – albeit over a four-week period – was the princely figure of 921 (clearly I wasn't making half the effort that I thought I was).

Before concluding this chapter about dive training, mention must be made of the fact that there are no female divers in the Naval Service Diving Section. The reasons for this are as simple as they are honest: since the late 1990s women have joined the navy either as cadets or on general enlistment. The physical standard, medical standard, and aptitude test is non-gender specific – it is, however, diver-specific. Similarly, there is no gender bias in the application and selection process; it is open to both male and female. The numbers of females serving in the Naval Service is small enough, and if you factor in that many of them may have no interest in becoming a diver in the first place, then the number of interested personnel gets even smaller. Thus, applications from females will be few and far between. However, the course is there to be undertaken, and it is more than likely that some day that there will be a female diver in the Naval Service. Time will tell, and good luck to whoever it is. On this subject, Lt Cdr O'Regan had this to say:

> This year 2014, we had 1 female attempt an aptitude in which she did not pass but we recommended her to come back next year. Diving wasn't the problem but the physical exertion was … The door is open for a woman to write herself into the history books.[58]

Today, the Naval Service Diving Section trains its divers to the highest national and international civil and military standards. Its equipment, facilities and personnel meet similarly matching national and international standards. It now has the personnel, equipment and facilities to train and certify its divers in the following courses:

1 Naval-diver course
2 Combat-swimmer course
3 Dive-boat-coxswain course
4 SDDE 50-metre, surface-supplied-diver course
5 Remote-operated vehicle (ROV) pilot-technician course
6 Side-scan sonar and handheld-sonar course
7 18-metre dive-supervisor course
8 50-metre dive-supervisor and RCC-supervisor course
9 Explosive ordnance reconnaissance (EOR) course.

Bere Island, west Cork

In recalling or recounting naval diving and the various places divers did or didn't
do their training or who trained who, it would be sacrilegious not to mention
Bere Island and what it brought to naval-diver training. Naval divers started to
go to Bere Island back in the late 1980s. It was felt that it would provide better
diving conditions for working up the student divers to their qualifying depths of
33 metres. And so it proved: diving conditions there were outstanding and indeed
still are. The area is safe, with little boat traffic and minimal tides, and it's pretty
much diveable in any weather, day or night, and its seabed contours are ideal for
work-up dives.

The facilities are excellent. The camp itself is well maintained and, while back
in the earlier days it was a bit rough, it was always clean, tidy and – with a liberal
dosing of coal in the fires – warm. Over the years the Department of Defence

*A course tradition
since 1989ish:
a good brisk run up
to the cross, middle
of Bere Island, west
Cork (twenty-first
NS divers course) -
diving gear optional!*

Rerrin village; BFW offices on the left

has invested money into the camp and its upkeep, and while many have decried the waste of the taxpayers' money during the recent recession, nobody could deny that whatever money was spent on the camp in Bere Island it was indeed money well spent. Similarly, special mention must be made of the local community in and around the village in Rerrin on Bere Island and the hospitality they afforded to the Naval Service Diving Section over the years. Everybody to a sinner was excellent. Mentioning names is by definition a dangerous pasttime, for if a person is accidentally missed then upset is caused – however, if I neglect to mention somebody, please accept my most humble apologies. Over the years there have been some notable persons; some have passed away while others are still with us, so to mention some of them: Patrick Murphy (RIP) of Murphy's Ferry Service, and his wife Carol, who still carries on the ferry business. Dessie O'Sullivan (RIP) of Dessie's pub and the way he would look at you over his bar counter. Vincie Moriarty, the BFW foreman who died tragically along with his daughter in 1994. Mention should also be made of Raphael McCarthy, the BFW foreman, and his co-workers in the BFW over the years: Danny McCarthy, Jim Crowley and Michael Leary. In Murphy's shop and post office, Brendan Murphy and his sister Mary must be acknowledged as must Kitty and Albert that used to run the restaurant and chipper back in the day. And finally, we must mention Mary 'Jackie' in the hotel in the west end of the island and Colum Harrington of Bere Island Ferries.

The one thing about our divers was when you were posted ashore after serving at sea and you were posted into the Diving Section you never rested. It was like being at sea again, because you were always on call, always training – if it wasn't training the guys that were there at the time, it was training new courses, always testing new equipment, personal training, ROV [remote-operated vehicle] pilot training, all that sort of stuff.

Former Commander Fleet Operations,
Commander Gene Ryan (retd) (2013)

A perfect day for a run to the cross – cold wet and windy.

Student divers enroute to dive site, Bere Island, west Cork

(above) Diving course jogging to dive site: supervisor on the left, Paddy Delaney
(below) Chief diver and supervisor, Fergy Cunningham, taking the divers' details before a dive
(facing page) Dive supervisor Paddy Delaney *(between divers)* about to dispatch the first diver into the water; the diver with the lifeline or floatline on him is always deployed first; his buddy standing behind him is next

THE CHIEF: A CASE OF MISTAKEN IDENTITY (A SHORT STORY)

The distance from the Diving Section to the Basin is about 1 mile. It would take the course approximately fifteen minutes to jog down to the Basin carrying their lifelines and float lines. They were more awkward than heavy. The chief stood at the doorway of the Diving Store and surveyed the diving course that had assembled awaiting his instructions. The chief and the other training staff readied themselves. The chief gave the order to move out. The course moved off in unison. There were two ranks of divers, four in each rank. They moved through the naval depot and out the main gate on the road to the Basin. Somewhere along that road this conversation occurred:

(Diving course is jogging along the road … there's a sound of heels dragging)

Chief   Diver Murphy, lift those feet like a good man, your heels are dragging.

Sound of dragging heels stops. Course jogging … a couple of minutes later, again the sound of heels dragging and the chief's a bit annoyed.

Chief   Diver Murphy, lift those bleeding heels, get them a bit higher …

Sound of dragging heels stops. Course jogging … a couple of minutes later, the sound of heels dragging again and the chief's getting pissed.

Chief   Diver Murphy, don't have me tell you again, lift those fucking heels higher.

Sound of dragging heels stops … course keeps on jogging until the heels drag again. Chief really pissed off now. He halts the course and closes the distance between himself and 'Diver Murphy' at an alarming rate.

Chief   Diver Murphy, just who the fuck do you think you are sunshine!

'Diver Murphy' looking a bit confused: What Chief!

Chief   You Murphy, are you yanking my fucking chain or what, Murphy. When I say lift your heels, Murphy, I mean *you* lift your fucking heels. I'm only going to tell you things just once from now on Murphy – have you got that!

Diver   But I'm not Murphy, Chief.

Chief   You're what?!

Diver   I'm not Murphy, Chief.

Chief   What … then who the fuck is Murphy, so!

A voice from a bent-over diver at the rear, heaving and panting, rope everywhere, hands on knees, sucking air …

                 I … am … Chief.

Chief looks towards the sound of the gasping voice and then back at the diver in front of him

Chief   Then who the fuck are you so?

Diver   I'm O'Driscoll, Chief.

Chief pauses … then with a deep intake of breath slowly rolls his eyes up to Heaven … pauses … breathes out …

Chief   For fuck sake … right … you O'Driscoll, you lift your bleeding feet up, OK.

And looking back to Diver Murphy …

Chief   And you, Murphy …

Diver Murphy Yes Chief?

Chief   Murphy, you tidy up that bleeding rope and try and keep up with the rest of us like a good lad, alright.

Diver Murphy Yes Chief.

Chief   Right you bleeding lot, jog on … fuck sake, we'll never get there!

3

OUR DARKEST DAY:
GERARD (GERRY) DISKIN,
25 OCTOBER 1989, RIP

Prior to 24 October 1989, it was left to an individual serviceman to be as fit as possible before commencing a diving course. At that time it was straight to diving from day one. While the physical fitness of an individual commencing a diving course is still very much left up to them, things have changed and moved on for the best since the tragic and untimely death of O/Sea Gerry Diskin at approximately 16:30 hrs on 25 October 1989 due to a diver-training exercise. Gerry was what the navy termed an ordinary seaman (O/Sea) and applied for the diving course while serving on board the LÉ *Eithne*, where his uncle was the senior NCO. Senior Chief Petty Officer John Walsh, the coxswain of the LÉ *Eithne*, was himself a CD2, and one of the navy's most senior and experienced divers. The untimely death of Gerry led to a naval court of inquiry, whose findings and recommendations were adopted in full in 1990.

Today, there is a pre-diving aptitude medical test, and a dedicated three-week pre-diving exercise phase, which is designed to prepare potential diving students for the rigours of a diving course through a dedicated diver-training programme. On completion of this phase, there is a diver-fitness test within which there are a series of pass/fail, go/no-go tests. Each student must successfully pass each test before proceeding to the next. Should a student not pass a test, that student is deemed to have failed the diver-fitness test and is precluded from progressing any further.

For Gerry Diskin and all diving students prior to 1989, this procedure was not in place. The norm at that time was that students, while expected to have a reasonable level of fitness prior to commencing the diving course, would be programmed for diver-fitness-training periods normally before a day's diving would commence. As part of that training regime, 'mud running' was considered to be the most arduous, but at the same time a normal training exercise conducted by naval divers under training. Mud running entailed a student diver being dressed up in his diving suit (either a drysuit or a wetsuit) and 'running' through the mud exposed on low water in Ringaskiddy, an area located opposite the naval base on its southern side. This mud running was a throwback to the Royal Navy training days. Depending on the consistency of the mud, whether it was soft or hard, the exercise would have been either relatively easy or difficult. The harder the mud, the better, as you didn't sink into it as much. Lighter students tended to have the upper hand in this area. 'Mud running' was a lung and leg-burning, energy-sapping, psychological nightmare for any student to partake in, but in an odd way was also the most enjoyable.

Importantly, enduring those mud runs or exercises like it had another purpose: by bonding a group of guys they built an *esprit de corps*. It also helped the student build up a strength of mind, to keep focused and to be determined – all the things that a student would need to pass the course and become a navy diver. So it was for Gerry and his nine classmates of the seventh naval divers course in October 1989.

On the morning of 24 October, the seventh naval divers course was programmed to conduct an early-morning mud run. They commenced their gym work at 08:05 hrs approx. with warm-up exercises and stretching, while at 08:30 approx. the class was directed to change into their diving suits (wetsuits). At 09:00 hrs approx. the course departed the Diving Section and jogged out of the depot lines and across the Irish Steel bridge towards the foreshore in Ringaskiddy. The course proceeded down onto the exposed foreshore – it was low water – and once there commenced the mud run along the length of the foreshore, approx. 1,000 metres, before reaching the old wooden pier in Ringaskiddy. Upon arrival the course rested for a few minutes, regrouped and then returned to the naval depot via the Ringaskiddy reclaimed land. On entry to the naval base the course stopped, put their hoods back on, dressed themselves and continued to the Diving Section. While jogging down the depot lines (roadway) Diver Diskin became very unsteady on his feet – so much so that he couldn't continue jogging, and he lagged behind. His partner was then told to return and assist him to make his way to the Diving Store. The rest of the course continued down the depot lines and completed the exercise. At this point Gerry had collapsed and was carried by other naval personnel back to the store.

In the Diving Store it was immediately clear that Gerry was in a serious condition. Exactly what was wrong with him was not clear, but he needed medical attention quickly. The base doctor was summoned and he immediately requested an ambulance to transport Gerry to a hospital. The naval-base ambulance was off the road, so the only ambulance available at that particular time was the Irish Steel ambulance. This was requested, and Gerry was dispatched to the South Infirmary at best speed. On arrival into the South Infirmary, Gerry's condition had deteriorated; he was in a very critical condition. In the meantime the parents of Gerry were contacted and apprised of the situation. They immediately travelled to Cork from their home in Merlin Park in Galway. Gerry was transferred to the Cork Regional hospital for a CT scan. During the latter part of the evening and into the night it appeared that perhaps his condition was beginning to stabilise and that he was rallying. His vital signs were stable, though his heart rate was still high. Gerry's parents had arrived, and though serious he was receiving some visitors that night.

During the early hours of the morning – at 01:00 hrs approx. – Gerry relapsed and his condition deteriorated further. He had suffered kidney failure. While in the Intensive Therapy Unit, Gerry was placed on a ventilator and was displaying no signs of movement. During the morning the Naval Depot OC, Cdr Eoin McNamara, the naval chaplain, Fr Des Campion, and the hospital chaplain met with Gerry's parents, Peggy and Bernie. The anaesthetist informed them that 'he was having difficulty holding onto Gerry', and at 16:15 hrs approx. Gerry arrested. Subsequent attempts to revive him were in vain. Gerry was pronounced dead at 16:30 hrs:

> On the Flag Officer's direction a Court of Inquiry was convened on 22 November 1989 'for the purposes of inquiring into and reporting in to the circumstances and events which resulted in the death of O/Sea Gerard Diskin'.[1]

The board consisted of four members: Lt Cdr R Ryan (president), Lt D. O'Callaghan, Lt R. Long and Capt. T O'Brien AMC (members). The terms of reference were set out and evidence was taken under oath. On 5 December 1989, the Cork City Coroner's Court was held. On 24 May 1990 the board members of the Court of Inquiry (CoI) concluded and signed off on their inquiry report and submitted it to the flag officer, Cmdre. Joe Deasy, for his perusal. The flag officer in turn submitted the report to O i/c A-Admin, DFHQ. On 27 July a communication was sent by the flag officer to D/Trg (director of training, Defence Forces), requesting the inclusion in the training circular 1/80 –DF Training Manual the newly devised diver-fitness test as recommended by the CoI. Among the CoI recommendations, which were implemented in full, were:

- A diving-aptitude medical examination (exclusive of the diving medical) which would in future be required for all personnel attempting the diving-aptitude test.
- A three-week diver-fitness training phase (pre-diving) with a series of pass/fail fitness exams at the end (to be added to the diving-course syllabus).
- A full and comprehensive diving medical for students who successfully pass the diver-fitness test. (To commence the diving course itself the student would have to pass the medical examination.)
- Mud runs were to be prohibited from all forms of training exercise (and remain so).

The following year, with the approval of Gerry's parents, the staff of the Diving Section instigated a perpetual memorial trophy in honour of Gerry's memory, to be awarded to the best diving student on a naval divers course. It wasn't much but it was an effort by the Diving Section to recognise Gerry Diskin's attempt to become a navy diver, and to acknowledge his death during that attempt. Indeed, the presentation of the trophy for the first time was by Gerry's uncle, S/CPO John Walsh, on what was a very moving occasion for him.

At that time the O i/c Diving Section and the course officer for the seventh diving course was Lt Chris Reynolds (since retired from the Naval Service), and it was only when researching material and interviewing Chris, that I realised that I had never actually asked him what he thought of the incident with Gerry at that time.

With the benefit of hindsight [twenty-five years later], what did he recall of the situation regarding the death of Gerry?

With hindsight, it was a very traumatic time for all of us. I was there at the time he died … we followed the processes that we thought were right, given the air temperature and his age. There was no reason to think that he might overheat; it was just one of those things that if we did that a thousand times, young Gerry would probably survive 999 times. It was a terrible tragedy that he passed away.

Could we have done more when the incident happened? I don't really think we could. Maybe if we took a hose, or if we had carried him down to the sea and physically immersed him in the sea to cool him down rapidly, that might have been a good thing to do, but we didn't know. I remember you looked around and I looked around and we said 'What the fuck's going on here?' … I think anybody that was involved in that [incident] did what they thought was the right thing … it was just so out of our understanding that this might have happened, that … obviously there was no way that if I thought there was any chance of a young twenty-year-old man dying from heatstroke would we have run the exercise.

The other side of it – and I think I've always said this – is that because the navy's so small and because we ask ship's divers, not MCDOs or CDOs, but ship's divers to do weird and wonderful things in horrible and strange places … we have to train our guys in a very pragmatic and robust way. If you don't stress a guy when he's on training and then take him out into the real world and stress him there, then you're asking for a lot worse. That's all we used to do on the course, the whole course. The reasons we didn't let up on the course when the rest of the world was enjoying a nice, soft, easy pace, and everybody's a winner and everybody has to get a medal, we never went down that road … we actually had to protect the people doing the work … our guys in many ways had to do it by the seat of their pants, in a fucking cold river, in the Blackwater off Lismore, where you couldn't see anything, and you'd run into vehicles underwater and prams and you're looking for dead girls – when you're doing that you have to be a bit robust in your training.

They always were and always are very robust in their training [diver-training staff] and they do stress their people both physically and mentally, and you have to do that if you want to protect your guys once they qualify, and, God bless us, unfortunately … in this case young Gerry Diskin died.[2]

In like vein, I spoke also with another student who was on the course with Gerry that morning. Declan Fleming was a lieutenant and at thirty-two years of age the oldest student on the course. I asked Declan what he recalled:

It was my first ever mud run and obviously that's not something you forget. I remember how testing and challenging it was alright … The thing I always remember is we went into the water by the pier in Ringaskiddy. How beautiful that was to get washed off at the end of the mud and then we ran back along the foreshore-reclaimed land and over the bridge. Everybody was obviously tired, there was no alarm, I was just hoping that I'd be able to get through it … so we went down the slip at the back of the NCOs' mess, 20 seconds later and that's how close he was. That's the one thing I always thought, and I'm sure others did as well, if he had only made it to the water, sort of like a minute earlier …[3]

Until 1989 mud running was part and parcel of any diver-training conducted by the Diving Section since 1982, whether naval or ARW training. It was also part and parcel of any Royal Navy diver-training courses attended by Irish naval personnel. It was something that was done quite routinely and matter-of-factly. Gerry's course was no different. The ten students who made up the course that morning on the mud run were as much the same as they were different. The oldest student was in his early thirties, while the youngest, Gerry, was twenty. They had various levels of fitness – some were stronger, others faster – and they were all doing the course for their own reasons. Gerry was just one of those students, a real nice young man just trying to better himself both as a person and as a Service man.

Still it depends on what you're training for and it's a subjective opinion but you have to prepare for everything … I remember my first job I did after the course and it was in January in Athlone. And I remember looking into the lough in Athlone and there was a huge surge through it as the river was in flood. You guys were all talking about getting in here or there, and you know I was thinking that you can't get into fucking that … and that's why the course is so hard … it has to be mentally and physically hard, and it does really put people under pressure, and the mud run was part of that … maybe it's just a bridge too far in today's health-and-safety world.

Declan Fleming (Lt; retd)

While in the process of writing this book, I made contact with a senior member of the Army Ranger Wing-course undertaken in 1983, and asked him what abiding memories of the course he had. Like the vast majority of the others interviewed, he answered 'Mud runs'. He mentioned it at the very start of our conversation and later on in more depth. I thought it interesting and frank that even after nearly thirty-two years he still vividly recalls his experiences on the 'mud flats', as he called them. So, having transcribed his interview, I felt that it should be included pretty much in its totality:

> Well, if you look back at what it was designed to do, you know you have to keep going back to why did the guys cope with that in the first place? Now, part of it was you tried to make the divers an elite group, give them some *esprit de corps*, so that meant it had to be a tough course. But secondly, the idea was that you had to be physically fit and that was all about oxygen and cardiovascular fitness, and running in the mud flats absolutely did that for you and tested you. But the problem was it was easy to overdo it. But in terms of what it actually achieved if it was done right, it was spot on. And it also meant, a little bit like Special Forces, you get guys who don't give up easily, which if you're underwater and there's trouble and people start to panic, well that's no good for you. You know you need people who are going to stay and endure and get you or themselves out of the shit. So from that point of view it does what it says on the tin … it was the toughest part from a physical point of view. I mean, it was one of those things where you drive people; you can literally kill them doing it. So I mean that's the point, that's why you remember it – it pushed you, and you knew it pushed you hard towards your limits. Now, for us I suppose it pushed us hard. You know, it would have been hard enough I suppose for someone to push us any harder than we had already been pushed [Ranger selection course], so you know the mud flats were doing it for us. We were all having to work hard, we were all fairly fit, but we still had to work hard running in the mud, so that's what you remember. [4]

Gerry struggled on the mud run – that was certain. On the return into the naval base, the course was stopped for a quick rest and to tidy themselves up. It was here that I spoke to Gerry as he was having difficulty pulling up the zip on his jacket – it wouldn't move. I tried to get the zip up myself but there was no moving it, and as I spoke with Gerry, I looked at him directly, when I asked him how he was, he said he was 'tired but good'. We resumed the jog in. The events that unfolded that morning after Gerry's collapse and his death the following evening were a very traumatic time for everybody concerned.

To this day, when I think of Gerry and that morning I still recall vividly holding him and wiping his brow with cold water and trying to, I guess, comfort him until better help arrived. The following evening, Gerry was dead. In trying to remember how I was told or who told me, I still can't recall. But for me even, after all these years, two things remain certain. I was the supervisor of that course and I was the supervisor of that mud run – that can never be changed. Every student that undergoes diving instruction must have complete faith in their instructors and in the instruction given, and if you follow that then everything should be OK. Gerry entrusted that with me, he did everything he was asked to do, and he did it well. I didn't spot Gerry's difficulty – I think I should have. I let him down; I should have done better for Gerry.

The loss of Gerry to his family must only have been incalculable. His memory lives on within the Diving Section.

When I spoke with Gerry's uncle, John Walsh, about this particular chapter, he told me a little anecdote about their time together on the LÉ *Eithne*. John – while serving as coxswain – would often, as his duty required, go around all the decks and cabins on the ship in the morning and 'call the hands' so as to ensure that all the necessary hands (ratings/crew members) were up and out of their bunks. Gerry was a junior rating and so was in a four-berth cabin, along with another three lads. John told me that every now and then – just out of 'divilment' – that he would often when 'calling the hands' tell the occupants of Gerry's cabin in no uncertain naval descriptive terminology to get up and out of their bunks while at the same time telling his nephew it was OK to take another thirty minutes for himself. Not surprisingly, Gerry never took his uncle up on his kind offer!

4

OPERATIONS: EXTERNAL

It is not the critic who counts; not the man who points out how the strong man stumbled, or where the doer of deeds could have done better. The credit belongs to the man who is actually in the arena; whose face is marred by dust and sweat and blood; who strives valiantly; who errs and comes short again and again. Who knows the great enthusiasms, the great devotions, and spends himself in a worthy cause. Who at the best knows in the end the triumph of high achievement; and who at the worst, if he fails, at least fails while daring greatly. So that his place shall never be with those cold and timid souls who know neither victory nor defeat'

Theodore Roosevelt

The period following Lt Deasy's arrival back into the naval base in November 1964 until the arrival of the minesweepers in 1970 was a very barren period for diving operations in the service. This was due to the simple fact that Joe was the only diver in the Naval Service during those years. In conversation with him at his home, Joe told me that his primary contribution to diving in the service during that period was his ability to write letters to Command outlining the further need for divers in the service, and highlighting that if he were to dive by himself he would be breaking all the rules in the manual. However, the arrival of the three minesweepers in the early 1970s forced the hand of the Department of Defence and the Naval Service, and in due course personnel of the Naval Service commenced formal training with the Royal Navy at their diving training centre in HMS *Drake* and, later, in HMS *Vernon*.

As courses were completed and the numbers of divers within the service grew, the ability of the Naval Service to respond to requests from the civil authority An Garda Síochána to assist in certain incidents also began to grow. In a sense the spotlight began to shine on the Naval Service divers and, by consequence, on the Naval Service.

I have deliberately made two decisions in relation to this chapter and the diving operations. One was to omit completely all those taskings and jobs that took place internally within and around the naval base throughout the entire period. Not because they were in themselves not important – indeed, they are, for they are the bread and butter of naval diving – but simply because they run into their thousands. Secondly, I have tried to keep the chapter as short as is practicable while at the same time trying to include those diving operations that show in their own way a natural progression of naval diving, naval-diving equipment and the divers themselves from the 1970s through to 2014. Clearly, not all operations are mentioned, for many more operations have been omitted than included, but I think the operations mentioned have in their own way helped to define what the Naval Service Diving Section is today.

The 1960s

On Sunday 24 March 1968 the Aer Lingus Viscount Flight 712 *St Phelim* suffered a catastrophic incident while en route from Cork to Heathrow, and subsequently crashed into the sea just south of the Tusker Rock, with the loss of sixty-one people. The presence of Lt Joe Deasy as a liaison officer during the initial search operations by the Royal Navy would be the first time that a diver from the Irish Naval Service was tasked with an official presence at a dive site, although no diving took place. It would not be until 1973 that Naval Service divers would be called upon, and that operation would involve the MV *Claudia.*

The 1970s

In March 1973 the MV *Claudia* steamed into Irish territorial waters. Within its hold were 5 tonnes of assorted arms, ammunition and explosives brought from Tripoli, Libya, where it had been purchased by the IRA. Its subsequent voyage back to Ireland was uneventful inasmuch as the crew were unaware that they were being tracked by other agencies after their passage through the Straits of Gibraltar. Having transited up through the Bay of Biscay towards Irish waters, the Naval Service and other elements of the state's security forces were put on alert, and an interdiction operation formulated. Elements of the Naval Service deployed a couple of days in advance and remained within striking distance as both the MV *Claudia* and fate were steaming towards each other. On the evening of 28 March 1973 the *Claudia* approached Irish waters close to the south-east coast and the fishing port of Helvick Harbour. The lead element, LÉ *Deirdre*, under the command of Lt Cdr Liam Brett, maintained radar watch on the *Claudia*, and as the vessel moved towards Helvick Head, another small radar contact was acquired – this one moving towards the suspect vessel. The *Irish Times* reported that

> The Claudia and the launch were kept under radar observation until finally the launch made contact with the Claudia. This appeared as a merging of the signals. The signals remained merged for 10 to 15 minutes before separating and the launch then went under the stern of the Claudia, before both vessels moved off towards the south-east and then turned towards Helvick Head and the small harbour there.
>
> They were followed at a distance by the naval ships and their course continued until they were about 1 mile from Helvick Head, when all three naval vessels turned on their search lights.[1]

A boarding party from the LÉ *Deirdre* intercepted, boarded and arrested the *Claudia* at 23:20 hrs approx. The small launch pursued by both the LÉ *Fóla*, under the command of Lt M.R. Murphy, and the LÉ *Gráinne*, under Lt E. McNamara, was making a determined effort to escape. The LÉ *Gráinne* slowed down to boat-launching speed and launched its Gemini craft with a boarding party under the command of Sub Lieutenant Frank Lynch (diver). Several warning shots were fired during the course of the pursuit. The Gemini overtook the launch, and finally boarded and arrested the three men on board shortly before midnight. During the operation it was thought that something may have been thrown overboard from the *Claudia* just prior to her being boarded. This then became the objective of the subsequent diving operation that would see naval divers being deployed to what possibly was its first ever external diving operation. Requesting the services of the naval diving team was not an issue; the problem at that time was the lack of necessary equipment, particularly a compressor to sustain them over an extended period away from base. However, this didn't prove to be a major issue in the end as Lt Peadar McElhinney, the base diving officer at the time, rang a Garda Inspector Gallagher at Garda Headquarters in the Phoenix Park– whom he knew through diving – and explained the situation.

At that time the Garda Síochána didn't have an established diving unit, so what they relied upon when it came to water or diving matters were the diving skills that some of their members had. When called upon to carry out diving duties, by way of remuneration they would only receive subsistence allowance when called, and as the whole situation hadn't been properly formalised it was leading to all kinds of difficulties for the members involved. Such matters came to a head between 1972 and 1974. The Garda 'divers' were in 'dispute' with their own department over these issues, and had ostensibly withdrawn their diving services until the issues were addressed to mutual satisfaction. For the moment, the Naval Service benefited from that situation as the inspector loaned whatever equipment he had at his disposal. No paperwork was asked for and none was given. Consequently, a truck was despatched from Naval Headquarters, based as it was just down the road in Parkgate Street in Dublin, and was duly loaded and driven to the naval base. The naval diving team loaded its equipment onto the LÉ *Gráinne* and sailed for Helvick Head to begin operations. The *Irish Times* of 2 April 1973 reported:

> It is believed that the divers are searching for a box or briefcase which may contain documents relating to the purchase and origin of the arms shipment and which may have been thrown overboard just before the Claudia was arrested by Naval minesweepers.[2]

However, the Department of Defence clearly did not want to give away too many secrets, with the *Irish Times* noting :'Other than confirming that the search had been initiated, both the Department of Defence and the Naval Service remain silent on its purpose.'[3]

Naval divers commenced searching in the general area on 31 March, and continued diving operations over the next several days. According to the officer leading that diving operation, Lt McElhinney, 'We marked out the area with buoys, Dan Buoys, and then we set up channels more or less to swim along, to cover the whole area, which we did.'[4]

With the extra equipment loaned by the gardaí, the naval divers were able to maximise their dive times, with little down time due to recharging sets. Diving continued until the operation was concluded on the afternoon of 5 April. Nothing relating to the arms shipment was found, though it appeared the diving team may have found some unexploded ordnance in the form of a sea mine left over from the war. The relevant entries from George Jefferies' diving logbook for this diving operation simply state:

> 31/3/1973 – Seabed search – Helvick Head operation, Claudia vis 10ft – sandy bottom – total times 210 mins.
> 5/4/1973 – Seabed search – Helvick Head operation, Claudia vis 3–4ft – sandy bottom – total times 380 mins.

Though there was nothing to show for their efforts at the end of the operation, the Naval Service Diving Section and its divers had received good coverage in the national newspapers and, more importantly, it put them firmly in the public eye for the future. The *Irish Times* reported the conclusion of the operation:

> After an operation which lasted more than thirty hours the five Irish naval frogmen have ended their exhaustive search of the seabed off Helvick Head, where the Claudia, was arrested on March 28th with a five-ton cargo of arms and explosives on board. Shortly after 4 o'clock yesterday evening the divers returned in two rubber dinghies to the naval minesweeper Gráinne which had been on stand-by alert near the harbour since last Sunday evening.[5]

On return to the naval base, Lt McElhinney reported to the commanding officer of the base, Capt. McKenna, to give him a verbal debriefing of the operation. It was here that the rest of the report on the diving operation found the light of day. Lt McElhinney went on to inform his captain that it appeared that they had found some unexploded ordnance. It was a mine – exactly what type he wasn't quite sure – but the owners were either British or German, or possibly even Irish:

> … we didn't find anything other than. I remember George Jefferies saying to me, 'Look we discovered that there's a mine at the bottom.' I said 'Are you sure it's a mine,' so I went down and had a look at it. It was the top of a mine, covered by the silt and the sand, but you could see it clearly, but it was fairly well embedded at that stage of the game.[6]

He went on to show Capt. McKenna the location of where they had encountered the mine, and at that Capt. McKenna went over to a chart in the CO's office that included a list of mines sunk during the Second World War by the maritime service. 'God,' he said, 'that's amazing – bang on where it was sunk.' So Capt. McKenna was satisfied that at the very least the divers were doing their job, and Lt McElhinney was delighted that the divers were at least keeping their eyes open. As a result of the diving operation the naval divers had received coverage on RTÉ news over the period and – in the words of Lt McElhinney – 'That more or less put the divers on the map for the first time.'[7]

The year 1974 was a lean year as regards external diving operations, but there were at least two operations that required the services of the naval diving team. The first of these was a diving operation in Lough Corrib, County Galway in June, and the second was in September of that year – a search operation for a missing person in the River Boyne, near Drogheda. The diving operation in Lough Corrib involved the divers searching a specific part of the seabed for hand grenades whose origin were unknown.

This description of the operation is best left to the diver involved, Johnny O'Neill, as there's a certain degree of style and eloquence in his words that would be lost if anybody else were to write it:

> I remember once we went to Lough Corrib … to retrieve grenades, and what it was, some professor had this oul' glass-bottomed yoke and he was searching for old bottles, and he saw these grenades and we were called out to have a look at them and take them up … but we were there and we were staying in Galway army barracks – I think we were there for about a week. We brought up fucking tons of grenades, fucking loads of them – they were all stuck to the rocks, and we were using our knives to prise them off the rocks … and they had loads of them onshore – maybe a hundred grenades or so. The army lads came down, and they said there's a bit of an island out in Lough Corrib, we'll put them out there and put a charge under them … so they brought them out to the island, and they blew them up. Only for the fucking island to disappear … the fucking grenades were all live … there was this fucking monstrosity of a fucking explosion and this lovely island that was there just went woooosh … and fucking thing disappeared … the fucking island had been there thousands years or something … everyone just started looking at each other going 'Here, fuck that', so we got in the trucks and fucked off saying 'Fuck that' … we were sticking knives in them and every Jaysusin thing … never had a grenade in me hand up until that time …[8]

On 9 September 1974 the Diving Section travelling to Drogheda, County Louth to conduct a search of the River Boyne close to the town centre for a young man. There had recently been a circus operating close by and, as part of an act, the circus had spanned the river with a tightrope. The young man who went missing had apparently been drunk and had tried to cross the river via the line. Unfortunately, he fell into the river and drowned. The divers stayed in Gormanston camp and travelled to Drogheda each day. The search was based close by the Greenhill's towel factory, whose manager at the time was a sister of a serving fitter in the navy, so she took it upon herself to look after the diving team. Diving ops only took place at low water. Close by the area where the searches were being conducted there was a sewerage outfall from the town, and added to that there was a cake and oil mill factory in the area as well – all this wasn't making the divers' task any easier. Diving operations had been conducted over a four-day period but with no success. One day the minister of defence decided to come down and say hello to the divers, to make them feel appreciated. George Jefferies recalled the scene:

> I remember one day we were coming down and Paddy Carolan and Noel Garrett were coming across the river, the two of them, and they were just exiting out of the water and Garrett was covered in sewerage – I mean covered in sewerage – papers and all kinds of shit hanging off him … he was a good oul' diver, and I remember Donegan came down, the minister of defence, with his welly boots and he congratulated and thanks us very much, so on and so forth … I remember Garrett saying to him … 'You are like fuck' … and Danno saluting him because he was the minister of defence.[9]

The body of the young man was found much later down the coast.

On 4 November 1975 the divers were called into action in Hare Island, Galway Bay, and again this operation involved old ordnance. The situation this time involved the finding of some projectiles by a civilian diver. The divers were tasked with locating and recovering shells. Weather conditions were poor, with a heavy groundswell. George Jefferies takes up the story:

> You could hear the banging below and I went down and here was Danno with the projectile between his legs, and he beating shit out of it with the handle of the knife … beating the shit out of it he was … the ordnance

officer took it over to Hare Island and blew even more shit out of it … frightened the life out of him … yeah, funnily enough the next one came up a bit differently.[10]

Johnny O'Neill (left) and Paddy Carolan with one of the offending shells in Galway, 1975

Another diver there that day, Paddy Carolan, described it thus:

> I hopped out of the boat, and I took it [the shell] off Johnnier and I handed it over to Danno, and I was walking up the beach behind to give him moral support and he dropped it … and we all shit a brick, we got up to the top of the beach … and their ordnance fella came out a put a small bit of explosive round it … there was no sign of it to be found anywhere after it, shell or anything.[11]

Lucky enough for the likes of Johnnier and Danno, it would be several more years before the Naval Service Diving Section would have to be getting familiar with any type of ordnance material.

On 5 October 1976, the diving steam headed up to Galway to a place called Lough Inagh at the request of the gardaí seeking a missing person, a young woman by the name of Mary Duffy, whose rape, murder and subsequent disappearance shocked the nation. The gardaí had managed to arrest two male suspects, Evans and Shaw, and after several hours of questioning the suspects confessed to the murder and informed the gardaí of where they had disposed of the young woman's body. They indicated the lake but not the location, and so it remained for both the Garda Sub-aqua Unit, led by Sgt Niall Bracken, and the naval diving team, led by Lt Dan O'Neil, to search the lake and to recover the body. Tommy Lavery recalled Evans 'coming out to the lake [boat house] and putting his hand out like that, and he was saying "Out there, out there."'[12] The search area was large and an exact location unknown. So both the navy and garda divers would search the lake in the time-honoured fashion, as trained, using a search technique called a jackstay. Simply put, it's a line laid along the seabed and weighted at intervals to keep it down, with a float line at either end to mark its start and end. If a series of two or more jackstays are laid parallel to each other, as determined by the size of the area to be covered, the area can be searched far more quickly and very efficiently, particularly if there are a couple of boats available. Having been briefed on the operation ahead, the divers laid their jackstays and commenced diving operations:

> The suspected area was approximately three-quarters of a mile long by 600 yards wide. The search was carried out by a systematic jackstay search scheme with five divers on a span each time. The jackstay was moved 15 yards after each sweep – an operation which could take one hour and required maximum cooperation and coordination from personnel involved.[13]

The bottom of the Connemara lake was typically soft, peaty and murky, and capable of hiding a missing person quite easily. The search by the divers had to be slow, steady and thorough, with each span overlapping. The depth of the lake varied but the maximum depth encountered was 40 feet, with visibility varying from nil to a couple of feet. Over the course of the next five days, divers from the navy, Gardaí and the army sub-aqua club searched the lake, some using the jackstay, others searching areas that had been deliberately missed by the jackstay and other areas of interest. On the evening of Saturday 9 October the last jackstay of the day was laid in preparation for Sunday morning, and all divers secured for the night. The following morning, it was determined that the navy and garda teams would search the deepest part of the lake while members of Galway sub-aqua club would search using the jackstay as laid the previous evening:

> … and on the Sunday morning there was a conference between the teams – Niall Bracken was the sergeant in charge – but Niall had a thing that the garda divers and the naval divers would do the deepest part of the lake, centre of the lake about 60 or 70 feet, and they would let the Galway sub-aqua club go across our rope … and three quarters of the way across they came across her … they wouldn't have known they came across her only the rope was moving, and she was covered in all the oul' brown things that come down from the mountains, you know … she was kneeling down, she was actually kneeling down with the cover, and the rope had cleared away all the brown shit off her and there she was, her bare back … and they found her.[14]

The body of Mary Duffy had been found, but she had still to be recovered; she had been murdered and this was a murder case:

> … and they found her, and we had to go down … myself, Danno and Martin Carroll and another garda diver took an 8-by-4 sheet [plywood] to the bottom and lifted the corpse on it and brought her up to the surface … there was a helicopter above taking photographs … of exactly how she was … she was beautiful.[15]

The diving report simply states: 'The body was lifted and brought ashore at 18:00 hrs. by the Garda and Naval Service divers.'[16] It was the first time that the naval diving team had worked with the Garda Sub-aqua Unit, but it certainly wouldn't be the last. The naval diving team – which returned to the naval base the following day – consisted of Lt Dan O'Neill, CPO George Jefferies, L/Sea Noel Garrett, L/Sea John Walsh, A/Sea Martin Carroll and O/Mech Behan.

It wouldn't be a long until the next operation. Less than two months later – on 25 November 1976 – the naval diving team made its way up to Glencolumcille, County Donegal for a search-and-recovery operation less than a mile off the coast at Rathlin O'Birne Island. The 65-foot Burtonport trawler *Carrig Una*, while returning from a fishing trip in the early hours of Tuesday 24 November, at 03:10 hrs approx. struck a reef and sank rapidly with the loss of all five crew members, Ted Carbery, John Boyle, Michael Coyle, Doalty O'Donnell and Anthony McLoughlin. This tragedy had all the hallmarks of a very similar tragedy less than two years earlier where on 7 January 1975 the newly built Burtonport trawler *Evelyn Marie* also struck the same reef, with the loss of all six of her crew. However, the weather was to play the leading role in this operation. The diving team spent a lot of its time looking out at the weather, conducting shore searches or waiting for word on conditions at the wreck site. Conditions were, to say the least, not good for diving. The Atlantic swell was rising and falling by as much as 30 feet, and even though the wind at stages was workable, the surge and resulting surf zone made the task of diving patently unsafe. The depth of water was reckoned to be in and around 80 to 100 feet. Sgt Niall Bracken (former head of the garda diving team) coordinated the search:

> Sgt Bracken [ex-head of garda diving unit and stationed locally in Donegal] coordinated the search with Mr Aloysius Bonner of Burtonport Co-Op and with Mr J. Murrin of Killybegs. There were teams of Garda, Navy and Army Divers. There was also a number … of local divers and a group of Queen's University divers who visited and dive regularly in the area on weekends. The officers in charge of the three main groups flew over the area and landed on the island twice a day to assess conditions. A joint decision was made after each recce.[17]

While all this flying and waiting was being played out, one of the naval divers was quite anxious to play his part in any recovery operation. L/Sea Paddy Carolan had known and fished with some of the crew when Paddy had been a trawler man himself. Paddy had come down to the naval base at one stage to do some training for BIM (Board Iascaigh Mhara), and afterwards transferred to the navy:

> I was annoyed, very annoyed at that stage, and you know I thought what the fuck am I doing here. I knew all them fellas that had perished, I fished with them, and I wanted to be in there searching. But we were there ten days and we weren't allowed dive and we were called back to base.[18]

So a decision was made in light of the relentless weather that was making any attempt at diving very unsafe:

The search was called off at 16:00 hrs on Sunday 28 November. There was a storm 10 blowing from the SW on the twenty-seventh. It veered NW on the twenty-eighth. The long-range weather forecast was continuing disturbed for the week. On Thursday 2 December 1976 the continuing disturbed weather produced even more hazardous diving conditions than those previously experienced.[19]

The naval diving returned to the naval base on 29 November, arriving at 22:00 hrs. The naval diving team returned to Donegal again the following day – 30 November – departing the naval base at 16:00 hrs and eventually returned to the naval base at 22:00 hrs on 3 December 1976.

Records for 1977 show three operations conducted outside of the naval base, with two of these operations Naval Service requirements. April saw a search-and-recovery job for an anchor lost by the LÉ *Deirdre* in Rosslare Harbour during a severe gale. John Walsh described the operation:

> Another open seabed search I remember in terrible, terrible, weather – Deirdre lost her anchor down in Rosslare and we had to do a dive for that. We spent three days there, 27–29 April 1977 … we managed to recover [it], just about; there was just a couple of links spotted sticking out of the sand.[20]

The anchor was recovered a couple days later.

In August naval divers went to Lough Swilly, County Donegal to search for equipment lost overboard from a naval vessel.

The year 1979 would live long in the memories of six naval divers, and in the memories of many others, too. In early January of that year, the Total-owned oil tanker *Betelgeuse*, while unloading its cargo, blew up, killing fifty people. When recalling this particular operation, one of the divers involved commented, 'It was where boys became men.'[21] (See Chapter 5: *Betelgeuse*, 1979.)

The 1980s

On 6 February 1981 members of an IRA active service unit boarded and set an explosive charge in the engine room of the coaster *Nellie M* in Lough Foyle, just off the shore from the small town of Moville, County Donegal. The ship was carrying approximately 1,000 tonnes of coal, and was at anchor awaiting the change of tide before heading up and into Derry port. When the charge detonated, it blew a hole in the sea chest sufficient to send the ship to the seabed. She sank in less than 9 metres of water, and luckily sat down in an upright position. Her bow and stern sections were above water at all stages of the tide. There was no one on board during the explosions, as the crew had been evacuated by the IRA when they were leaving the ship.

The declared intention of the IRA was to disrupt the maritime traffic in and out of Derry. The sinking of the *Nellie M* achieved this aim only for a few hours, but the point had been well made by then. It showed a lack of security awareness by both sets of authorities, North and South. However, the ship had sunk, it was by now an eyesore, an embarrassment, a constant reminder, and something had to be done to get rid of it. As there was no crew lost in the incident, the involvement of the Naval Service divers was considered unlikely, even with the possibility of explosive charges remaining on the vessel. This was 1983 and as such it would have fallen very neatly into the laps of the Army Ordnance Corps. However, it appeared an explosive-ordnance-disposal officer, based in the Southern Command, had a different viewpoint. As he saw it, it was a ship, it was in water, and it was sunk and on the seabed, and for that he required the navy. Gerry O'Donoghue described the subsequent events – which saw the first clearing of such a vessel – and the consequences:

The *Nellie M* was a great job in that it was the first explosive-ordnance-disposal job for the naval divers. At that stage I and divers in general were still under suspicion because Maloney was flag [Commodore Maloney, Flag Officer Commanding the Naval Service]. He had a commander in the naval base interview me before I left to find out what I planned to do when I got there. As I had no clue until I actually arrived on scene, the final direct order was given: 'Please don't do anything dangerous' … So there was this great commandant from the Ordnance Corps who said, 'I'm fucking not going up to that unless I get a navy diving team', and we said 'No problem.' I met him in Dublin and we flew to England to meet the engineer … now the flight was delayed so we laid into a few whiskeys. We arrived over to this poor engineer's house in England, feeling a bit shook, so we chatted away to him but he could tell us fuck all really. Meanwhile, the team had arrived up … the usual suspects … we did a dive on her hull and then a number of dives into the engine room … I was down on a line, I had boots on which

was the dumbest thing I ever did, and nearly drowned myself once again …
We were making it up as we went along … the thing was to do something,
we had to do a dive. We found nothing, so we certified her clear … when
they raised her they found the control box, the detonating box, but that was
only a bunch of wires, so we did OK. We came good out of that … we came
out looking smooth … it was our first EOD job.[22]

As a direct consequence of that particular job, there was a round of letters from
one commander to another with a view to having the MCDOs qualification by
the Royal Navy recognised, and to receive further qualification by the army EOD
school. Gerry elaborated:

The result of the *Nellie M* was the army Ordnance Corps, who were sus-
picious of us before, then said, 'Oh, we won't accept the MCDO bomb
disposal qualification but we will let him come on our EOD course.' So
then they let me come on their EOD course even though I wasn't a university graduate. I didn't have a zoology degree, so I did the three-month
course with the Ordnance lads, so I could use explosives in Ireland.[23]

Just over a year later – on 23 February 1982 – members of the Provisional IRA
again boarded a coal-carrying vessel. Like the *Nellie M* before her, the *St Bedan*
was lying at anchor in Lough Foyle awaiting the tide before heading up to Derry.
Clearly, what had worked for them previously was working for the IRA again. The
similarities between the vessels, the cargo and the methodology of the operation
were incredible. An explosive charge was placed inside the engine room and in
similar fashion they departed the ship. The charge detonated a short time later,
but this time the vessel heeled over onto her starboard side and settled down on
the seabed in 10 metres of water.

This time there would be no flying to England for the MCDO. The diving
team arrived on site on 10 March. The information at the time was that there had
been more than one charge placed in the engine room. This made sense as two
charges were better than one, and increased the chances of success. The placement
of any charge would be most successful if placed to blow out the sea chests, and
the previous year's operation showed that they had already got those tactics right.
But what's not always possible to tell in these matters was what exactly the truth
was. Did they plant two or more charges, or only one? If they did plant more

than one charge, where were they placed? This was the dilemma facing the diving officer and his team of divers. So after a series of extensive searches by the diving team in areas that were accessible to them – the bridge and afterdeck areas particularly – the only thing left was the engine room. Gerry described the scene:

> The *St Bedan* was the first time we actually blew a hole in a ship … and we didn't know what the fuck to do now as she was on her side. So we decided to blow up the port sea chest on the educated guess that there was more than one charge placed in the engine room. One had gone off on the starboard sea chest then the port sea chest was as good a place as any … so we shimmied down the hull 'cos she was awash, found the port sea chest intake, and we packed a bunch of plastic explosives into the sea chest [from the outside], and you know there wasn't much point in doing it, but sure feck it, we were there – why not! There might have been explosives behind the sea chest so basically we were just counter-mining … we lit the fuse with a flare, got into our very dodgy

Divers standing on the port side of the sunken St Bedan, *Lough Foyle, 1982*

Gemini to get away … That was good because it worked, no one gave us any shit over that, which was good also.[24]

The diving team concluded operations and returned to the naval base on 19 March. The operations conducted on both the *Nellie M* and the *St Bedan* were notable firsts for the Diving Section, the *Nellie M* being the first EOD operation and the *St Bedan* the first time that 'we actually blew a hole in a ship'.[25] But much more important than that, the Diving Section had now moved on again in its development,

> … and that was the next big step, 'cos technically I could blow shit up … I'm not sure if I did a sea mine after that. The army were always nervous about sea mines – they were kinda almost happy to have us around. So then we moved on to the next level … that was because of [Cdr] Joe Deasy I think, or whoever – maybe [Capt.] Brett was there at the time. Wally – given a choice – wouldn't have let me within 2 miles of explosives … that put us into EOD – that was a huge stepping stone because the lads [meaning us] could work with me.[26]

On 6 January 1984 naval divers were involved in another extended lake search, having been called in to assist the Garda Underwater Unit in searching for two missing persons in one of the bigger lakes in the north-west. Lough Gill, in County Sligo, is the location of the Isle of Inisfree. The lake itself is about 5 miles long by 1 mile wide, and at its deepest is about 120 feet deep. It was here that the naval diving team commenced a search for four young men: two brothers and two army privates. The four men went out fishing on the lake on 2 January and drowned when their boat overturned when caught in very strong winds. Two bodies – those of Private Michael Rooney and Mr John McLoughlin – were subsequently recovered shortly after the incident, while the search continued to locate the remaining two men, Private John McGowan and Mr Patsy McLoughlin. The diving officer leading the operation was a young S/Lt Chris Reynolds, who was essentially leading his first real diving-operation team away from the naval base, and had with him some of the navy's most senior divers. But Chris was nothing if not determined and undaunted:

> The very first day we arrived, we had driven most of the night and into the

day in a bloody Land Rover, a truck and a minibus. Half of the guys were in the back of the truck, some in the minibus and meself and Walshy, who was in the back of the Land Rover all the way up. Anyway, we got to Lough Gill and there was a garda inspector there … we didn't have any proper fatigues or combats – just all dressed in bits of gear 'n' pieces. Anyway, we all hop out, coughing and spluttering and spitting, like fucking war-torn guerrillas getting out of the car. The inspector – whose all dressed up – goes 'Who's in charge?' looking around hopefully, and I go 'I am,' and he goes 'Ah no son, who's in charge?' and I go 'It's me, it's me,' and he just looked at me, rolled his eyes and goes 'Ah now, you're really taking the piss.'[27]

Diving operations there were not difficult for the divers – after all, it was a fresh-water lake – but what proved to be the most difficult aspect of the diving were the very cold temperatures both in the air and especially in the water. Temperatures of 3 degrees both in and out of the water were the norm, and groups of sodden divers huddled around the campfires after a dive with cups of soup and sandwiches in hand were regular scenes – indeed, the hospitality shown by the local community in Sligo town undoubtedly made the operation tolerable for all those involved. Unfortunately for all concerned, no bodies were recovered during that diving operation, with the naval diving team concluding its operation on 21 January, making it one of the longest searches of its type in Ireland at that time:

> 6th–21st Jan 1984 – Diving in Lough Gill for 2 bodies. Diving with gardaí and army divers – jackstay search pattern using snagline – depth varied, vis nil, tide nil – nothing recovered, good diving – 0/80ft – total time 664 mins.[28]

On 12 Sept 1984, the LÉ *Emer* arrived off the northern side of An Blascaod Mór, the Great Blasket Island. For the next three days the ship-borne diving team conducted a search of a submerged wreck of a ship that had foundered there during the Great War. That ship was made famous by Peig Sayers in her biographical book about her life and times on the Great Blasket. The ship – the SS *Quebra* – foundered against the northern side of the island close by an area known locally as Lochar Rock in heavy fog on 23 August 1916. She was carrying a general cargo of foodstuffs, meat, flour, tinned food, metals of various types and artillery shells. These shells were bound for the Western Front.

During the early 1980s this wreck and area had been dived quite frequently, and the presence of the shells was well known. But with the passage of time it had still not been determined if indeed those shells were inert or if they or part of them were fused. That would not in itself be a problem if they were left alone, but it could be a problem if the shells happened to be live and were raised and taken home as souvenirs. When a member of the Garda Sub Aqua Club (not to be mistaken with the Garda Sub-aqua Unit) raised the matter with the relevant authorities, naval operations tasked the LÉ *Emer* to the scene to conduct a survey of the wreck and site to assess the situation. Over the next three days or so – 12–14 September 1984 – a series of dives was conducted and assessments made on the nature and quantity of the shells. Two charges of 5 lbs of PE4 were placed in two areas, and following successful detonation subsequent dives resulted in further assessments. It was not possible to declare categorically that the munitions were inert. It would require a larger and more extensive survey by a full diving team in an operation that would need to be several days longer. Until then the wreck was placed off limits to civilian divers until its safety was determined by the navy.

It took a while to plan and coordinate, but on 8 August 1986 a ten-man naval-diving team under the command of the diving officer S/Lt Chris Reynolds, complete with all necessary diving and camping equipment, made camp on the Great Blasket for just over two weeks. The sight chosen for the campsite was the only piece of terrain flat enough to pitch a tent. On a good day it was beautiful, especially the view from the makeshift toilet located in the corner of the field where the camp was established.

The first series of dives conducted were a mix of recce dives and mapping the wreck site. This was important as it would not only build up a mental and pen picture of the actual wreck site and its important features but, in doing so, allow the divers to maximise their somewhat limited 'bottom time' due to the depth of water the wreck lay in. Also, to assist the divers the initial recce dives saw the divers laying ground lines from feature to feature, which also would greatly assist the divers when travelling around the wreck. The operation saw the divers operating alone on the island without any vessel support. Great emphasis was put on good timekeeping regarding dive management, and over the course of the first week a large number of dives were conducted on the wreck. However, the weather was not always conducive to diving, and a day or two were lost. Even on the bad days the sight of the Kerry mainland, Dunquin and the Blasket sound – home to the Spanish armada wreck the *Santa Maria de la Rosa* – was just beautiful. On one or two occasions a couple of divers would take the island ferry that ran tourists out and back over to Dunquin pier, and from there it was straight to the nearest shop where they would promptly clean it out of rashers, sausages, pudding and any fresh bread that may have been there.

Luckily enough, down days didn't feature too much in the first week of diving. Slowly but surely a detailed picture was being drawn up on the condition and lay out of the wreck. More importantly, and central to the operation, the location and approximate number of artillery shells were also being established. When the boss was sufficiently happy with the bottom picture that had developed over the dives, the second part of the operation was implemented. Contact was made with Command, and the ARW provided the necessary detail for the

Blasket Island –SS Quebra *Operation outdoor toilet with fantastic views – probably excluding this one though. Brendan Cotter modelling the latest portable naval stores-issued toilet.*

explosives that would be used to counter-mine the rather large stockpile of artillery shells located through the wreck. During the final couple of days of the operation several counter-mining charges were placed amongst large amounts of the projectiles, and while all the charges successfully detonated, no sympathetic detonations were deemed to have occurred.

However, the diving operations as conducted during the period of 8–21 August 1986 – whilst a successful and hugely informative operation – didn't fully survey the forward section of the wreck. Before the wreck could be fully cleared and certified as clear, this area would need to be surveyed. This, then, would be the objective for the following year's diving operation to the Blasket Islands. Details of the 1986 operation was recorded in the author's diving logbook:

> Diving operation took place on west side of Great Blasket Island –British MV Quebra was wrecked on the 23 Aug 1916 – carrying general cargo and supply of munitions … information from Lloyds registry of shipping – diving took place over 3 weeks working out of campsite on north side of island – All diving took place on air (scuba)- neg RCC - 1st and 2nd week, plotting, charting and checking of no of shells, sizes, disposition on wreck etc … 3rd week involved explosives P.E.4, 2lbs to 18lbs charges initiated from surface, diving involved placing charges beside suspect shells and detonating – operation took place in good weather – with campsite facilities – principal diving officer S/Lt Chris Reynolds. Max depth – 113 feet, Total time – 272 mins. Equipment – SCUBA.[29]

On 19 March 1987 the diving officer, Lt Shane Anderson, wrote a letter of request through the school commandant to OCNBAD Capt. Joe Deasy requesting permission to return to the Blasket Islands to survey the bow area with a view to finally clearing the area of potential ordnance hazards. The necessary permission and authority was granted, and on 10 August a naval diving team descended on the Great Blasket Island and established camp there. Over the next twelve days they dived and surveyed the wreck, particularly the forward section, which was the main objective. In the subsequent post-operation diving report, Lt Anderson concluded:

> Para 12. The operation successfully achieved all the objectives laid out in Ref 'A'.

Para 13. The for'd area of the ship including for'd magazine was thoroughly checked and charted. No fuze storage area was located and it is presumed at this stage that no fuzes were held on board.[30]

This concluded the diving operations on the *SS Quebra*. They had their origin with an initial reconnaissance dive back in 1984, and finally concluded after two full diving operations in late 1987. The Naval Service Diving Section has not returned to the Great Blasket Island to date. However, in the intervening year of 1985 a tragedy of epic proportions took place not that far away from the Blasket Islands, in which over three hundred people were killed on a flight from Canada to India. The flight, Air India Flight 182, a Boeing 747 cruising at an altitude of 33,000 feet, when approaching the south-west coast of Cork was blown out of the sky by an explosive device contained within its cargo hold. (See Chapter 6: Air India Flight 182).

On the evening of 15 February 1989, at Lismore Bridge, County Waterford, a young girl by the name of Aileen Daly was 'flung' from the bridge into the river by her father. The bridge lies over the River Blackwater in the shadow of Lismore Castle. The picturesque scene belied the poor diving conditions on the day of arrival of the naval diving team. The river itself wasn't in flood, as the weather prior to the incident had not been bad, but it was freezing and the flow was significant. When the diving team arrived on site late in the afternoon, they were greeted by members of the Garda Sub-aqua Unit. As the flow of the river passing through the legs of the bridge was quite fast, an initial dive was made by a diver in the middle of the river just downstream from the bridge to assess the conditions, such as the speed of the flow, visibility and nature of the seabed.

The Blackwater is a river of varying depths, speeds and widths. The next six days would see the naval diving team and the Garda Sub-aqua Unit work together in some of the most trying conditions on the river, yet also some of the most peaceful. The river at some points was probably 30 to 40 metres wide and 8 to 9 metres in depth. When searching the wider stretches of the river, the teams split up, with one team searching one side and the other team the opposite. Sometimes the two teams would combine and search one side together, and then return upstream and do the other side. Other times the teams searched stretches of the shallower parts of the river by wading down them. The method of searching was for the most part a 'modified snag-line search'. The snag line was simply a length of rope with hand loops placed at equal distances along its length, onto which the divers could hold. If the visibility was good, the divers could move outwards a bit more along the line to cover more ground, and if the visibility was poor they could move in to ensure that nothing was missed. The term 'modified', however, was a euphemism for going with the flow of the river, because, in general, once you left the surface with the loop in your hand, the divers would then proceed to search the stretch of the river according to the flow of the river. The two hardest-working divers on the snag lines were both the inside diver nearest the river bank – who had to try and keep the river bank close to him as best he could – and the outside diver, who had to try and keep the snag line with the divers attached in a reasonably straight line, and all this while trying to search for a little girl.

The river was home to many a submerged tree, and the greatest fear from both a diver's and a supervisor's point of view was getting fouled up in one. If a diver did get fouled up, the sound of snapping and breaking branches could be heard through the generally black visibility, and once free the diver would continue. On more than one occasion divers had gloves pulled off their hands by being snagged on something and being unable to free it in time. The temperature of the freshwater river slowly told on the divers as the naval diving team were using 7 mm wetsuits. Endurances began to decrease over the course of the operation, and once a chill or shiver set in, there was very little chance of recovery, and this could be very dangerous for the divers.

Over the course of the operation – from 19–26 February 1989 – it was estimated that the diving teams involved covered approximately 8 miles of river banks by either diving or wading stretches of the river. Unfortunately, and much to the sadness of the divers, Aileen's body was not recovered during the diving operations. A joint decision was made by both garda and naval authorities to conclude the search, and on 26 February the operation was concluded. The author's logbook for the last two days of the search operation report

> 25/2/89 – Continuing search – Snagline search in use – due to severe current at all times diving conditions were dangerous – 0/30' – 90 mins – SCUBA.

> 26/2/89 – Search for girl ends today – Approx. 8 miles of river searched – Total of 13 divers involved – Nothing found – 0/30' – 90 mins SCUBA.[31]

Several weeks later the remains of young Aileen Daly was recovered near Dromore,

Villiarstown, County Waterford. Her father subsequently was charged with her murder and stood trial. He was found guilty but insane.

The 1990s

On Sunday 9 June 1991, two Mk 17 sea mines, remnants of the Second World War, were hauled up in fishing nets by a trawler operating out of Dunmore East. As the mines were being hauled onto the deck, they were recognised for what they were and the danger that they could possibly pose. Incredibly, both mines appeared to be relatively intact, with contact horns still showing and some wires exposed, with both mines having large holes in the sides of the shells. These holes were large enough that the fishermen could see inside and positively identify the large, cylindrical explosive charges (similar in shape and size to a beer barrel) contained within each mine. Faced with not one but two mines in his nets, and discretion being the better part of valour, the trawler skipper managed to attach a float line to each of the mines so that they could be located later, and then duly returned the mines to the safekeeping of the seabed. The mines were dropped in approximately 50 feet of seawater between Dunmore East and the entrance to Waterford estuary. Weather conditions on this particular day were not good, to say the least: there were high seas with a strong south-easterly wind blowing

The members of the naval diving team were called back into work that Sunday morning, and having assembled in the Diving Store they set about organising the necessary equipment for the counter-mining operation. Taking into consideration the weather conditions, the potential scale of the operation and the necessary logistic support involved in dealing with two mines simultaneously, it was determined that travelling down by ship would be the best and more sensible option. The ship involved was the LÉ *Orla*, under the command of Lt Cdr Mark Mellett, and the diving officer for the operation was Lt Cdr Gerry O'Donoghue MCDO.

After what can only be described as a hammering on the transit down, the *Orla* finally anchored off Dunmore East and the diving team assembled on the bridge of the ship. As surface conditions were not good, it was not unreasonably felt by most of the diving team that the boss would say that the operation would be delayed until the conditions and wind moderated. But that's not what the boss had in mind when he mustered the team:

> I remember lying on the settee in the senior-rates' mess on the way down

and remarking that the weather was just shite for this type of op … finally, after what seemed like a lifetime, the ship went to anchor off Dunmore East and started to roll in the swell. A pipe went out calling all the diving team to the bridge. When I got up to the bridge I just couldn't believe my eyes. What I was seeing from the bridge windows, the sea was just pure muck. Whitecaps everywhere, no bleeding way where we going to go diving in that crap.[32]

Instead, the details of the operation were hammered out. The mines were to be treated as individual operations but happening at the same time. The diving team was split into two smaller teams. The mines were then to be recce'd, with the initial intention of raising them to the surface and towing them into more sheltered waters for counter-mining; for this *Orla*'s two SeaRiders would be manned by members of her crew.

It was necessary to conduct the operation without delay as the mines were now encroaching on the shipping lanes in and out of Waterford. So with the decision made, the divers completed their preparations and commenced diving operations. Both teams located

(left): Main-filling charge from a Second World War mine (origin unknown);(right): a demonstration contact mine similar to those found off Dunmore East; this demonstration model was photographed outside the Diving Store. To its left is a demonstration depth charge.

their mines quickly enough in the heavy swells due to the attached marker buoys. The mine nearest the shore was dived first, as the second mine was a bit further offshore by a couple of hundred metres. Visibility on the seabed was poor, and this only added to the difficulty of the operation. A lifting bag was brought down by the two divers, and after a while the divers surfaced and indicated that they had attached the bag and had opened the air cylinder to begin inflating it. After a short while, the bright-yellow lifting bag appeared on the surface, comfortably supporting the mine. This mine was taken in tow by the SeaRider and slowly towed towards the sheltered waters inside Kilcredaun Head. When they got into the sheltered waters, the divers then re-sank the mine in preparation for counter-mining operations later.

Dealing with the second mine proved to be a far more stubborn operation. The mine had no real strong points where the divers might safely attach the lifting bag, and the poor visibility necessitated the divers making a couple of dives more than they had planned. They were feeling the effects of the very poor surface conditions, and communication was proving very difficult between the divers and the supervisor while the divers were underwater. In the end they managed to attach the lifting bag. However, the low-pressure air hose connecting the lifting bag and the air cylinder used to inflate the bag didn't seal properly. So when the bag inflated, it only barely made the surface due to lack of air supply, and towing the bag with the attached mine therefore proved very difficult. The surface conditions were playing havoc with the SeaRider as well. Waves broke constantly into the boat – so much so that the petrol tanks had become contaminated with seawater, leaving the SeaRider operating on only one engine. The extremely slow progress being made with just the one working engine led to the decision to cast the tow adrift. The boat returned to the LÉ *Orla*, where the fuel tanks were replaced, thus enabling the boat to return to the area.

It the meantime it had been decided that the first mine would be counter-mined in situ while the second was being searched for. The counter-mining of the first mine proved to be very much textbook, and a full-order detonation was achieved when counter-mined. However, the second mine was proving to be a bit more problematic. After searching for a while, the barely visible lifting bag was found, and as the afternoon turned to early evening, the boss – not wanting the operation to progress into the night – decided to deflate the lifting bag and counter-mine the second mine on site. This necessitated stopping any shipping traffic for the duration of the operation. Eventually, the counter-mining charge was made up by the boss, and handed over to the two divers that were hanging onto the side of the SeaRider in foul surface conditions. The two divers left the surface and descended the float line to the mine below. As they descended, both divers could hear what they would later describe as a rumbling noise, like something rolling along the seabed. Visibility was down to inches, and as both divers made their way to the mine they realised that it was the mine itself rumbling along the seabed in the groundswell. The method of counter-mining the charge involved the placing of the small 5 kg PE4 charge onto the main filling charge of the mine. Both divers wondered if indeed they might not be able to complete the operation given that the mine was essentially doing a 'Siege of Ennis' along the seabed:

> It was funny – myself and Gerry were heading down the downline to the mine, the vis was getting progressively poorer, and as we were getting deeper we could both hear this sort of dull noise coming at us, like … badummm, badum badum badummm – a bit of a silence then it would go again, badumm, badum badumm … both of us looked at each other – you know that sort of 'What the fuck is that' look – the two of us just looked at each other then probably came to the same conclusion, 'That's the fucking mine – I don't believe it!'[33]

However, with time and air running short, the divers – with the help of a roll of insulating tape – managed to reach into the mine, grab a hold of the main filling, and strap the PE4 charge to it with several hastily wound turns of the insulating tape. Not necessarily happy that the PE4 would remain where it was taped, given that the mine was doing its own thing, both divers signalled the surface and left the bottom. On the way up they ensured that the Cordtex train was at least intact, and had no kinks in it.

Once on the surface, both divers were recovered into the SeaRider. After a quick debrief to the boss about the state of the charges, preparations were made to initiate the charge. A couple of minutes later and with the necessary radio calls made, the safety fuze was lit and burning confirmed. The det board (detonator board: a floating polystyrene board on which the safety fuze is placed to keep it clear of the water) was cast adrift, there was nothing left for the divers to do except leave the immediate area and move to a safe stand-off distance. At the time the boss remarked to both myself and Gerry that 'We've managed to achieve in the last ten minutes what the Germans couldn't achieve in the five years of World

War Two, and that was close down Waterford Port.'[34] Two minutes later, and with a loud, sharp crack emanating from underneath the boat, a large plume of water rose upwards from the dive site a few hundred metres away. All in the dive boat agreed that the main filling charge had indeed detonated. The dive site was given a few minutes to calm down, and there was a quick recce dive of the seabed to ensure that there had been a full detonation. In the meantime the SeaRider crew gathered up the stunned fish before returning to the LÉ *Orla*:

> 9/6/91 – Explosive ordnance disposal – 2 Mk 17 British contact mines – Dunmore East – both exploded – severe conditions – 0/50 feet – total time 80 mins – SCUBA.[35]

Subsequent to the return of the diving team to the naval base, it was determined by the diving officer, the OC LÉ *Orla* and Command that the six members of the diving team and the two SeaRider coxswains were to be recommended for Distinguished Service Medals for their conduct during the diving operations that Sunday. The subsequent paperwork, relevant reports and individual recommendations were all promulgated and sent up through the chain of command to the relevant authority. None were awarded.

In 1992 the Naval Service Diving Section engaged in another long search-and-recovery operation, this time in Lough Derravaragh, County Westmeath, made famous by the Children of Lír. On the evening of 23 December 1991 three men went out duck shooting on the lake and, following an incident, all three drowned. Two bodies were recovered but the third person, Philip Moffat, remained missing. On Friday 3 January 1992 the naval diving team consisting of eight divers and two drivers, with Lt Declan Fleming in charge, departed the naval base and proceeded to Mullingar Barracks, which would be the base of operations during the diving operation.

The Garda Sub-aqua Unit, led by Sgt Thomas 'Tosh' Lavery, was on site, and together both teams would scour the seabed in an attempt to recover the body. Conditions both above and below the surface over the duration of the search were good. Visibility on the bottom was good, but – like all lake diving – as long as you didn't stay in the one place and kept moving, the visibility would in general always be good enough to do an effective search. The search schemes employed were governed essentially 'on the basis of witnesses reports, information supplied by the gardaí, and as a result of items found'.[36] So, with no particular starting point, the operation began in earnest. It focused more towards the northern shore, which ran in an east–west line. The favoured means of searching the lake was by a 'towed diver' search. This was a very efficient method of searching the seabed, particularly over such a large area and especially when there was good visibility. In no small way was the usefulness of this type of search helped by the ability of the local fishermen and their ability in driving their boats. They were invaluable.

The method itself was simple enough, but it did take a bit of getting used to, and indeed would lead to some lighter moments. This involved a length of scaffolding pole or suchlike, about 10 to 12 feet in length, with a length of line passing through it. The two ends were then brought together and joined by another line to the surface, much like an inverted Y, but with the bar going between two parts of the Y. The line was then taken into the boat, where it was secured to the stern. One of the divers would have a lifeline up to the boat, and when the divers were ready he would signal the surface to start the engine and commence the run. This was done at a reasonable speed – perhaps three to four knots. The divers would be spaced along the bar, normally three to a bar, and depending on visibility would scan the lake bottom looking for any evidence of the missing person.

The start of a search involved the divers getting to the pole and organising themselves when there. Sometimes the pole would be dropped to the seabed and lie flat awaiting the divers to go down. If the lead diver happened to get turned as he travelled down the line, so as to be facing the opposite direction to the way the boat intended to travel, he wouldn't necessarily be aware of it. He would then direct the other divers along the bar and indicate to them which way to face. However, as he himself was facing the wrong direction and there was no way he could know, when the signal was given to the boat to start the search, chaos would ensue as the divers would be facing the wrong direction with the bar coming back over them at speed. All that the divers could do when that happened would be to hang on and try and turn around and face the right way. Sometimes, two divers would be facing each other, both believing that they were facing the correct way, which was fun, and sometimes the boat driver would get the signals wrong and start the boat and move off before the divers were ready, which was even more fun. Sometimes the pole, the divers and the line would all be lined up and correct, only for the boat to move off at a complete right angle to everything. When that happened, the pole would dig in on its end, and pitch pole the entire lot upwards, with everyone holding on for dear life.

But in the end a very large tract of the lakebed was searched, and, indeed, as the

Lough Derravaragh dive site

days passed there was firm evidence that the search technique was working well
as there were always tell-tale signs that the towed divers had previously passed
through the area. There were scour marks from poles, divers' hands, divers' fins, and
sometimes it would be some item of diving kit. When the availability of civilian
divers become plentiful, particularly at weekends, the search scheme would change
and a long search line comprising of up to thirty divers would be used, with a
boat either end to assist in keeping the line straight and moving. On these occasions there were many competent and experienced civilian divers; however, like
all things in life, these occasions also happened to attract a few well-intentioned
but less than helpful divers to the site:

> I remember a particular morning – I don't recall if it was a Saturday or
> a Sunday – but either way there were loads of divers available, so it was
> decided by the guards and ourselves that the best way to keep good control
> of them and also make use of them was to do a long swim line and keep
> them all going in the one direction. Anyway, two guys stood out like the
> proverbial lighthouse on a dark night because they had just the best of gear.
> Brand new drysuits, black with a sponsor's logo emblazoned in yellow let-
> tering across the backs of their suits, absolutely no doubting where these
> guys came from and who sponsored the gear. Let's just say that they were
> from Cork … these guys just looked like the dog's bollocks, except they
> couldn't dive. Tosh Lavery was the supervisor for the dive … everyone got
> numbered off for their place on the swim line, and off into the boats goes
> everybody. I think maybe seven to eight boats full of divers and all off to
> the dive drop-off point. On arrival everyone got into the water and all onto
> the line … Tosh wasn't wasting time so he told everybody to stand by. Once

Tosh checked that everyone was well, he told them to leave the surface. The dive commenced but the two lads were still struggling with their gear, all sorts of problems developed. Tosh loitered over to them and between the jigs and the reels, after about five minutes Tommy got a pain in his arse with the two of them, pulled the two guys out of the water, got a boat to come over to him and ordered the two lads into it. We were close enough to hear Tosh chewing the two lads' new arseholes and telling them in no uncertain terms that if he 'finds them on the dive site when he gets back' he'd 'fucking arrest the pair of them for impersonating divers.'[37]

Tosh also recounted a couple of other moments:

There was a big fire out at the lake and the grub; Jaysus ... there was fellas coming out of the pubs in Mullingar for their fucking dinner and they were telling their wives they were involved in the search ... they weren't involved in the search, they were on the beer all week ... three fellas came from Cork, they made a huge collection, they drank all the money in Mullingar, went back to Cork and they never got in the fucking water ... [Finally], the army came in and laid roads and put up tents. The Civil Defence came in and fed everybody – they fed half of fucking Ireland there ... it was like a war zone in fairness.[38]

Sometime during a dive on the first Saturday, while leaning over the pole and being towed through shallow waters close enough to the shore in 5 metres of water, the author spotted what looked like a spearhead lying on the lakebed about 3 metres in front of him. As the tow passed over it, he picked it up and shook off the silt. It was a spearhead – no doubt about it – but where did it come from and how long had it been there? It seemed to be around a couple of hundred years old – probably from the 1798 rebellion. A week later, Derry McMahon (brother of navy diver Chris McMahon), after viewing the spearhead for himself, informed me that he reckoned it was much older – possibly Bronze Age or thereabouts.

On Monday 13 January 1992 the naval diving team concluded diving operations without having recovered the body. A lot of effort, dive time and resources had been involved, and to fail to recover the body was disappointing:

Diving operations ceased 17:30 hrs this date. Nothing further located.

Approximately 40 divers on search over week-end. 8 NS, 8 army SA, 6 GS, 18 civilian.

… A total of 124 hours [7,440 minutes] bottom time was accumulated by the eight diving members of the team.[39]

In an epilogue to the diving operation in Lough Derravaragh, the body of Philip Moffat was recovered in May that year, and the spearhead – which was subsequently handed over to the National Museum – was sent for carbon dating. It turned out that Derry McMahon was correct:

The National Museum of Ireland is pleased to announce the acquisition of a large socketed bronze spearhead from Lough Derravaragh, County Westmeath, through the good offices of the Naval Service. The spearhead, which dates to the later Bronze Age period, between about 800 and 500 BC, was found on the lake bed by naval diver Martin Buckley, in the course of official operations. The spearhead is in fine condition and measures almost 50 cm. in length.[40]

The cutting edge . . . from the Bronze Age

• Chief Petty Officer Gerry Duffy, of the Irish Naval diving team, testing the sharpness of a large socketed bronze spearhead, dating back to between 500 and 800 BC, on his companion Naval Officer Martin Buckley, who found the spearhead in Lough Derravarragh, Co. Westmeath, during official operations. They were at the National Museum yesterday to hand the spearhead over to Pat Wallace, director of the Museum.

In 1995 the fishing trawler *Carrickatine* sank without warning and without trace sometime on 15 November. The vessel had been fishing in an area known as the Stanton Banks, some 50 miles north of Malin Head, County Donegal. Weather conditions in the area were poor, and a number of vessels also fishing the area made their way back to port. The *Carrickatine*, it was assumed, was doing the same thing. It was known that she had been experiencing engine-room difficulties but that the skipper was not unduly worried about it. When the vessel failed to make Greencastle later that night, the alarm was raised. On 20 November the LÉ *Deirdre* with members of the Naval Service Diving Section embarked was tasked with assisting the IMES (Irish Marine Emergency Service, a forerunner to today's Irish Coast Guard) in the search for the *Carrickatine*. The *Irish Times* later reported

> … what may have been the most detailed and comprehensive sea search operation in the history of the State. Units of the Irish Marine Emergency Service, the Naval Service, Air Corps, Irish Lights, the RNLI and local fishing vessels, were involved, with Naval Service patrol ships and the Irish Lights Tender, Granuaile, continuing well into the new year.[41]

While the LÉ *Deirdre* worked offshore, a second diving team had proceeded to Donegal by road. Over the course of the next several days, both the sea area and the coastline bordering it were extensively searched. It proved fruitless. Although items such as shoes and a lifebelt were recovered ashore and fish boxes recovered at sea, none of these items were positively identified as having come from the fishing vessel, though the fish boxes were possibly from the *Carrickatine*.

On Thursday 23 November 1995 the LÉ *Deirdre* berthed alongside Rathmullen pier in County Donegal, and embarked personnel and specialist sub-surface search equipment. This equipment consisted of a remote-operated vehicle (ROV), a side-scan sonar, a magnetometer and a video plotter. It was a very rare event that a side scan and mag would be used from an Naval Service vessel, and the equipment – though used extensively during the subsequent searches – failed to locate the fishing vessel. Both the weather and the nature of the seabed conspired during the search to make an already difficult task harder. The weather constantly ran strong winds and heavy seas, while the nature of the seabed in the area was such that it contained previously uncharted Second World War wrecks later identified as U-boats. The magnetic anomaly detector was also working overtime in an area full of magnetic lodestones and large quantities of Second World War munitions. So all these uncharted wrecks and anomalies had to be considered as possibly the *Carrickatine*, with each one having to be individually checked out by the ROV. It was both time-consuming and painstaking work. On 7 December the LÉ *Deirdre* berthed back alongside Rathmullen pier and disembarked the search equipment and personnel, and on completion returned to the naval base.

Unfortunately for the families and the search personnel from all the state agencies involved, the *Carrickatine* remained elusive and remains so today. In the post-incident report submitted by the OC LÉ *Deirdre*, Lt Cdr Tom Touhy, in his 'conclusion' he states that

> The search operation highlighted a number of shortfalls in equipment aboard NS Vessels. Whereas it is accepted that our primary role is surface detection, it would be prudent to have at the very least knowledge in sub-surface detection and accurate sub-surfacing plotting.[42]

In the 'recommendations' section, he states:

> That the Service procures sub-surface detection equipment, i.e. side-scan sonar and ROV [remote-operated vehicle] so as to ensure that there is:
> Knowledge of the operation of this equipment in the Service.
> That the Service has the ability to respond to requests for sub-surface searches.[43]

On Sunday evening 4 February 1996 the Irish-registered fishing vessel *Jenalisa* went missing with the loss of its three crewmen without discharging a distress message or signal of any kind. The weather on the night in question was poor. In the immediate aftermath of the incident, one body was recovered by a passing fishing vessel oblivious to the incident that had taken place. It was the recovery of the body that sparked off the subsequent search by trawlers form Dunmore East and the emergency services. On Monday 5 February the naval diving team was dispatched from the naval base to Dunmore East under the command of Lt Eddie Mulligan to assist in the search for the missing vessel. Also arriving into Dunmore East that evening was the garda underwater unit. As the weather was not conducive to diving, the diving team returned to the naval base on Wednesday, only to find themselves returning to Dunmore East again, at 05:00 hrs on Thursday morning. On Thursday 8 February the missing vessel was located after a series of searches by fishing vessels using fishing sonars and echo sounders to identify probable targets. On one such dive of a probable target, as determined by the *Coronia II* skippered by a Mr Taylor, the *Jenalisa* was located by members of the naval diving team in approximately 38 metres of seawater. Now that the vessel had been found, the search for the two missing fishermen would begin in earnest.

Given the nature of the wreck and the amount of trawl net in the immediate vicinity of the trawler, all subsequent dives were conducted principally using surface-demand diving equipment (SDDE). In fact this operation would be the first time that a full survey and search of a sunken trawler using only SDDE would be undertaken.

The surface-demand equipment used by the navy at this time was the EXO 26. It was a good functional piece of equipment and it was what the Naval Service Diving Section could afford at the time. The post-diving operation report, as submitted by Lt Mulligan, stated:

> Due to the fact that combined dives which would entail 'in water' decompression stops were planned, the recompression chamber was embarked on board the LÉ Aoife. As surface-demand diving equipment and camera equipment were being embarked, a vessel was required to moor or station directly over the wreck. A local half-decker, the 'Silver Bell', proved ideal for this. Diving operations were carried out on the 'Jenalisa' from the 'Silver Bell' as dive platform, and supported from LÉ Aoife, which remained within 300 metres of the dive site at all times.[44]

Having conducted a comprehensive series of dives using the SDDE and a handheld real-time video camera, the naval diving team completed its diving operations. No bodies were recovered and all compartments bar the engine room space had been searched and video recorded. While the divers couldn't access the engine room space given the location of the door into it, they did manage to insert the video camera into the space and to record the area as best they could. No bodies were seen in this area, though it couldn't be ruled out definitively. On Friday 16 February the naval diving team returned to the naval base.

However, it was not to be the last involvement of the naval diving team with the *Jenalisa*. The Department of the Marine had decided to raise the wreck and required the presence of members of the Diving Section to act in an advisory capacity to the salvor. On 27 February members of the Diving Section returned to Dunmore East. Weather and technical difficulties with the salvage vessel caused the naval divers to return to the naval base, but not before the possibility of the Naval Service Diving Section raising the vessel was mooted by a senior official at the Department of the Marine. As Eddie Mulligan stated in his post-operation dive report:

I referred him to SO OPS. A subsequent telephone call with FOCNS on the matter transpired and it was decided that the NS Divers would NOT be lifting the vessel'[45]

It's very probable that this had been an extremely short conversation, and with it everybody breathed a sigh of relief.

Lifting operations began in earnest on 3 March, and after a couple of unsuccessful lift attempts and a couple of mishaps, the *Jenalisa* broke the surface on the morning of Wednesday 5 March. A subsequent inspection by garda divers revealed what had been suspected: that the bodies were not on board. That evening, the barge with the *Jenalisa* attached berthed at Waterford at 19:45 hrs approx. In the post-operation diving report to Command, Lt Mulligan made several recommendations based on experiences during the search-and-recovery operation. The one that would have significance for the Diving Section was the recommendation that 'The present SDDE EXO 26 headset be replaced with KMB 18 helmet/BandMask'.[46] This wouldn't be cheap: a Kirby Morgan BandMask, or helmet, is an expensive item, and at least three would be required. It would take another two years before the new KMB 18s arrived, but they were well worth the wait.

There was a funny moment one morning when three divers were making their way from Waterford to Dunmore East in the diving truck:

> This particular morning we were after a late night: Gerry was asleep, I was in the middle and Browners, the driver, pulled in and went over to a shop across the road. He then came back with a few bottles of water and a packet of Solpadine. I'll never forget it – he was leaning across the driving wheel and he popped two tablets into his mouth. Not taking much notice as I'm there trying to keep him awake and Gerry's in another world. Next minute I get this elbow into the side of me ribs ... and all I could see was Niall pointing at his mouth and saying 'Spit in me mouth, spit in me mouth.'[47]

Niall:

> Yeah, I couldn't get the fucking water bottle open quick enough – the fucking things were sizzling away in me mouth.'[48]

Another first for the Diving Section was its involvement in a drugs Joint Task

Force (JTF) operation in Moneypoint, County Clare, conducted from 14–20 August 1996. The naval diving team, under the command of Lt Declan Fleming, was deployed to join the JTF in searching the hull of an ore bulk oil carrier, the *Front Guider*. Her draft was 17.5 metres loaded and 8 metres when in ballast. At 06:45 hrs on the morning of 20 August the naval diving team, having travelled through the night, arrived at Moneypoint power station. After attending the operation conference involving all the main players, the diving team prepared to commence diving operations on the hull. The main search areas, as determined by the Customs officer, were the main seawater-inlet chests, the rudder stock and housing, and the ship's hull along the keel line from stem to stern on the outboard side.

Diving conditions in the Shannon at Moneypoint are sometimes not the best, and visibility can be a bit of a lottery. Trying to determine slack tide was difficult, visibility was poor and it was only possible to dive on the slack tides. Over the course of the next few days, the diving team located the seawater-inlet chests, removed the protective grids and searched the inlet chests and valves. The rudder stock housing was investigated and found to be clear, while the ship's hull search would take place later when the ship had been unloaded. During the course of the hull searches, which were only taking place at the slack tides whenever they occurred, the Customs and Excise rummage team on board had much greater success. According to the post-operation report, as submitted by Lt Fleming,

> The operation was initiated by the C&E [Customs and Excise] on the basis of international information that they had received … as is widely known, 40kgs of 80% pure cocaine was discovered hidden inside the deckhead of the ship's exercise room … It transpired later that the cocaine was taken on board while loading in Columbia from a boat on the offshore side right forward. It was taken down the duct-keel and later brought aft through the duct-keel and concealed in the accommodation space.[49]

The first Naval Service Diving Section involvement in a JTF Customs and Excise-led operation was a great success both as a diving experience on a vessel of that size and, of course, because of the operation's discovery of the cocaine. It was the first of many similar operations.

In a follow-up diving operation related to the *Carrickatine* lost in 1995, the Naval Service Diving Section returned on Friday 5 September 1997 to the area of possible loss of the *Carrickatine* to investigate a location of another uncharted wreck that was found by a pair of trawlers while fishing in the area. The *Father McKee* and the *Brendellen*, whilst pair trawling in the area, had snagged their trawl several times on an unidentified hazard. Fearing that it may have been the *Carrickatine*, they reported the position to the Marine Surveyor's Office. Mobilised, the naval diving team boarded the trawler *Father McKee* in Rathmullen on 5 September, and proceeded to the area with the objective of diving the wreck and verifying its nature. The LÉ *Aoife* had sailed the previous day from the naval base with the RCC embarked to rendezvous at the position and to provide dive-support facilities. The weather forecast for the period was not good, and diving on the site was not possible. In light of the costly logistics involved by both the navy and the *Father McKee*, it was decided that the only possible way to check the nature of the hazard was to jury rig the divers' live video camera and to strap it to the on-board crane wire on the *Father McKee*. The camera was taped to a flat steel bar bent at an angle so that the camera would be able to look ahead and downwards. The bar was then taped to the head of the crane hook, which in turn had a length of heavy chain hanging from it to keep it steady. With considerable skill, the skipper of the *Father McKee* moved the vessel into position and moored it over the wreck site. The crane wire and attached camera were then lowered down to the seabed. Visibility was good, and with a combination of slewing the crane and manoeuvring of the *Father McKee*, good video footage was achieved. It was soon clear that the wreckage was unfortunately not that of the *Carrickatine*.

Following the operation, in a very rare display of appreciation, the secretary general of the Department of the Marine wrote to the secretary general of the Department of Defence to express his department's appreciation of the conduct of the naval diving team. In turn, the secretary general of the Department of Defence wrote to the chief of staff of the Defence Forces, who also commented on it, and who in turn wrote to the Flag Officer Naval Service, Comdr. John Kavanagh. The flag officer then had the letters and comments sent to the diving officer, Lt Eddie Mulligan. The flag officer himself remarked:

> 1. With reference to the comments in the attached correspondence for the Sec. Generals of the Dept. of Marine and Natural Resources and the Dept. of Defence as well as the notation by the Chief of Staff, I wish to also again express my own appreciation for the excellent work which you

and the members of the Diving Team carried out in the investigation of this wreck off the Donegal coast.

2. The remarks by the Sec General of both the Depts and the Chief of Staff speak for themselves … well done on the manner and level of professionalism once again displayed by you and the Naval Service Diving Team during this difficult operation.[50]

The *Carrickatine* remains missing, and with it the six bodies of her crew:

The largest search and rescue mission ever mounted off the Irish coast, involving 400 people and more than 40 vessels, the Air Corps and the Royal Air Force, covered an area up to six times the size of Ireland between November 1995 and February 1996 without finding the boat.[51]

Sometime during the afternoon or early evening of Saturday 14 March 1998 former minister of defence (1994–95) Mr Hugh Coveney TD tragically fell from the cliffs by Roberts Cove, just outside Cork Harbour, while walking his dogs. Later that evening the alarm was raised and the emergency services activated. Rescue 117 from Waterford airport and the Crosshaven RNLI boat arrived on scene. Darkness forced the suspension of the search until the following morning (Sunday).

Earlier – on the Saturday evening – Lt John Leech, who lived close by in Roberts Cove itself, having returned home from a mine-disposal operation in Skibbereen, noticed the search-and-rescue activity and went to investigate. Having been told by neighbours of the situation and the identity of the missing person, he immediately informed the duty coxswain in the naval base, itself not too far away from Roberts Cove. With authorisation to mobilise a diving team by the operations officer for the following morning, Lt Leech notified his team to meet at 09:00 hrs in the Diving Store. Having assembled the team and necessary equipment, they proceeded by boat and road to the scene of the accident. On arrival the diving team prepared the equipment and boat, and stood by to receive the pre-dive brief by the chief in charge of the operation and by dive supervisor, CPO Martin Carroll:

… At 1045 on completion of a pre-dive brief, we proceeded to Roberts Head where we commenced a progressive swim-line search in the direction of the ebb-tidal stream. At 1149 located Mr Coveney's body in 12 metres of water. We recovered his body into our RIB and subsequently transferred it to the LÉ Emer. ...

LÉ Emer recovered the body on board by hoisting our RIB and landing it on the afterdeck. Lt Leech handed the body over to Sgt. __ __ [gardaí] at approximately 1345 whilst the ship was alongside the oil wharf.[52]

Several years previous to his death, Mr Coveney as minister of defence visited the naval base and the Diving Section for a review of the equipment and so on. The day was poor – when it rained it came down like steel rods. The minister and entourage had made their way to the Diving Section and, having been shown around the gear laid out outside the store, made their way into the diving truck, where the underwater-camera television monitor was situated. As if on cue, it began to rain quite heavily. On the roof of the diving truck were two skylights, both of which were well beyond their sell-by date. Minister Coveney was a tall man and was towering over most people in the truck. He casually remarked that it was lucky for all of us that we were inside the truck rather that outside, whereupon I noticed he was standing directly beneath one of the skylights. I thought to myself that it won't be long now before he has cause to regret that statement, and sure enough it began to rain inside the truck as well, right around the seal of the skylight directly above him. All he could do was laugh.

The 2000s

On 3 October 2000, at approximately 04:00 hrs, while running before severe weather off the coast of Galway, the British-registered Spanish fishing vessel *Arosa*, while transiting towards Rossaveal for shelter, ran bow first onto Doonguddle, one of the largest rocks that make up the Skerd Rocks, approximately 13 miles southeast of Slyne Head. On board the trawler that morning were thirteen crewmen, of whom only one would survive the subsequent sinking. The weather was foul, with southerly winds blowing gale-force 8–9. Visibility would have been very poor, and no doubt the vessel would have been taking a beating from the seas. There was very little the crewmen that weren't on watch could do except take to the bunk. According to the only survivor, Ricardo Arias Garcia,

> At around 4 o'clock in the morning we felt the ship hit a rock, we didn't take much notice of it as we thought it was a heavy wave, but after about

a minute the boat began crashing against other rocks. Everyone woke up, the alarm started to sound and we were worried that the boat was going to sink … Some of the crew threw the life rafts into the water and the rest of us began clinging onto the trawler. There were seven of us. With every wave that came, we had to hold on very tight but some just couldn't. Then I was the only one holding on, and a huge wave came and swept me away, too. In between the waves I tried to look up, calm down and organise myself. I saw another wave coming; I closed my eyes and took a deep breath. When that wave had passed, I felt rocks beneath me. I dragged myself up along the rocks, I looked up and saw the light of the helicopter …[53]

Several bodies were later recovered by the rescue helicopter and lifeboats – however, several more remained to be found. While the diving team was mobilised and directed to proceed to Galway, the diving officer, Lt Darragh Kirwan, knew that for the moment it would be a fruitless journey. Weather conditions in the area would preclude any diving operations for several weeks to come. The diving officer recalled the road journey up and was probably the highlight of the trip:

I remember the *Arosa*, a funny side to the *Arosa* job, because we were given a garda escort on the way there. I remember there was a big deal that the *Arosa* had sunk, and there was a big gale blowing up there even though we knew that we wouldn't be going diving. So anyway we were sent up in the blue truck and SO Ops had arranged a garda escort around Cork, around Limerick and Galway. I remember the Cork escort was grand – it was at the right time and we flew through it. In Limerick, your man actually put on the siren and we flew through it, and then we got to Galway during rush hour and we just sat there behind the garda bike. He didn't put on his light, so he just sat there and we just sat there looking at him; it took us an hour to get through Galway.[54]

Indeed, the lieutenant was correct in thinking that they wouldn't be doing much, and it would be at least three months before a civilian diver from Carna, County Galway managed to get down and survey at least part of what was left of the *Arosa*, as reported in the *Connacht Tribune*:

A group of people led by Gardaí in Carna went to the scene last Saturday and Carna diver, Pádraig Ó Maoilchiaráin, went to investigate. He reported that the boat was badly broken up, at the stage. There was no sign of bodies … this was the first time since the tragedy, which happened on October 3, that diving could take place at the scene. Gardaí in Carna say that a further dive may be undertaken later in the year, when the weather calms down.[55]

Following that dive, it would be another five months – on 16 May 2001 – before the Naval Service Diving Section got the chance to return and dive the wreck of the *Arosa*:

> So we based ourselves in Rossaveal and drove out [by boat] to Doonguddle – I think was the name of the rock, if my memory serves me – out by Skerd Rock. Doonguddle was the actual rock the vessel had foundered on. Depth wise I think it was around 10–15 metres and there were kinda like large crevasses … the *Arosa* itself had been folded up like a concertina in places and just jammed into a crevasse by the Atlantic swell coming in. When we did get to actually dive it, we recovered one body. That was partially submerged under a load of shale and broken rocks, sand and little bits of metal and so on. I think it was Catcher [Colm Cotter] who found him, and it took several dives to dig the body out … the body was essentially skeletal remains from the chest up and the rest was buried, so we dug down. When we dug out the rest of the body, it actually still had flesh on it, probably because the sea life couldn't get at it … that job wasn't done in one go, we had to wait for the weather to abate, but it was a lovely dive.[56]

Subsequent detailed searches of the area failed to find any other traces of the other missing crew members. The *Connacht Tribune* of 7 Sept 2001 reported that:

> The human remains which are being examined now were found by Navy Divers on May 16th, this year. It is understood that a human hand, found in a field in the Muigh Inis area of Carna, three months ago, is also being DNA tested and is being assessed in the context of the Arosa tragedy.[57]

16 February 2002: 'Father, son and grandson feared drowned'

> Thirty-six small boats, many of them fishing trawlers, were among the search party yesterday for three generations of a family after they failed to return from a fishing trip off the County Down coast. They were 54–year-old Michael Green, his 33–year-old son and 10–year-old grandson, who were also called Michael Green.[58]

This was the background to the sub-surface search for the *Tullaghmurry Lass*. The vessel had sailed from Kilkeel Harbour at 03:40 hrs approx. on Thursday 15 February 2002 to go prawn fishing in the Dundalk Bay area. Having failed to return by 20:00 hrs that night, the alarm was raised. It was reported that surface conditions at the time were good, with visibility of several miles and sea conditions calm. No Mayday was broadcast, making the disappearance of the *Tullaghmurry Lass* all the more baffling. However, there was some indications of where the vessel may have sank, though nothing of a positive nature: there were reports of oil slicks and flotsam from an area to the south-east of Kilkeel. These waters fall under the Northern Ireland/UK Coast Guard area of responsibility. The first couple of days' extensive searching of the waters failed to recover any bodies or a probable location of the sinking.

Several days after the sinking of the *Tullaghmurry Lass,* the Naval Service received a ministerial direction to deploy the Naval Service Diving Section to assist in the search for the vessel:

> I remember getting the heads up that we were probably being called into the search operation and that we'd initially have to attempt to locate the wreck site with the side-scan sonar and if found – depending on the depths – either dive or use the ROV [remote-operated vehicle]. This didn't present any particular problem for us as we were well used to it, but it would be the first time that the side-scan sonar would be used in anger, so to speak. Mucking about with it in training was one thing, but employing it as your primary search tool in an operation is another because then the pressure is really on, there's no room for error.
>
> Then we were told to pack our bags and prepare to travel on the *Eithne* for the job. I was thinking that the job was in Northern Irish/UK waters and when they see us arriving over the horizon on the *Eithne*, they'll have

a shit haemorrhage and then tell us to fuck off. So pack a bag [clothing/ training gear] for about three days … Jesus, little did I know nineteen fucking days later … lucky enough we were stuck at sea.[59]

The subsequent sub-surface search operation was conducted by the naval diving team and led by Lt Darragh Kirwan. It took place over a three-week period, and was neatly summed up in the following section of a report by the then officer commanding of the LÉ *Eithne*, Cdr Pat McNulty. In it he gives a background description of the search operation to senior command in relation to a separate matter:

> The search took place between about 4 miles and 12 miles off the County Down coast, with the LÉ Eithne remaining on task for the full 19 days, with the exception of 2 separate overnights in Dublin. The ship had a full NS Diving Team [9 members] on board. The search was conducted around the clock by Towed Sonar, with the diving team watching the monitor, set up in the hanger. Weather was w'ly [westerly] gale force 8–9 for most of the 3 weeks [the LÉ *Emer* spent a full twelve days sheltering in Lawrence Cove at this time], but being on the Irish Sea, and having the bigger unit, made the search quite feasible – and comfortable.[60]

The weather was indeed poor, and on more than one occasion it felt that the ship had been stopped dead in the water when it had pitched into a heavy swell. The towing speed for the side-scan sonar was about 5 to 6 knots, depending on the sea and swell conditions, and it was a constant juggling act for the officers of the watch to adjust. The control panel unit (CPU) that controls all the operational functions of the side-scan towfish itself was based in the hanger. It was here that the Diving Section members – in two teams – manned the CPU four hours on, four hours off, around the clock. Cdr McNulty stated in his report that the only breaks over the nineteen-day period were when the LÉ *Eithne* left her station to go to Dublin for two separate overnights to facilitate some crew change and spare-part replenishment. The video-display unit on the CPU is only about 8 inches square, and it displays an image of the seabed in black and white or different shades of grey. To sit and watch the picture on a screen this size was very tiring for all concerned. The search-grid pattern was about 8 miles wide by 12 miles long, with the central position being the best guesstimate of the probable

location, though there was no real evidence to prove it. However, a possible/probable datum point had to be determined for any sort of reasonable and logical search pattern to be conducted. The grid-search area settled on after discussion between the OC LÉ *Eithne* and the diving officer was entered into the ship's navigational computer. The search area was then overlaid by a search grid, which showed the various legs of the search and the start and end points of each run. Thus, when the ship approached the start point of the first leg to be searched, its was placed into autopilot mode, thus enabling the ship's DGPS navigational computer to guide it along the search leg. Each leg searched and the overlapping of the various legs were shown on the navigation screen so that each officer of the watch could see how the ship/search was progressing. As the ship approached each start or end point, the bridge would contact the sonar-watch team by radio and inform them that the ship was approaching an end point and would be turning. This allowed the watch to reel in the towfish cable sufficiently to allow the ship to turn without the towfish hitting the seabed. It didn't happen often, but if the bridge forgot to warn the watch crew, then only when the ship would begin its turn would the watch crew be alerted by either the ship heeling over or slowing down, or – as was normally the case – the image on the sonar screen showing the seabed coming up to meet the towfish. Either way, when this was noticed by the watch team, there would be a scattering of the chairs in the hanger and two or three guys running as fast as they could down to the quarterdeck to pull the tether in by hand, while the remaining

Black strip at rear houses the sonar transducers (either side); black/red connector block on top is for the umbilical, and angled steel feature is for securing the umbilical to the towfish

guy would be watching anxiously to see if the towfish would hit or miss the seabed. It would be fair to say that the towfish bottomed out a couple of times.

In an incident that led to the side-scan towfish being out of commission for several hours, it must first be explained in very simple terms how the towfish maintains or alters its depth, and how things can change very rapidly on the CPU screen (for a more informative account in layman's terms of how a side-scan sonar works, see the section on equipment). The towfish depth is maintained by either the towing vessel keeping its speed constant once the depth has been set, or, similarly, the depth setting can be altered by the towing vessel either speeding up or paying out more telemetry cable, depending on which is more suitable – generally, it is the latter option. The CPU display screen is only about 8 inches square and shows a digitised grayscale image of the seabed. Generally, the screen image will be in two halves left and right, representing port and starboard sides either side of the centre line – the centre line of the display being the trail of the towfish as it travels through the water. The depth at which

Side-scan sonar about to be deployed from stern of LÉ Eithne; *note original tail fin; (l–r): Frank Cunningham, Courtney Gibbons*

the towfish is operating and the range setting on the screen determines how far either side of the centre line the images begin to define on the screen. So when the images either side of the screen begin to merge with the centre line, it is an indication of a couple of things: either the seabed is rising up to meet the towfish or the towfish is getting lower to meet the seabed. Either way, the towfish needs to be raised, and raised quickly.

During one early-morning watch at sea, the towfish met with the seabed. Sea conditions were quite rough and gale-force 6 to 7 winds were blowing. Why it met with the seabed wasn't immediately known, but what was known was that there was something wrong with the towfish. When it was raised the answer became immediately clear to the watch: the circular tail fin that was normally attached to the towfish, and which was required to keep the towfish flying straight and level, wasn't attached anymore. In fact it was lying on the seabed several hundred metres behind the ship and getting further away every second that we looked at the place where it should have been. It was a case of end of operations as regards the side-scan sonar for the time being:

> I actually remember that there was something like 60 knots of a wind came down off the Mourne Mountains that morning and the ship was just doing about 3 or 4 knots. We were flying the towfish at about 6 metres above the seabed and the ship just ground to a bit of a halt … and the fish took a bit of a nosedive. I remember how we got around it with the mayonnaise tin. I always remember Pat McNulty [Cdr Pat McNulty; retd] was the captain, and it cemented in his mind the kind of can-do attitude of the divers.[61]

A trademark of the Naval Service Diving Section – something never open to dispute – is the ability of a navy diver to think outside of the box, to think laterally and, much more importantly, to think on his feet. However, this time it looked as if things were beyond them. The lost tail fin was the only one that the Diving Section had – there was no spare. The nearest available tail fin was over three and a half thousand miles away in the US, and it would take at best around three days before it arrived into the country. The naval stores officer made the necessary arrangements to purchase and fly in the tail fin on the first available flight to Ireland, with customs clearance and a garda escort awaiting its arrival. However, it was still three days away, and it meant three days' down time from the search, which couldn't be afforded:

Just about to get wet

I had it in my mind that maybe we could fabricate something that might be used as a replacement tail fin but nothing really was coming to mind. Then, while in the galley and chatting to the chef, I just happened to be looking at some empty 25-litre catering mayonnaise drums, and thinking maybe they might just about do. They looked like they were the same size, give or take. Take the end off of one, dickie it up a bit, reattach it to the tail end of the sonar, and it might work. Then it sort of grew arms and legs to be a full-on piece of engineering. It was incredible to watch the lads beavering away at the bits 'n' pieces. We had guys on angle grinders, grinding the ends off an oil drum as a replacement for the plastic mayo drum. There were guys cutting perspex sheeting to size to fit inside the circular drum as we needed to be able to secure the drum to the actual towfish. There were braising rods, duct tape, rivet guns, prayers and a healthy debate about the best way of doing things. So the upshot of the next two hours' work or so in the after workshops of the *Eithne* was a tail fin. In fairness it was looking a bit rough and ready, but it looked sturdy enough that it just might do the job. So the Mark 1 Naval Variant Tail Fin was attached to the towfish.

The OC LÉ *Eithne* was then informed that we were ready to trail the towfish again. So the ship was slowed to towing speed, all the necessary pre-deployment systems checks were conducted, and the only thing left to do was to trail the fish. Into the water it went and the tether paid out to the required length. In the meantime, while the towfish was being paid out, back in the hanger at the CPU all eyes were glued to the screen and, sure enough, one look at the screen and we all knew straight away that it was flying straight and true. So we were up and running and back in the game, so to speak. In fact it flew so well that when the new replacement tail fin arrived on board, we felt that there was no need to change them, so it remained in its box for a few more days. We were rather proud of that little bit of ingenuity.[62]

Unfortunately, as the search continued there was nothing to report by way of a probable contact that might have been worth investigating with the ROV. So after a search of nineteen days, the naval diving team along with the LÉ *Eithne* were stood down by naval operations and directed to return to the naval base on 7 March. Nineteen days were spent on station, making it one of the longest operations conducted by the Diving Section to date. Sometime during the first week of April, Police Service of Northern Ireland (PSNI) divers located what they believed to be the wreck of the *Tullaghmurry Lass*, as reported in the *Irish Times*:

> Police divers believe that they have located bodies in the wreckage of the Tullaghmurry Lass, the Kilkeel [County Down] fishing vessel which sank with three generations of one family on board … based on video footage taken at the location of the wreckage, divers now believe that they have discovered bodies of some or all of the missing members of the Greene family.[63]

Subsequent dives by the PSNI diving team searched and located the remains of the missing bodies and returned them ashore for burial.

On Saturday 24 May 2003 the naval diving team was tasked to Kilrush, County Clare to partake in an annual Coast Guard (CG) SAR exhibition, departing the naval base at 09:50 hrs. While preparing for the day's SAR display on Sunday morning, the diving officer, Lt Darragh Kirwan, received a phone call from the Coast Guard requesting the assistance of the Naval Service Diving Section in recovering the body of a woman who had fallen from the Cliffs of Moher the previous Monday. Information was also relayed to the diving officer that earlier that morning two members of the Doolin CG had swam into the cliffs, and it was their opinion that the location of the body meant it was unlikely it could be recovered intact. This information was passed on to the senior naval officer on duty in Naval Operations. Darragh gives this account:

> I remember that job because the Coast Guard had asked us that if from what we had heard from the two Coast Guard fellas when they went in that 'she won't come easy' and therefore we had to investigate if we could cut her in order to extract her. I remember discussing it with yourself in the jeep on the way down and there was a general consensus that 'Sure, if that's what we have to do …'. I rang the SDO back, who rang the flag officer 'cos I had to make sure that I got 'top cover' if this was how it might transpire … there was nearly a kind of disbelief on the phone: 'Sorry, you've been asked to do WHAT!', and I said, 'Look it's just an option, but I won't be able to talk to you from the base of the Cliffs of Moher, so we have to have all this racked and stacked beforehand. So that if we go there and it isn't an easy job and we still have to recover the body, that all this has been discussed beforehand and people know that this has been discussed …'[64]

above: Many hands can screw up a good thing, but not this time. Fabricating the new tail fin for side-scan sonar, Tullaghmurry Lass *operation (aft workshop LÉ Eithne) (l–r): Unknown, Trevor Murphy, Darragh Kirwan (diving officer), Martin Buckley, John Robinson*
below: Fitting the tail fin: John Robinson (left), Paddy Delaney

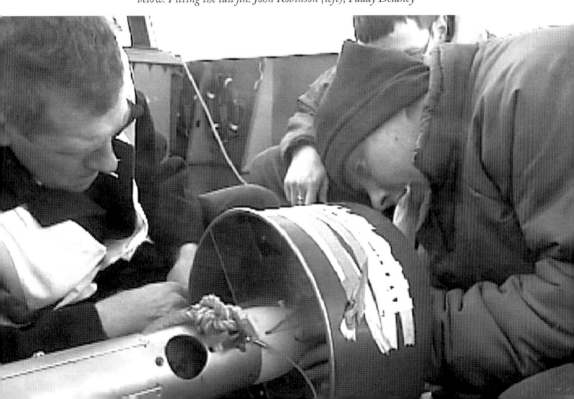

The naval diving team was directed to proceed to Doolin and to liaise with the CG there. The naval divers had never before conducted operations in that location – this operation would be the first. The Cliffs of Moher at their lowest are about 350 feet high and at their highest over 700 feet. From there one can see the Aran Islands in Galway Bay to the north and to the south Loop head. Such was the backdrop to the diving team's next recovery operation: spectacular views and beautiful weather. However, there was to be a downside to the job: the body had to be recovered that day as the weather was due to break soon. The body could not be left there for all to see. So with that information to hand, the diving team, the gardaí and the Doolin CG all arranged to meet at Doolin Coast Guard Centre, where a plan would be formulated as to how best to effect the recovery. Introductions were completed and members of the diving team were shown over to the edge of the viewing area and handed a couple of pairs of binoculars. Lying down on the viewing platform, members of the Doolin CCRS pointed out the area where the body was located. What could be seen of it was on the shore amongst rocks, or at least that's how they appeared from 600 feet up even through binoculars:

> One of the members of the Doolin CG was lying down beside me up at the viewing platform showing me where the body was located, and he was saying 'Do you see the boulder?' and I was 'Yeah, have the boulder,' and he was 'Do you see the pebble to the right of it?' and I was 'Yeah, have the pebble' … 'Well that's where she's wedged in and we can't get her out of there.' Anyway, I remember thinking, boulder, pebble, boulder, pebble, and then we swam in and the fucking boulder was the size of a double decker bus.[65]

The plan, such as it was, involved no diving but would require a surface swim. With the naval divers would be the two members of the Doolin CG along with some equipment loaned by the Fire Service. So with a plan in place and all the necessary equipment to effect the recovery of the body, all divers embarked by boats to be ferried the 2 miles or so to the cliffs. What was not expected by the naval diving team was the sheer size of the cliff face now that they were looking up, and the sheer size of the rocks that they had earlier been looking down upon, which were immense – the size of large cars and decent-sized vans, even from offshore. More ominously for the divers, the surface swim would prove to be more challenging than first expected. The breakers and the surf were much bigger than had been thought, and the foreshore was full of broken-down seaweed and wrack that essentially turned the water there into near treacle. While standing offshore and preparing to deploy, a small rethink was necessary by all the divers about the swim-in. When waves and breakers break onto a shore, there is generally a sequence, or cycle, to them. They break very heavy and then, as the sequence of waves continues, they get smaller. Normally there is then a quieter, or flatter, period, and then the cycle will start over again, with the waves getting higher and more powerful. So the divers stood off for a while and watched and counted until they identified the general cycle of the waves that they would have to be swimming through before the waves would break onto the shore. At 15:20 hrs approx. – once it was determined that the heaviest waves had passed, and when the waves should get flatter – all divers deployed into the water and began the surface swim in as fast as they could. As luck would have it, the decision to leave behind the lifting equipment loaned by the Fire Service was a good call. Things went reasonably well until the divers began to swim through the treacle-like water that was closer to the shore, when they slowed to a crawl. This treacle-like substance was in fact seaweed that had been broken down by the waves breaking onto the shore. It wouldn't have been so bad except the waves began to grow again and increase in energy, and as the divers tried to either maintain their position or swim back out they were getting carried bodily with little or no control towards the shore and to the awaiting rocks. Eventually, as the waves reached their strongest, the divers got nearer and nearer their destination. All a diver could do to protect himself was to curl up into a ball and hope for the best as each diver in turn was literally bowled upwards onto the rocky foreshore. With a few lumps and bruises to show for it, all the divers survived that experience.

Now it was time for the recovery of the body. The divers would worry about getting off later. Unfortunately for all concerned, the body – which had fallen some 600 feet – had in fact been wedged quite spectacularly between two large boulders and would make for a difficult extraction. All necessary provisions had been made by the diving team to ensure that the body would not stay there another day, and it was hoped that the worst scenario would not be played out:

> The legal position was still being researched regarding the possible dismembering of the body. It was hoped that the presence of more personnel would be able to move and recover the body intact.[66]

The extraction of the body – while it proved somewhat difficult and unpleasant – was achieved within a short period of time. It was placed into a body bag and prepared for removal from the shoreline. This was where things would again get somewhat hairy: nobody was looking forward to the journey out. It was initially discussed as to whether or not the Shannon SAR helicopter might be tasked with the removal of the body, but for whatever reason it was felt best to remove it by sea. But one thing was very certain: the divers couldn't swim the body out – some other way of doing it was required. So once again, the situation called for a small bit of lateral thinking by the Diving Section.

There's a seamanship exercise conducted by naval vessels that allows them to transfer stores, personnel and fuel between two ships while they are underway at sea: it's called replenishment at sea (RAS). At its simplest it involves passing lines back and forth between the ships, so while one ship pulls in on the line, the other ship pays out on the same line, and in this way the package is transferred from one ship to the other. So while it would not be quite an RAS, it would be along those lines. First, the casualty cradle that was on the Doolin inshore lifeboat was required, along with the longest length of line that was available to the divers. The only line long enough to complete the task was the divers' light jackstay search line housed on its reel and held in the diving boat. With the line passed into the lifeboat, the next question was how to get them passed to the divers. The lifeboat men had a device called a Schermuly Speedline – a line-throwing apparatus housed in a plastic cylindrical container with a long, thin but very strong braided-nylon line attached to the end of a rocket. When fired, this rocket pulls the line over a distance to another person or vessel. Normally, this works very well, but it also has the capacity not to work so well, and when that happens the outcome is unpredictable. In the navy it is classed as a pyrotechnic and falls into the category of ordnance, and with good reason. So when the lifeboat men prepared to fire the Speedline, the divers took cover – not that they doubted the lifeboat men or their accuracy, but because they would have seen the results before of Speedline rockets going wrong. So with everyone behind cover, the rocket was fired. It hit the water about 5 metres in front of the lifeboat, then ricocheted upwards at about 50 miles an hour and hit the cliff face a couple of hundred feet above the divers. With a loud report from the rocket, there followed a mass exodus of screeching gannets, terns and any other bird in residence there. Normally, this might have been interesting to watch, but the rocks that began to fall from the impact of the rocket put paid to any such ideas. The divers beat a rather hasty and undignified retreat from the area – if it hadn't been so dangerous it would have been hilarious. Darragh Kirwan recalled:

> So they fired the rocket with the line attached and I remember hiding behind a big boulder and I'm thinking this isn't a fucking good idea at all. You know, firing a rocket into a cliff face where you had this boulder that used to be up there probably a year ago, halfway up the fucking cliff face, so it wouldn't take too much to blow a few more down … I remember the first one kinda hit the cliff face, it disintegrated and we didn't get the line, but for the second one we saw the error of our ways and none of us were hiding behind any rocks. We all had gotten as far away from the cliff face as we could so we were actually in the firing line, but it was safer to be in the firing line. I remember we were actually laughing like giddy kids with the firing of the rocket, saying this was fucking nuts.[67]

Anyway, in due course a second rocket was fired and the results proved much better. The light line made it ashore and was taken in hand by the divers, who proceeded to pull in the floating cradle and the heavier divers' search line. The cradle was prepared and the body well secured into it for its passage out to the waiting lifeboat. The plan was simple enough after that: once the cradle and body made the lifeboat and were recovered into it, the heavy line would be passed back to the divers' boat, the divers would then enter the water and, while holding onto loops they had made on the line, would be pulled backwards from the shore by the divers' boat. The plan was good in theory and, in fairness, worked not too badly in practise. Once again the sequence of the waves outpaced the evacuation of the divers, and while hanging on for dear life the divers were eventually dragged backwards off the foreshore to the relative safety of deeper and calmer water. At 17:00 hrs approx., with all the divers recovered back into the boats and the operation successfully completed, all returned back to Doolin CG station, where the body was handed over to the local gardaí. The diving report as submitted simply stated:

> Six NS divers swam in onto the foot of the cliffs at approx. 15:20 hrs at low tide. On the swim in, all body bags etc., were lost in the surf zone due to strong swells. Two members of the Doolin CG unit were also in attendance to direct the divers to the location and assist where possible. On arrival on

the rocks divers set to work moving the already broken limbs of the body to assist recovery. At approx. 16:00 hrs the body was removed intact from the rocks. The body was secured into the bag and stretcher at approx. 17:00 hrs and towed from the rocks with all divers and CG personnel in attendance. The stretcher was recovered into the CG RIB and recovered in Doolin.[68]

So ended the first participation of the naval diving team in an operation at the Cliffs of Moher, but it wouldn't be the last for less than a month later the diving team would be back again and in very similar circumstances, though this time it was a male. On 16 June 2003 the diving team was tasked with proceeding to Doolin to effect a recovery of a body from the base of the cliffs. This operation was in essence a mirror image of the previous operation; however, the weather was to hamper the initial attempt at recovery. The diving team returned to the naval base to await better weather conditions at the dive site. On Friday 20 June the divers returned to Doolin and on Saturday the naval diving team, with two members of the Doolin CG again in attendance, swam in and effected the recovery of the body. Unlike the previous operation, the divers were prepared this time and both the swim in and the recovery was without incident. The body was recovered again to Doolin CG station. This time even the relevant paragraph in the post-operation dive report was shorter than the first one:

> Divers returned to Doolin pm Fri 20 Jun 03 due to unfavourable weather. On the Sat 21 Jun 03, four NS divers accompanied by two Doolin CG members swam onto the rocks with the stretcher. The body was recovered into a body bag and secured into the stretcher. The stretcher was then towed from the surf to deeper water, with the divers on a towline. The stretcher was recovered into Doolin CG RIB and landed ashore at Doolin Pier. Divers returned to the Naval Base Sun 22 Jun 03.[69]

Around 15:00 hrs on the afternoon of 29 November 2005, about 2 miles south-east of the Saltee Islands, County Wexford, a twenty-six-foot fibreglass fishing vessel the *Rising Sun*, out of Kilmore Quay, sank while engaged in potting, forcing its three-man crew into the water without time to raise the alarm. The skipper, Pat Colfer, was lost immediately, but the remaining two crewmen, Jimmy Meyler and Ian Tierney, survived by clinging onto the upturned hull before it finally sank at around 19:00 hrs. The two crewmen then managed to stay afloat until rescued by a passing fishing vessel, the *Napier*, at approximately 21:34 hrs. Both men were taken ashore to hospital; unfortunately, Mr Meyler died in hospital later that night. A request from the Coast Guard to the naval authorities for assistance in searching for the missing vessel was received at 23:00 hrs. The following morning, members of the naval diving team commenced deployment to the scene:

> We were in Limerick diving the Shannon up towards Ardnacrusha, Raheen, and Mary's Island – that side of things – not too sure of the location, but looking for a missing fella there. We were searching there for a good few days and it was all less than 10 metres, everything was less than 10 metres. We came back and we de-rigged, and de-briefed and got sorted for the next job, and then the *Rising Sun* hit.[70]

And from the diving report for the operation:

> Diving team of 7 personnel responded on Wed 30 Nov 05 with side-scan sonar [SSS] and air-diving capability to 35 metres. Three members of the team were transported by CG helo from Cork airport to Kilmore Quay, Co Wexford with SSS equipment. Remainder travelled by road to RV on scene. A 3 man team operated from Kilmore Quay RNLI boat 'The Famous Grouse'. Search centred on area where oil and diesel observed on surface. Charted depth range 45–47 metres.[71]

Following the initial search by the side-scan sonar and other vessels in the area, the diving officer, Lt Darragh Kirwan, made the decision to recall the initial diving team to the naval base and to prepare and pack the necessary diving equipment for deep-diving operations.

The subsequent search to locate the *Rising Sun* and the events following its location were unprecedented in the history of the Naval Service Diving Section. This search, survey and recovery would add a few other firsts for the Diving Section. It would involve the biggest number of naval divers ever recorded on a job, and it would involve the use of the remote-operated vehicle (ROV) as a primary search tool not only in relation to surveying the vessel but also in searching for a missing diver; the joint use of both the divers and the ROV ensured the maximum use of dive time and resources. The search also involved the Irish Coast Guard helicopters and the Irish Lights vessel *Granuaile*, and it would be

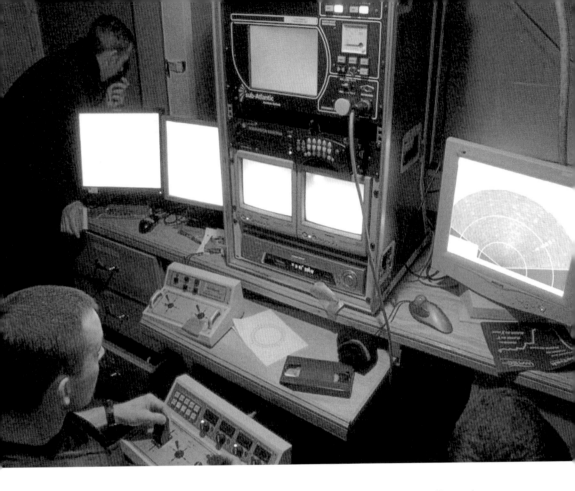

the first time the ROV recovered a missing person. Over the course of the operation, the Naval Service Diving Section and other agencies of the state would come in for unwanted and unwarranted criticism, particularly during the initial stages of the operation. However, quite apart from the initial tragedy that sparked off the search, another equally tragic incident would compound the situation, but would also put an end to any misgivings some people may have had about the conduct of the search operation. That incident was the unfortunate death of a local diver, Billy O'Connor, during a dive on the *Rising Sun*.

The *Rising Sun* had been located and an exclusion zone was placed around it by the Coast Guard. The tidal stream in the area is quite strong during normal tides; however, as the tidal streams were coming off the back of what is termed 'springs', the ebb and flow of the tidal stream would only have been added to in terms of strength and speed, making any form of diving and station-keeping difficult. The charted depth in this area was about 53 metres. The Naval Service Diving Section, according to its own rules and regulations, can only dive to this depth on surface-demand diving equipment and must have an RCC present on site. There is no latitude in these regulations – period. Hence the return of the diving team to Cork on the evening of Thursday 1 December. But another scenario was being played out ashore. Earlier that morning emotions were running high in Kilmore Quay amongst family and friends of Pat Colfer, the skipper, and the perceived inactivity of the naval diving team and, by extension, state agencies only added fuel to that particular fire. All that could be seen by the family, relatives, friends and acquaintances was the trawler lying on the bottom and no one diving to investigate it to see if the body was there. Billy O'Connor, a friend of the family and a well-known technical diver, offered his services with another friend, Harry Hannon, to dive the wreck, and to try and ascertain if the body was on board. The Coast Guard and the Naval Service both cautioned quite strongly against it. However, the dive went ahead later that afternoon. All appeared to be going well for the two divers, but at some stage while ascending from one decompression stop to another, and less than 10 metres, the divers became separated and lost sight of each other. Billy O'Connor failed to make the surface. His partner completed his decompression stops as required. There was now another casualty:

> … SSS [side-scan sonar] was transported on Thurs 01 Dec 05 to LÉ Emer, off Kilmore Quay … I had a brief meeting with Mr Charlie Colfer, brother of the missing skipper. I outlined the nature of the diving operation and the time frame involved. He asked me for my advice regarding an offer from local civilian divers to dive the possible wreck, on behalf of the Colfer family, to determine whether the body of Mr Pat Colfer was on board. I told him that it is a Coast Guard operation and the NS were acting in aid to the civil authorities … I told him that I hoped the divers brought some answers for his family but that the nature of the NS involvement would not change and that I expected to be diving on Sun 04 Dec 05 … the Diving Team departed Kilmore Quay at approx. 15:30 hrs. While on the return to the naval base, I was informed by both Mr Chris Reynolds (CG) and CFO [commander Fleet Operations] that one of the civilian divers had not surfaced from the dive and was presumed missing. The team continued to the naval base.[72]

So while there was a trawler to be positively identified, surveyed and its missing skipper to be searched for, now there was also a missing diver, presumed dead. Over the next couple of days the naval diving team – supplemented by divers from other naval units – began conducting deep-diving work-up dives in the RCC and SDDE-system work-up dives in the specialist tool-training tank at the National Maritime College of Ireland in Ringaskiddy, close to the naval base. It would stand the divers in good stead. On Saturday 3 December 2005, all the necessary equipment – the ROV container, the SDDE container and RCC and ancillary equipment – were loaded aboard the *Granuaile* at the naval base for deployment to the dive site. On completion of loading, the ship sailed for the dive site. The *Granuaile* was by far the most suitable platform for this operation. On Sunday 4 December, with the *Granuaile* (under the command of Capt. Dermot Grey) moored in position over the wreck site, naval divers commenced diving operations. Given the resources now available to the diving officer and with an ROV to operate, the plan was for diver searches in daylight hours during the high and low slack-tide periods, and for the search to be conducted during the night by the ROV team during similar tidal periods. However, as sometimes happens during these types of operation, the first day's series of dives and the use of the ROV didn't go too well. The ROV sustained damage and had to be recovered for essential repairs, with a replacement umbilical and winch being required from the naval base. The following day the necessary spares arrived by sea and another three-man team of ROV operators arrived via CG helo. The days that followed saw more dives completed by the team, with both 'in water' and 'surface decompression' requirements conducted. ROV operations followed on during the night time hours. On Friday night 9 December at approximately 22:00 hrs, the ROV team deployed the ROV into the water to commence another video survey of the wreck, and on completion of that survey continued to conduct a visual survey of the wreck site, searching for the missing diver. Over the next hour or so the ROV operators conducted the required survey as directed by the diving officer, surveying the starboard side, the aft area and wheelhouse. On completion of this video survey, the diving officer directed the ROV to carry out a search of an area using the on-board sonar, and to interrogate any contacts of interest:

> It was turning out to be a long day for the three of us, myself, Gibbo [Courtney Gibbons] and Woody [Ciarán Woodward], and it was going to be at least another two hours, but at least we weren't diving and piloting.

Anyway, we set up the ROV to scan the sectors and to see what would turn up. Every now and then we'd pick up a contact x number of metres away, and we'd drive out to it using the sonar and the cameras to keep us on track, and invariably the possible contact would turn out to be a large rock or large sand ridge, so while trying to keep ourselves orientated with the wreck so as to keep our own relative bearings, we'd set up again and scan another sector, and so it went over the next hour or so.

Sometimes we'd keep the ROV working away even with the strong currents pissing past the ROV – it wasn't great but it was workable. Finally, I had had enough and decided to quit while we were ahead … I told Gibbo that we'd wrap it up and to bring home the ROV while I info'd Woody, so that he could start hauling away on the ROV umbilical … suddenly we quite literally drove over something – next thing I know, myself and Gibbo are looking at

ROV being recovered back to the deck of the Granuaile *after spending nearly twelve hours continuous thrusting while holding onto the lost diver during the search-and-recovery operation on the* Rising Sun

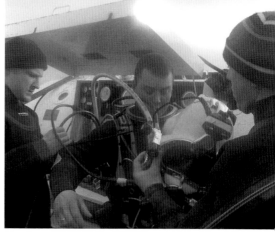

Noel Dunne (left), Paddy Delaney
Having located the body of missing diver on the Rising Sun *operation with the ROV the previous evening, early the following morning the two divers are tasked with diving to attach a recovery line to the body, depth 53.8 metres.*

a fin, or what appeared to be a diver's fin, and then we saw the unmistakable outline of a gloved hand. 'Fuck me, that's a hand, Gibbo.' With that we applied full downward thrust on the thrusters to ensure that the ROV didn't move from that spot. So the next few seconds passed with the pair of us holding our breaths to see exactly what we had seen, and then we tilted the cameras upwards and the face appeared and then we knew. 'Well fuck me, we've found him.' I don't know what Gibbo thought, but I fucking couldn't believe it. We spent the last couple of hours trying to be scientific about our searching, et cetera, and when bringing the ROV home we drive over him – crazy! … We manoeuvred the ROV off him, making sure that we kept him in the cameras, and then manoeuvred the ROV to a position where we could use the manipulator to grab him. I knew once we had him grabbed by the jaws of the manipulator, we could essentially rest for a while and call the boss to let him know.[73]

The following details from the diving-officer's report outline the remainder of the story for the search for Billy O'Connor's body: how the body was recovered to the surface and then to the deck of the *Granuaile* for some forensic detailing by the gardaí, and the subsequent passing of the body into the Hook Sub-aqua Club boat for his return ashore. The diving report remarked:

ROV established firm contact with the manipulator arm on to the diver and remained in the water overnight, with ROV team monitoring situation throughout. Strong tides recorded during the night and ROV required to be driven at full thrust in order to maintain station with the body of lost diver.

Sat 10 Dec '05. Divers deployed down ROV umbilical at 11:49 hrs during slack tide. Divers made bottom beside ROV and lost diver in 53.8m of water … ROV used to monitor progress and record operation … using both the ROV manipulator arm and the recovery line, the body of the lost diver was recovered under control to 16m below the surface … recovered into the [divers'] RHIB by the team at approx. 13:30 hrs … Mr O'Connor was lowered into the local RHIB of the Hook Sub-aqua Club, as per CG and GWU agreement with club. Granuaile weighed and proceeded to A/S Rosslare to embark equipment.[74]

On Sunday 11 December 2005 the *Granuaile* repositioned over the *Rising Sun*, and the search and survey of the wreck site continued in earnest. The following days saw more dives by both divers and the ROV, with no sign of the missing skipper, Pat Colfer. The ROV confirmed by camera that both the life raft and the EPIRB (Emergency Position Indicating Radio Beacon) were still on board and stowed, thereby clearly indicating that there must have been no time for the crew to deploy them. Having completed the search of the *Rising Sun* and the surrounding area of the wreck on Tuesday 13 December at 17:00 hrs, the search of the *Rising Sun* and for Pat Colfer was concluded, and on the following day the naval diving team disembarked the *Granuaile* and returned to the naval base.

This operation was the largest operation ever conducted by the Diving Section, and it was notable for several reasons. It was certainly the deepest sustained diving operation conducted by the Diving Section to date; it involved the largest number of divers and technicians on a job – nineteen in total: sixteen divers and three ROV technicians. It also involved planned surface decompression dives and the first planned use of the ROV as a search tool that was integrated into a daily search schedule so that the maximum use was made of the tidal slacks. The operation also involved the use of the Coast Guard SAR helicopter on two occasions to transport personnel and vital equipment to the dive site, and the use of the *Granuaile*, which was the only vessel in Irish waters that could possibly have provided the necessary platform for both ROV and diving operations over a sustained period of time. While the diving operation failed to find the body of Mr Colfer, the operation in every other respect was considered a success. As with every other diving operation, there are always lessons to be learnt, and this

Rising Sun having been salvaged and recovered back to the deck of the Granuaile for investigation by the MCIB

operation proved no different, but perhaps the biggest lesson that was learnt was not in the area of diving but in the area of public relations and the press.

2006: *Maggie B*

On Wednesday 29 March 2006 at 23:00 hrs approx. the fishing vessel *Maggie B*, with three crew on board – skipper Glen Cott, Krzysztof Pawtowski and Jan Sankowski – while fishing off the Waterford estuary on the south-east coast encountered some very rough and turbulent sea conditions due to conflicting high winds and spring tides, and sank within minutes, with just enough time for the skipper to raise the Mayday alarm:

> Krzysztof Pawtowski, who survived without a life jacket or survival suit six degree temperatures by inflating the boat's liferaft and clinging to it, was reported to have said that the vessel sank in minutes some 8.6 km south of Hook Head. He was plucked from the water by Dunmore East lifeboat just 51

minutes after the emergency was raised by the boat's skipper. Neither Cott nor Sankowski were so fortunate.[75]

The sinking of the *Maggie B* occurred a little over four months after the *Rising Sun* tragedy and in loosely similar circumstances. On Friday 19 May 2006 'the Department of Transport on behalf of the Minister of State Pat "The Cope" Gallagher requested the Naval Service Diving Section to carry out a thorough survey of the *Maggie B*.'[76] On Sunday (21 May) all the necessary SDDE equipment, RCC and ROV containers were embarked on board the *Granuaile* under the command of Capt. Dermot Gray,while alongside the naval base, and on completion of loading the *Granuaile* sailed for Dunmore East with four naval divers of the ROV team embarked. At 08:00 hrs Monday 22 May the LÉ *Niamh*, with Lt Darragh Kirwan and diving team embarked, slipped and proceeded to rendezvous with the *Granuaile* off Dunmore East. An operation similar to that conducted on the *Rising Sun* four months previously would be carried out on the *Maggie B*, with the lessons learnt during that operation put into effect. The *Granuaile* located the position of the wreck and moored up over the site. Once again this vessel proved to be the only suitable platform from which to conduct this type of operation. In similar fashion both divers and ROV worked in support of each other, particularly

Dive Plan for the day's diving ops on the Pere Charles

in inclement weather. Over the course of the week comprehensive visual and video surveys were conducted on all accessible areas. No bodies were sighted or recovered during the operation. On Friday 26 May the Diving Section was released from its tasking by the Department of Transport. At 17:00 hrs the *Granuaile* arrived alongside the oil wharf at the naval base and all equipment was unloaded. On completion the *Granuaile* was released to resume her normal operations:

> This is the second operation of this type that the Diving Section has been tasked with. The lessons learnt during the Rising Sun had been addressed … however, with the possibility that this depth of diving will become more prevalent in the coming years, the shortcomings, regarding a suitable platform, highlighted during the Rising Sun operation still hold true. The Diving Section needs to be diving to 50 metres on a frequent basis and to date has not been able to do so. NS ships are not designed as a dive platform and have limited space for the proper equipment to be embarked. Short of acquiring a role-specific tender, the use of the Granuaile should be investigated for training purposes.[77]

2006: *Pere Charles*

On Wednesday 10 January 2007, at 18:00 hrs approx, the fishing vessel *Pere Charles* sank while making its way back to port at Dunmore East with the loss of all five crewmen on board: skipper Tom Hennessy, Pat Hennessy, Billy O'Connor, Pat Coady and Andriy Dyrin. The naval diving team under Lt Darragh Kirwan was placed on standby to deploy to Dunmore East when weather conditions moderated to the point when diving operations could commence. On Monday 15 January SDDE equipment and RCC was embarked aboard the *Granuaile*, and on completion of loading, the *Granuaile – under the command of Capt. Harry McClenahan – * sailed for the dive site. At the dive site the vessel established itself over the wreck, and a series of dives were conducted by the naval diving team. Poor visibility of less than half a metre hampered the divers' search, with no bodies being sighted or found during the dives. It was established that 'both life rafts were observed missing from their storage',[78] and that the *Pere Charles* was lying well over on her starboard side to an angle of approximately 110 degrees, and that there was a lot of crush damage. The weather had by then deteriorated to the point

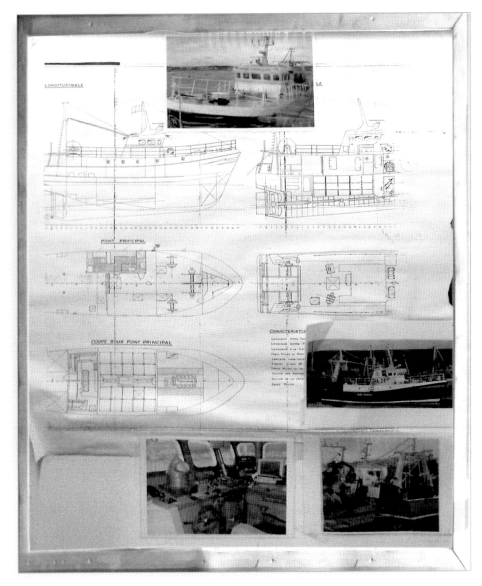

Familiarisation briefing board for Pere Charles *operation*

where the naval diving team and the *Granuaile* returned to the naval base to await a moderation in weather conditions. On Monday 22 January, having again loaded the *Granuaile*, both the vessel and the diving team returned to Dunmore East and re-established themselves over the wreck of the *Pere Charles* the following day. The next four days would see a total of seventeen dives to 34 metres conducted by the

Having been recalled to the naval base to conduct an urgent recompression therapeutic treatment table on a civilian diver, the quickest way back was courtesy of the Coast Guard's S61 from Sligo

naval diving team, with all dives carried out in pairs. Comprehensive searches of all accessible areas of the vessel were conducted by the divers both visually and by video camera, and for the first time the use of a small, portable mini-ROV, courtesy of the *Granuaile*, was used to access and video the more difficult and inaccessible areas of the vessel:

> The Video Ray mini-ROV from the ILV *Granuaile* was used to access the accommodation spaces of the wreck and found to be clear. No crew members were located within the wreck or in the immediate vicinity of the wreck or seabed.[79]

On Sunday 28 January 2007 the *Granuaile* and the naval diving team concluded diving operations and returned to the naval base to secure the equipment.

2012: *Tit Bonhomme*

On the morning of Sunday 15 January 2012 the small fishing vessel *Tit Bonhomme*, while making its way into its home port of Glandore–Union Hall in west Cork, at 05:45 hrs approx. struck and foundered on Adam's Rock close by the entrance to the harbour. On board were

six crew members: skipper Michael Hayes, Abdou Mohammed, Said aly Eldin, Wael Mohammed, Shaban Attia and Kevin Kershaw. Of the six crewmen, only Abdou Mohammed would survive, apparently after having being sucked out of a bridge window, such was the force of the waves breaking through the wheelhouse. The weather that morning was poor, with south-easterly winds blowing force 6 to 7, visibility down to hundreds of metres and heavy seas running. There appeared to have been some confusion, with the first distress call made from the *Tit Bonhomme* to the Irish Coast Guard at 05:46 approx., but at 05:49 hrs approx. a second distress call was received by the Irish Coast Guard and with greater clarity, instigating a huge search operation involving three lifeboats, a naval vessel, two Coast Guard Sikorskys and numerous local trawlers and smaller boats. Sea and weather conditions hampered constructive surface searching, except that undertaken by the helicopters. The diving officer in charge of that operation was Lt Conor Kirwan:

The following morning, with one satisfied customer gone to the hospital and a good fry-up devoured, the Air Corps duly flew us back to Mayo, where we were required for duty later that day in their lovely EC135 P2. (l–r): Tony O'Regan, Noel Dunne, Paul McCarthy and the pilot

> The diving team were up in Galway searching for a body. Fergy [Frank Cunningham] was running the show up there and the call came in on the Sunday that the *Tit Bonhomme* had gone missing … I travelled from Cork and the team travelled down

Tom Kennedy (left),
Martin Buckley.
It's not always
about diving …
searching the dykes in
Wexford's sloblands
for a missing person

from Galway and we all met up on the quay wall in Union Hall. When we got there I knew the weather was going to be shite for the next five days. So going into the meeting of the different parties, the families, etc., I knew it would be a job managing the expectations of the local community and the families … to go in there and say that we'll be on that vessel in the morning or that we'll have that vessel cleared first thing … it wasn't realistic and from a political point of view we would have been pulled apart … So therefore while we were dealing with the Coast Guard and the families, we immediately made it clear that we wouldn't be able to get anywhere near the wreck due to its exposed position over the next five days or so – although we dived the areas that we could and we dived them until the weather calmed down enough to allow us to dive on the *Tit Bonhomme*.[80]

The weather would continue to hamper the search efforts of all parties throughout the entire operation. It was not until Thursday 19 January that naval divers could commence their diving operations on and around the wreck of the *Tit Bonhomme*. The vessel was lying in 7 metres of water and at an acute angle on her port side. Searching the wreck and clearing it would be critical:

> The problem with the fishing vessel – talking to the locals at the time and the local fire brigade – was that the *Tit Bonhomme* was recognised as a very tight vessel in terms of compartments and trying to get into the accommodation space, and was actually used as a training vessel by the local fire brigade because it was so tight. So it was like a worst-case scenario for the fire brigade as to what they would encounter if there was a fire there and that was why they used that vessel. But that indicated to us at a very early stage that it was going to be a very difficult operation in clearance terms …[81]

When Conor Kirwan, earlier in the interview, alluded to the fact that he knew the pressure from the families of the missing fishermen would begin to ramp up after a short period of time, especially when there no results from the search, he was correct. Local media were reporting that the relatives were convinced that the remaining bodies would be located in the accommodation space. This type of pressure and anxiety by bereaved friends and family members was entirely natural and understandable in any incident of this type, but in its own way it was also unhelpful:

> In between all this, on the quay wall, family members were adamant at that stage – though it was contradicting what the survivor had said – they were adamant that all the bodies were down below in the accommodation area. So therefore the pressure and the focus were very much on us to get down into the accommodation area and to clear it … but even with surface demand there was always a possibility that we might not be able to get down through the hatch into the accommodation. So what we looked at was getting an ROV down there … Paddy O'Driscoll from the Marine Institute came down with the Video Ray … the problem was that the Video Ray once it got near the accommodation area, [and because] there was so …[many] little bits of insulation in the water column, that the thrusters of the Video Ray kept getting snagged up pretty much straightaway, so it never actually got into the accommodation space.
>
> What happened next was we got to the point where Gordy went down

Two chiefs working their magic:
Fergy Heaton (left), Tom Kelly

Diver in full SDDE dress, with camera
and light mounted on helmet

[and] he actually got so pissed off with the Video Ray getting fouled that … in trying to recover the Video Ray, [he] actually managed to fit through the compartment … size-wise, once I knew that Gordy had managed to fit through, then the rest of us would fit through [Gordy is a big guy]. And that's how over the next few days we cleared all the accommodation area, and we cleared the engine room space as well, all on surface demand.[82]

So the *Tit Bonhomme* would be cleared over the next couple of days, and with it the possibility of any members of the crew being on board resolved. During the course of the clearance of the vessel by the naval diving team, the Garda Underwater Unit – while clearing an area of seabed adjacent to the vessel – recovered a crew member, Shaban Attia, one of the three missing Egyptians. The following day the Naval Service Diving Section, whilst diving another area close by the vessel, recovered the body of Kevin Kershaw. During the weekend following the accident another body was recovered by local divers supervised by an ex-naval diver from Baltimore, John Kearney, while diving on the opposite side of the island. This was the body of another Egyptian, Wael Mohammed. There were now only two remaining crew members missing – that of the skipper Michael Hayes and the remaining Egyptian, Ali Said Yeldin. The recovery of the bodies in the vicinity of both the vessel and the island would lead both the garda and naval diving teams to focus their coordinated searches in those areas. The longer the searches went on without any results led to the agencies expanding their search areas. Over the next several days' diving, no further bodies were recovered. The Naval Service Diving Section concluded diving operations in Union Hall on 5 February 2012, after twenty-two days of operations and with the remaining two bodies still unrecovered.

On Wednesday 8 February the body of missing skipper Michael Hayes was recovered from the sea close by Union Hall. Two days later, on Friday 10 February 2012, the remaining body was recovered – that of Egyptian Ali Said Yeldin.

Conclusion

The operations recounted in this chapter provide, it is hoped, a reasonable account of the progression of the Diving Section and its capabilities as newer and better equipment became available. It is not by any stretch of the imagination a definitive account of operations, and is not meant to be. In fact, it couldn't be, for there were thousands of external operations over the years, and I couldn't have begun to account for them all. Over the years, particularly since the *Betelgeuse* operation in 1979, diving operations have expanded in complexity, depth and endurance both above and below the water. Critically, too, the operations have expanded in terms of technology and equipment. Gerry O'Donoghue back in the early 1980s described diving in its most basic terms: 'It's real rope-and-brick stuff – fuck the brick in the water, when you make the seabed cut the rope.' Gerry would agree that those days have well and truly gone.

Mention, too, must be made of the technical support the Diving Section has benefited from over the years, especially in the areas of information technology and in the fields of electronics and communications (and everything else in between). Since the arrival of the SDDE, and in particular the sub-surface search equipment, the requirement for technical support to assist, maintain and repair this equipment mushroomed. Personnel such as Barry McCormack – himself a diver – and Dan Laffan from the Naval Computer Centre were of immense help when it came to computers and laptops. In the electrical and electronic support areas, CPOs Tom Kelly (now warrant officer) and Fergy Heaton were tremendous also – indeed, it was typical of both these chiefs when on operations that they would often assist the divers when their primary services were not required. I recall on more than one occasion over the years the guys would be charging up diving sets and squaring away gear and so on. It's not an exaggeration to say that many an operation over the last decade or so would have had a sticky ending had it not been for the knowledge, skill, resilience and sometimes imaginative approach to repairs that all the support staff brought to the Diving Section.

Like Bere Island, an unseen part of the history of the Naval Service Diving Section was the outstanding assistance given by the Slua Muirí cadres based around the country, primarily in Dublin, Waterford, Cork and Limerick. Diving operations were often only a phone call away and usually occurred late at night, and though times have changed and the logistics involved in maintaining a diving team on the road have improved immeasurably, the assistance given by the staff of the cadres was sometimes the difference between a successful operation or not. In Dublin there was Ray Delaney, Stephen Dempsey, Paul Daly, Mick Boland, Pierce Power, Harry O'Neill, Mickey Johnson (brother of Tommy) and Paul 'ZIP' Nolan. In Waterford we had Tom Burke, Phil 'Stretch' Molloy, Paddy Maher and John Collins. In Cork there was D.P. Cronin, Henry Malone and Gerry O'Shea, and in Limerick there was Kevin Hartley, Charlie Coleman and Seanie Burke.

To conclude this chapter on the operations of the Naval Service Diving Section over the years, I will quote Capt. Dermot Gray, master ILV *Granuaile*, and, again, Rear Admiral Mark Mellett:

> As Master of the Commissioners of Irish Lights vessel ILV *Granuaile* I have worked with Irish Navy divers on several operations. We were always impressed with their professionalism and attention to detail to ensure that divers were safe and confident in all tasks set to them in extremely difficult situations at times. Because of this it is always a pleasure for all of our crew to work with the Irish Navy divers.
>
> Capt. Dermot Gray, Master ILV *Granuaile*, 2015

> 'Never has so much been done by so few, for so many' … in stealing Churchill's words – but for such a small unit the output was extraordinary!
>
> Rear Admiral Mark Mellett[83]

5

BETELGEUSE, 1979

We judge ourselves by what we feel capable of doing, while others judge us by what we have already done.

Henry Wadsworth Longfellow

During the evening of 6 January 1979 the Total SA French-owned oil tanker *Betelgeuse* berthed alongside the discharging berth at Whiddy Oil terminal in Bantry, County Cork. Later that night, at 23:30 hrs approx., she commenced the discharging of her cargo to the tank farms on the island of Whiddy. Her cargo for discharging was 114,000 tonnes of mixed Arabian crude oil, and it was expected that this operation would take about thirty-six hours to complete. Sometime between 00:45 hrs and 01:00 hrs on the morning of Monday 8 January an event occurred causing a massive explosion, followed by a series of further explosions big enough to split the *Betelgeuse* in half. The explosions and the resulting fire killed everyone on board and the workers on the adjacent jetty: fifty people died (forty-two French, seven Irish and one UK national). Five months later, during salvage operations, another person would die. A Dutch salvage diver working on the wreck on 22 May was killed, bringing the final casualty total to fifty-one persons. With the explosions, much of the oil on board ignited and generated heat in excess of 1000°C, causing further massive damage both to the ship and to the berthing dolphins alongside. Once the fire was finally extinguished it would be several days before any search-and-recovery operations could be mounted due to the presence of toxic and highly inflammable gas in the area.

On 15 January the Naval Service diving team was directed to assemble and report to Bantry. Lt Dan O'Neill was the diving officer on this operation, and his team consisted of CPO George Jefferies, CPO John Walsh, L/Sea Martin Carroll, L/Sea Noel Garrett and L/Mech. Gerry Duffy. The scene that met them upon their arrival was unmatched in terms of their collective experience during any previous diving operations. A transcription of the directing signal reads:

DTG; 152155 Z Jan [1979]
From: CONS
To (Action): COH
To (Info): OPC Bantry
Requests have been received for the services of six naval divers to assist garda divers at Bantry.
The request has been acceded to.
Naval divers will be under the direct control of Lieut. D. O'Neill, N.S. who is to ensure the availability and serviceability of a decompression chamber on site Naval Service divers operate at a depth in excess of 100 feet.
All diving operations are to be conducted strictly in accordance with diving manual BR 2806 and divers for which are qualified.
Diving team should depart for Bantry as soon as possible tomorrow morning.
ACK.

A further signal amending para 4 was sent the following day:

Delete all after BR 2806 and insert the following: And divers are not to operate to depths in excess of depths for which they are not qualified.[1]

Naval Command was ensuring that all its bases were being covered in the event of an accident. It wasn't off-loading any of its responsibility – it couldn't – but it was ensuring quite clearly and pointedly where it understood any responsibility lay in the event of mishap. Very probably for the first time the navy was being seriously challenged as to its perceived capabilities, but the naval Diving Section would rise to the occasion.

The divers departed the naval base at 14:00 hrs as directed and proceeded to Bantry. They established their base and prepared themselves and their equipment for diving operations. They established communications with the Garda Sub-aqua Unit consisting of Tommy Lavery, Mick Carr, Jim Brennan, Donal Gibbons and John Harrington and under the command of Garda Sgt Paddy Morrissey. After consultations with Sgt Morrissey, it was agreed that

The search area was confined to the area around Dolphin 22 which was the boat dolphin and around which the remains of eight bodies were found following the disaster.[2]

MESSAGE FORM

SIGNALS REF. NO	
	GR

Lt. O'Neill.

PRECEDENCE—ACTION	PRECEDENCE—INFO	DATE—TIME—MONTH	MESSAGE INSTRUCTIONS
P	P	152155 Z Jan	

FROM	SECURITY CLASSIFICATION
CONS	

TO (ACTION)		
COH	DELIVERY INDICATOR	ORIGINATOR REF. NO.

TO (INFO)   OPC Bantry

1. Requests have been received for the services of six naval divers to assist garda divers at Bantry.
2. The request has been acceded to.
3. Naval divers will be under the direct control of Lieut D. O'Neill, N.S. who is to ensure the availability and serviceability of a decompression chamber on site before naval service divers operate at a depth in excess of 100 feet.
4. All diving operations are to be conducted strictly in accordance with diving manual BR 2806 and dives for which are qualified.
5. Diving Teams should depart for Bantry as soon as possible tomorrow morning.
6. ACK.

Page...... of...... Pages	Does this Message refer to a Classified Message?	☐ YES ☐ NO	RELEASING OFFICER'S SIGNATURE AND RANK	

	Date	Time	System	Op.		To	Date	Time	System	Op.
R	15/1/79.	2253	CL	NT	D					

Signal for Lt Dan O'Neill directing diving team to Bantry

Naval divers commenced diving operations on Whiddy Island the following day at 10:00 hrs. Lt O'Neill established the whereabouts of both the chambers currently available in the recovery zone:

> On arrival at Whiddy I immediately established the fact that 2 no. recompression chambers were available in the event of a necessity.
>
> Gulf had hired a small 2 man chamber from Mr J. Butler, Dunmore East, which was available on Whiddy Island for the duration.
>
> The garda divers had made contact with the Dutch registered Smit-Tak salvage tug 'Barracuda' and had established that their chamber if not in use and in the event of an emergency would be available.[3]

With the necessary RCC facilities established and confirmed available – at least

*Lt Dan O'Neill
(centre), Noel
Garrett (right)*

in an emergency – diving operations could now commence.

The diving officer's subsequent report was perfectly written. It was succinct and to the point. I have transcribed the relevant sections pertaining firstly to the search areas and procedures, and secondly to the search schemes use. It is important these are known and understood, particularly in relation to the conditions, the dangers and the equipment used not just by the naval divers but also, it must be stated, by the Garda Sub-aqua Unit. It was a pity that the report was a bit short on its description and dive information as it didn't reflect in any great detail the actual difficulties and conditions in which the divers were operating, nor the effort that each diver was making:

> The depth in the area was measured using shot lines and was found to vary between 100 ft. and 120 ft. Due to the depth involved and the fact most of the naval divers had not dived to that depth for some time, I restricted all diving 'bottom time' to the no-stop decompression limits, and thereafter carried out all diving in accordance with the rules and procedures as laid down in BR. 2806 for diving at that depth and in prevailing conditions.

In other words, Lt O'Neill aimed to ensure that all dives conducted by the naval divers would be of a duration that would not incur a decompression penalty or require scheduled decompression stops – hence the 'no-stop' limits:

> In the region of Dolphin 22, I adopted a circular search scheme using two divers buddied together and where possible a short jackstay search (30/40ft), as with the amount and type of construction debris on the bottom, I felt that it was the safer and more reliable search scheme. As the search area extended south i.e. towards the shore, it became possible to use a longer jackstay search (150 ft.), again using two divers. The underwater visibility throughout the duration was negligible.[4]

The divers searched the areas indicated throughout the week, with both Naval Service and garda divers diving to their limits both in

(left, l–r): John Walsh George Jefferies;
(right): Gerry Duffy

depth and times. However, the equipment in use was nothing short of disastrous. Seven-millimetre wetsuits were the standard diving wetsuit – all very well in summer but not suitable for winter diving, particularly when the suits themselves were not up to scratch and especially when diving to 30 metres or more. The standard diver's life jacket at the time was the Fenzy. The diving sets would have been the Spiro or Aquarius twin sets, complete with a single-hose demand valve/regulator of Poseidon make. Half face masks or Avon full-face mask's depending on choice. They were diving in depths that made the wetsuit compress to a point where its inherent buoyancy was all but gone – likewise, any thermal properties it might have offered. Runners with socks were worn in lieu of booties. Any visibility was poor to nil, and any chance of getting some heat into the body through swimming was not a possibility. They were operating in a demolition site with oil

Body recovered and being passed to the Barracuda

on the surface and any amount of potential hazards awaiting the unsuspecting divers on the bottom. They were attempting to locate and recover multiple missing persons amongst a debris-strewn seabed covered in a layer of oil many inches thick, and all this in 120 feet of seawater:

> *Betelgeuse* was a dirty job, a lot of oil – everything was covered in this thick oil. The company down there gave us overalls to wear over the wetsuits to keep the oil off, but you just got totally covered. We were diving there … it was quite deep – 30 to 35 metres. We did grid searches around the jetty – both us and the guards. We found two bodies … we did a lot of diving there … then I had the accident down there when the first stage packed in, jammed up with oil and stopped working … I free ascended then. It worked [said Dan laughingly], then I spent about six hours in the chamber then, no problem as such but I tore the retina in my eye which came back to haunt me a few weeks ago … imagine thirty-five years later!
>
> Noel [Garrett] gave the signal [to the surface] on the lifeline and watched me all the way up. He grabbed me and came up with me nice and slowly. He said the free ascent went fine … and that was that. About a month later they promoted me to lieutenant commander …[5]

John Walsh recalled the *Betelgeuse*:

> The day after we arrived, a commercial team arrived from Portsmouth … they arrived with all the best of gear – they had SDDE, the whole lot, and we were still with our scuba gear and lifeline signals and the whole lot … they arrived and they looked, stayed twenty-four hours and left … so we were still there, had to endure floating oil, all our suits were destroyed and we were working with the guards … it was frustrating at the time – we were told to do it and get on with it, and we did it and we got on with it. We even paid for our own digs and claimed back afterwards, such were the times … anybody that was in the Diving Section was in it because they loved it … anybody else wouldn't have put up with what we put up with and went back and looked for more because that's what we did …[6]

In an interview with George Jefferies, he echoed pretty much what John was saying, and added:

I'd say this – that job was the turning point for the navy, definitely. Definitely the turning point for the navy … we were diving in 126 feet of water with 7-millimetre suits, Fenzy life jackets and max bottom time fourteen minutes … There was a crowd came over from Southampton to look for all this stuff that had fallen down around Dolphin 22 … they had a million pounds worth of stuff. You'd want to see the diving equipment they had, it was unbelievable this stuff … and here was us diving with 7 millimetre suits … and the guards were expected to this as well, that's what I can't understand, like. I mean they were expected to do this as well, and they got nothing out of it … but Bantry really was to me … the defining moment that the navy needed to move on in diving, and it moved on.[7]

Martin Carroll added his perspective:

The gear situation was shite. It was actually shite up until 1979 after the Bantry disaster – that changed fucking things around … and the 7-mm suits we had – the fucking oil used to go right through the them … we washed down in Swarfega every night, even showered with Swarfega for fuck sake.[8]

Gerry Duffy:

It was deep, it was dark and it was dirty – everything you never wanted in diving was in that job … but I think – and I include the gardaí in this – I think the pride of the place at that time took an awful lot of the blunt edge off the brutality of what happened. The pride of everybody on that job, like you know, the wetsuits, the socks, the runners, you know. I remember on one dive, myself and George were going down and halfway down I was left with the demand-valve tit in me mouth, the valve disintegrated, not a nice thing when you're going to 30-odd metres. We came back up, changed it out and went back down again … there was boys became men on that job.[9]

I interviewed Tommy 'Tosh' Lavery, retired garda sergeant and former head of the Garda Sub-aqua Unit. Tosh was involved in the garda operation on the *Betelgeuse*, and, indeed, on many other operations that both the navy and gardaí would work together on over the years. I asked Tosh what his thoughts were when he arrived down to Whiddy Island. The garda divers had been there several days prior to the naval team arriving:

> We had the boat rolled and tied up, carrying it, so when we got up over the hill, the first thing I remember is the big sign over Whiddy, so many days, no injuries in the work place, someone put a line through it and had written … 50 dead … so we climbed up over the hill, and I remember carrying this bit of fucking rubber. When we went over this hill I saw this fucking thing sticking up out of the water [the huge bow section of the ship] … be fucking Jaysus to Christ, I didn't know what we were facing, you know what I mean. We were going out to this thing in a fucking rubber dinghy, scuba gear and wetsuits, what the fuck was going on like … we were just sent down there, get down there quick …
>
> The *Betelgeuse* was one of the worst jobs of all time … in the unit. Because of the depth, because of the conditions, because of the equipment … the worst job ever.[10]

Dan O'Neill's equipment failure (see Chapter 7: Naval Service Diving Section Recompression Chamber) occurred on Friday 20 January. Operations continued

Navy/garda diving teams (front, l–r): Sgt Paddy Morrissey, Gerry Duffy, George Jefferies, Tommy Lavery, John Walsh, Noel Garrett, Donal Gibbons, Mick Carr; (back, l–r): John Harrington, Martin Carroll (looking over George's shoulder), Jim Brennan (behind Martin)

until Friday 27 January, when because of the tanker having become 'inerted', diving operations were suspended until the following Tuesday (30 January), when inerting operations were due to be finished. The naval diving team cleaned and secured their equipment and returned to the naval base for the weekend, pending recall. The following Monday, 30 January, both Danno and George returned to Whiddy for an update and reassessment of the situation, and they learned that the inerting operation would continue until Friday 2 February, with the guards also returning to Dublin to await a recall:

> I then indicated that I also proposed returning to base with our equipment. I requisitioned transport and finally departed from Whiddy Island at 14:00 hrs on 31.1.1979.[11]

And so the Bantry Bay *Betelgeuse* diving operation concluded, but the legacy of the *Betelgeuse* and the conduct of operations around it would rumble on a lot longer. Not least was the need to sort out sooner rather than later the issue of the severe lack of suitable resources for diving operations such as Bantry. But big wheels turn slowly. Gerry O'Donoghue remarked in an email to me when recalling his MCDO's course during which the disaster occurred:

> While I was away the Betelgeuse operation took place back in Ireland. I returned to find a group of divers rightfully proud of their achievements under horrendous conditions. A diving structure that did not exist, equipment that would have embarrassed a rural sub-aqua club and a Naval Service Command oblivious to the fact that they missed having to provide a funeral guard of honour for a diver by the proverbial skin of their teeth.[12]

6

AIR INDIA FLIGHT 182: TORONTO, CANADA TO BOMBAY, INDIA, 23 JUNE 1985

On Sunday morning 23 June 1985 at 08:00 hrs approx. an Air India Boeing 747, Flight 182, flying at 33,000 feet while en route from Toronto, Canada to Bombay, India, and carrying 329 persons, suffered one and possibly two on-board explosions. The resulting damage was catastrophic for the 747, which plummeted to the waiting Atlantic Ocean below. All 329 persons on board died. The incident happened approximately 100 miles off the south-west coast of Ireland.

Not too many miles away was the *Laurentian Forest*, en route from Quebec, Canada to Dublin with a cargo of newsprint. To the north of the *Laurentian Forest* was the Irish naval vessel LÉ *Aisling* P23, under the command of Lt Cdr Jim Robinson. The ship was in the process of arresting a Spanish fishing vessel, having stopped and boarded it an hour previously. Both vessels were oblivious to the air disaster that had taken place more than 6 miles above them. A distress alert was broadcast from the Marine Rescue Coordination Centre informing all ships of the disappearance from the Shannon radar screens of the Air India 747 at 08:44 hrs approx., and providing the coordinates of the last known position of the flight. The *Laurentian Forest* immediately turned her helm hard over, and the ship reversed its course and made her best speed back along her track to the location some 22 miles away. The LÉ *Aisling*, having received notification of the disappearance, immediately informed the boarding officer and NCO on board the fishing vessel to proceed to Castletown Bere. Having recalled the Gemini, the LÉ *Aisling* proceeded at her best speed to the same coordinates.

Muiris Mahon was involved in the recovery operation that day, and was subsequently awarded a Distinguished Service Medal. He recalled the operation:

Chris [Chris Reynolds] was the gunnery officer and a fella called Timmy Heinhold … was the SPO dusty [senior petty officer, Supplies] – they were on a trawler we were boarding, we were just doing a routine boarding … after the boarding the ship was going into Bantry for the Sunday night … and we did this routine boarding early in the morning. Chris was over there and they arrested her for whatever, and in the process of arresting her word came through that there was a plane gone missing so many miles off the coast and we were to go the area immediately. So Jim Robinson informed the captain [of the trawler] that he was to make his way into Castletown Bere, I presume, that would have been the closest to him, with Chris and Timmy Heinhold.[1]

At 10:00 hrs approx. the *Laurentian Forest* closed on the position, and entered into a debris field. Ahead lay wreckage, seating, clothing and bodies. The tailpiece was jutting out of the water and still more bodies were seen. The *Laurentian Forest* lowered it ship's boat to recover what bodies it could. Meanwhile, the LÉ *Aisling* was making her best speed to the same position, while on board the crew were making what preparations they could in the event of having to assist survivors. She arrived shortly after the *Laurentian Forest*. The OC LÉ *Aisling*, Lt Cdr Jim Robinson, immediately assumed the role of on-scene commander (OSC) for the incident. They were ill prepared for what awaited them but in true naval fashion they steamed on:

I was on the bridge [en route to the crash site] for the whole period of it, listening and watching … we thought we were looking for a 747 that maybe had landed in the ocean somewhere out there … beautiful day, absolutely beautiful day, like, it was June, late June 23rd … so Joe Sheridan [senior petty officer, Supplies] was out collecting blankets, and clothing, spare clothing around the place … would you fucking believe it … we actually were so naive we thought we were gonna just come across this bloody big thing sitting there in the water … that's how naive we were … little did we know what we were sailing into, into just a graveyard.[2]

The LÉ *Aisling* lowered its Gemini craft, whose crew commenced its own recovery operation. They would recover many bodies by the time they were finished that day.

By day's end, aircraft from the Air Corps, the RAF and the United States Air Force would be engaged in the search. An RAF Nimrod coordinated the aerial-search patterns. Long-range Sea King helicopters from RNAS Culdrose and RAF Brawdy in Wales together with RAF Chinooks and USAF HC 53 Jolly Green Giants were also involved. Lifeboats from Valentia, Baltimore, Courtmacsherry and Ballycotton, cargo vessels, rig-support vessels and Spanish fishing vessels all were engaged in the search-and-recovery operation as coordinated by the OSC:

> … what they were doing on the bridge was unbelievable, they were coor-dinating everything, apart from fifteen helicopters, there were ships and trawlers, lifeboats – they were working flat out – I mean every time I went to the bridge, I'd take a look and say "Let's get the fuck outta here" … it was crazy.[3]

The search area extended over some 25 square miles. Mossy recalled the scene:

> I don't think the skipper knew, I actually don't think they knew. I think the information was very varied until we got very close to the area and we got in touch with the ship called *Laurentian Forest* … she was the first ship on scene. There was just debris everywhere … and after the first run we pulled in a couple of bodies, four or five bodies – when we came back in I said, "There's too many of us in the boat guys", so they dropped the bowman … there's an amount of bodies, 'cos when you put six bodies in a Gemini there isn't much room for anybody else and it's not as if you could sit on top of them. So we were like coming in and taking an average of four to six each trip, with the white sheets covering them up, and the Gemini would go on the deck, and they would hand them out one by one and put them in place …
>
> It was a mistake bringing them indoors into the ship, but again it was a warm day and where do you put them – we had nowhere to put them … not equipped … Jaysus … it took six months to clean up most of that which had gone into the deck heads … anyway, that was the Air India disaster.
>
> … there were sharks in the water and they were having a ball. I never forget the first time we went to pull a body and it was pulled off of us, and "What the fuck" … we pulled in the body, and the two legs were pins, stripped bare of flesh, just bone, first time to see that … fuck … after that

(l–r): L/Sea John McGrath, Lt Cdr James Robinson OC LÉ Aisling P23, PO/Sea Muiris Mahon, A/Sea Terry Brown, recipients of the Distinguished Service Medals for their part in the Air India SAR operation, 23 June 1985

you were passing bodies with chunks taken out of them … but that was just the way it was.[4]

A total of 198 bodies remained lost to the sea, while 131 were recovered. The LÉ *Aisling* recovered twenty-nine bodies that Sunday, and as a consequence of their actions during that day, the on-scene commander, OC LÉ *Aisling* Lt Cdr James Robinson, and the three-man crew of the Gemini, PO/Sea Muiris Mahon (D), L/Sea John McGrath (D) and A/Sea Terry Brown, would be awarded Distinguished Service Medals a year later, in February 1986:

> It was incredible, just incredible … yeah I do believe that Jim just used us because we were divers and that's what we did … unfortunately, its part and parcel of what we do. I had picked up a few [bodies] at that stage of my diving career, not too many, but by the end of that day, it was quite a lot.[5]

In the aftermath of the bombing, the next phase was to attempt to recover the flight data recorders if possible. On 4 July the LÉ *Aoife*, along with other specialist vessels, whilst searching for wreckage on the seabed detected a faint signal believed to be coming from the plane's black boxes. On 12 July the two flight recorders were handed over to Indian government officials and subsequently flown back to India for examination. Towards the end of July the Canadian Coast Guard vessel the *John Cabot*, with a deep-water Scarab ROV embarked, departed Cork Harbour with a specialist recovery team and three Irish naval divers on board – Lt Cdr Gerry O'Donoghue, CPO John Walsh and PO Gerry Duffy – and proceeded to the crash-site debris field. Their job was to assist in the recovery of any debris that may have been brought up by the Scarab. Should the debris be too heavy for the Scarab to bring up to the surface, the divers would be deployed to attach lines or strops required before the wreckage would break the surface:

> Gerry O'D, myself and Walshy went to the *Cabot* for about three weeks and didn't do a whole lot because not a lot was happening. Then some weeks later, after we got back from that, I went back out on a deep-sea tug for another couple of weeks or so, to recover some bits and pieces.[6]

In February 1988 armed police stopped and arrested Inderjit Singh Reyat on his way to work at the Jaguar car manufacturing plant in Coventry, England. He was extradited to Canada in 1989. He pleaded guilty to manslaughter and bomb-making charges concerning another bombing in Narita Airport, Japan. In May 1991 he was sentenced to ten years for those offences. The Canadian authorities then spent several more years attempting to prove that he was also involved in the Air India Flight 182 bombing. In 2000 Ajaib Singh Bagri and Ripudman Singh Malik were arrested in connection the bombings in Narita Airport (Flight CP 003) and Air India Flight 182. Inderjit Singh Reyat cut a deal with the Canadian authorities in which he would be charged with the lesser charge of manslaughter in relation to Air India Flight 182 in return for giving evidence against his co-accused. All three then stood trial in British Columbia, Canada in 2003. However, Reyat failed to implicate his co-accused, and was sentenced to five years for his involvement while the other two walked free. Having served his five years, he was released in 2008. However, in 2010 he was tried on perjury charges relating to the 2003 court case, and found guilty. He was sentenced to another nine years. In November 2012 lawyers for Inderjit Singh Reyat lodged an appeal to the Canadian Supreme Court in relation to the perjury charges. This appeal was rejected and Reyat remains in prison.

7

NAVAL SERVICE DIVING SECTION
RECOMPRESSION CHAMBER

The only source of knowledge is experience

Albert Einstein

Naval Recompression Chamber, 1983–2008

When Lt Joe Deasy arrived back from the UK in November 1964 after successfully completing his torpedo and anti-submarine course, he could not have been impressed with what awaited him. Having come from a very sophisticated naval organisation – as the Royal Navy was, with what could arguably have been the best of facilities, equipment and support – Lt Deasy found himself once more back in Haulbowline, and it could not have been a pretty sight. He wasn't a dreamer; he was nothing if not pragmatic. The best he could have hoped for at that time was that his end-of-course report to his commanding officers might had convinced them in their wisdom to follow up his recommendations and to further pursue diver training of more officers and men, and in due course build up enough manpower with the necessary skills to constitute a diving group or section. Lt Deasy was to be disappointed, as for the best part of the next six years he would write letters on the matter several times to the school commandant – the officer in charge of training in the Naval Service at that time – and to his superior officers, only to have his requests for further diver training turned down. No doubt chief among those reasons was the lack of money. But Lt Deasy's particular knowledge gained from his

Joe Deasy (Cmdre; retd)

training as a TAS diving officer was not to be wasted, and for the first time his knowledge was to be officially called upon. This request for assistance would be the first of its type for the Naval Service, and indeed would be the first time that the requirement for a facility that would be able to offer the necessary advice and expertise in the area of diving illnesses and recompression would be mentioned, and also that it should be facilitated at the naval base.

On the night of 29 August 1967 the duty coxswain (a senior NCO manning the operations room out of hours) received a call from Bantry, County Cork. On the other end of the line was the colleague of a diver who had suffered a diving illness as a result of a work dive conducted earlier that day, and who had been treated at the on-site recompression chamber; later, however, he had suffered a reoccurrence of the symptoms. Having gained all the necessary and pertinent information, Lt Deasy advised the colleague of the diver to contact the duty Diving Section at the Royal Naval Base at Devonport, which kept a twenty-four-hour watch and which would be familiar with such cases. On their advice the diver was subsequently re-compressed in an attempt to alleviate the symptoms, but this would not prove successful. The following day the diver was flown by Air Corps helo to another recompression facility in Derry. It is not known if the diver recovered after his treatment there. It is important to note that the subsequent report Lt Deasy wrote to his commanding officer mentioned for the first time a need for specialist equipment in the treatment of diver illness, and, furthermore, highlighted the need for the navy to take the lead in this area:

> … a relief or advisory service with qualified divers and medical personnel, where information or assistance could be sought … this incident further illustrates the need for a Diving Section in the Service where the information sought by the Bantry diver would be readily available … I believe that this latest episode in the incident further pinpoints the need for a specialist information and services in this country, preferably in the Naval Service.[1]

Naval Command's direct response to this letter is unknown, but what is known is that it would be at least another twelve years before the case for a recompression chamber would be made again, and in a more dramatic manner.

The early 1970s saw the arrival of the three minesweepers LÉ *Fóla*, LÉ *Gráinne* and LÉ *Banba* as replacements for the defunct corvettes. As the construction of a minesweeper was essentially timber planking built around a shell of aluminium, this necessitated frequent ship's-hull inspections by divers as part of a detailed ship's-hull maintenance schedule. Naval divers were being trained by the Royal Navy from 1970 onwards, and by the middle/end of the 1970s some twenty-five officers, NCOs and men would have qualified as ship's diving officers and ship's divers. The period between 1970 and 1979 would see the naval divers become more operational as the decade unfolded, and their operations taking them deeper and longer whereby they would be making maximum use of their 'bottom time' as allowed by regulations, 'bottom time' being the period of time from the diver leaving the surface to the diver giving one pull (on the lifeline) to indicate he's left 'bottom'. Diving operations conducted where the nature of the seabed was not of a uniform depth often led the diving supervisors to have very trying times indeed, to such an extent that they would where necessary build in their own cut-off times and depth restrictions as another safety margin to try and offset any possible depth/time overruns. January 1979 and the Bantry Bay tanker disaster would bring this to a head and in a rather dramatic fashion for the Naval Service Diving Section.

The *Betelgeuse* diving incident

The search-and-recovery diving operations that followed the destruction of the Gulf Oil Tanker *Betelgeuse* during the early hours of 8 January 1979 were the toughest, deepest and most enduring that the naval divers had experienced up to that point. Involved in those recovery operations with the Naval Service Diving Section were members of the Garda Sub-aqua Unit. Importantly, also on site was the Dutch salvage vessel *Barracuda*, complete with a recompression-chamber facility on board.

Early on the afternoon of 21 January, Naval divers were conducting a routine search-and-recovery dive operation just off Dolphin 22. Two naval divers were tasked with conducting a large circular search of an area marked with a deep-diving shot line. After a couple of minutes into the dive, one of the divers, Lt Dan O'Neill, suffered an equipment failure. His demand valve failed, and Diver O'Neill informed his diving buddy and began to make a controlled free ascent. His buddy – clearly understanding the urgency of the situation – grabbed his partner and ensured they were facing each other as they ascended. As they passed through the last few metres to the surface, Diver O'Neill felt a sharp pain to his sinus area. On surfacing, he presented with a bloodstained face mask, and while it was suspected that only his sinuses had ruptured, the diving supervisor could not take a chance and so the diver was treated as having a suspected air embolism due to rapid ascent. Both divers were recovered into the diving boat, and Diver O'Neill was immediately put into the necessary body position in the bottom of the boat to offset any possible further migration, or creep, of air bubbles to the head, while the boat proceed at best comfortable speed towards the *Barracuda*. Once on board, the diver was attended to by the on-board Dutch diving medical technician, Evert Hendriks, who determined from a thorough medical examination that while the diver had suffered a severe shock to his system, an embolism in all

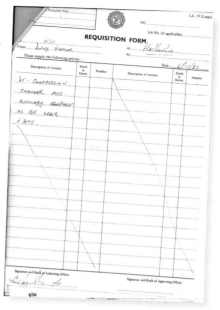

Requisition form LA 19, dated 6 December 1983, requesting the draw down from stores of (1) decompression chamber; requesting officer was S/Lt Chris Reynolds

probability could be ruled out, and that in fact all Diver O'Neill had suffered was a ruptured sinus. It was decided that in order to offset any possible chance of a 'bend', however unlikely, that they would recompress Diver O'Neill on a suitably short therapeutic recompression table. A couple of hours and a few cups of tea later, Diver O'Neill resurfaced and, on completion of another satisfactory medical assessment by Mr Hendriks, all personnel were secured for the day.

> Then I had the incident down there when the first stage packed in, jammed up with oil and stopped working … I free ascended then … it worked [said Dan laughingly] … then I spent six hours in the chamber then, no problems as such but I tore the retina in my eye which came back to haunt me a few weeks ago … imagine, thirty-five years later! … they stuck me in the chamber, nothing would have happened if they hadn't, but by the time you're in there you're straight down and then they tell you there's nothing wrong, that you didn't have an embolism … I just had burst sinuses …[2]

When the diving operations were concluded in Bantry, the diving officer in charge of the operation wrote his report. In the 'Conclusion and

Recommendations' section, Lt O'Neill mentioned probably the two most important things for the future development of the Naval Service Diving Section: not for the first time, the requirement for a recompression chamber and for permanent naval-base teams of divers. Lt Joe Deasy had mentioned the same requirement in his report twelve years earlier, and now the requirement for a chamber was coming home to roost. The incident concerning Lt O'Neill could have had a more dramatic outcome for the diver and, indeed, the Naval Service in general and Naval Command in particular. According to the 'Conclusion and Recommendations' section of the report,

> … the operation throws a new light on the N.S. diving duties both in terms of safety and operational standards. To that end the following recommendations are submitted … the diving incident of 20.1.1979 re-emphasises the necessity for a semi-transportable recompression chamber facility in the Naval Service and in particular in the Naval Base, where all diving aptitude training, continuation training for divers and the majority of diving duties takes place.[3]

Furthermore, and rather interestingly, Lt O'Neill went on:

> Naval base – permanent team of divers:
> This exercise in reality at Bantry again emphasises the necessity for a permanent team of divers in the naval base for both general service duties and if required as an aid to civil power.[4]

Clearly things were coming to a head for the future of naval diving. The *Betelgeuse* operation had passed. All taskings and dives were concluded, and all personnel had returned to the naval base, safe and sound. Just. The operations in Bantry were conducted in depths of water that the naval divers had rarely worked in before. Diving operations were conducted using wetsuits and Frenzys, single sets with single-demand valve regulators, no communications to the surface other than lifeline signals, and ultimately and equally as important no Naval Service-owned recompression chamber. It appeared that the Naval Service Command and indeed the Naval Service divers had all played their 'get out of gaol free card' on that operation, and everyone knew it, particularly Lt Dan O'Neill. It now required a dedicated effort to secure through the various budgetary systems in the navy the wherewithal to procure the necessary equipment. The Naval Service and Command now had to embrace diving and all that it entailed, for it knew it wasn't going to get a second chance.

While the Bantry Bay disaster was being played out, a young sub-lieutenant from Buttevant, County Cork, Gerry O'Donoghue, was in the middle of completing a diving course with the Royal Navy. This course was the international long mine warfare clearance diving officers course, thankfully shortened to the ILMCDO course, and thankfully shortened even further a couple of years later to MCDO and ultimately to CDO. S/Lt O'Donoghue – having arrived back from the UK in March 1979 – immediately assumed the mantle of diving officer, and with gusto set about the business of putting order into the organised chaos that was diving within the service. Naval Service diving at that time was not a formally constituted group or, indeed, even a section; it was at best a phone extension in a room that officially at least passed for an office, and was manned only if someone was in the room. Equipment was in short supply and really not fit for purpose. The newly appointed diving officer had bigger plans and saw a vision for diving within the Naval Service that far outstripped anything until then. What he did know was that he had a group of divers that were equal to, if not better than, most he had encountered in his time in the UK. Bantry Bay had proved this. He knew that he was working with a group of divers that were as like-minded and driven as he was, particularly when it came to diving. He also knew he was dealing with seasoned NCOs, not only with regard to their Naval Service experience but, more importantly, their diving experience. All the sub lieutenant had to do was provide direction, and he provided that in spades – leadership was a group thing. He needed money, he needed equipment, but what he really needed was a recompression chamber owned by the Naval Service and on site in the naval base. He knew that once he had that, the rest, as they say, would follow:

> The importance of a recompression chamber cannot be overstressed. It will:
> Save lives in the event of an incident
> Raise the professionalism of the Diving Unit
> Give diving supervisors and divers a peace of mind which at present they
>   do not have.
> Enhance the image of the Naval Service as a serious maritime agency.[5]

However, it is said that big wheels turn slowly, and indeed that is true, particularly for the Naval Service. Not for the first time, money was the stumbling block, but there was a growing need for the Naval Service to train its own divers, and the cost saving would be considerable – sending personnel over to the UK was an expensive business. The ship's divers course was not particularly cheap, nor indeed were flights, trains, accommodation and subsistence – it all added up. But apart from the cost saving to the Naval Service, there was also a real sense that training our own was the way of the future:

> It is pointed out that an expenditure of £500 at this stage will result in a net saving of approx. £16,000 if the course had to be carried out abroad.[6]

The elements necessary for the service to train its own were falling into place. The required approval from the director of training Defence Forces was in hand. The MCDO was in the service though serving at sea as navigating officer on board the LÉ *Gráinne*. The training NCOs and supervisor were already working within the Diving Store, such as it was. What was needed now was for the Naval Service to find the necessary monies to cover the cost of purchasing its own recompression chamber.

The decision to commence the training of divers in the naval base was taken in 1982, and 17 December saw the successful completion of the first Naval Service divers course, with four students passing. The recompression chamber that was such a necessary training requirement for the course was hired in from a civilian diving company for the duration of the course:

> For safety reasons a recompression chamber is required on site. As the NS does not, at present, possess one of these there are two possible solutions. A chamber can be hired from a local diving contractor for approx. 10 days at £50 per day.[7]

The hiring of the RCC, while very necessary, was also forcing the issue with Command on the urgent need for a dedicated Naval Service RCC. This point was not lost on anyone in command, and certainly not on Lt Gerry O'Donoghue MCDO, since he went away and hired another chamber for the second course held a year later, in 1983.

Working away behind the scenes during the late 1970s and into the 1980s were a core group of senior naval officers – all qualified ship's diving officers – and one civilian. The officers – Cdr Joe Deasy, Lt Cdr Peadar McElhinney, Lt Cdr Frank Lynch and Lt Cdr Dan O'Neill, along with Lt Gerry O'Donoghue MCDO – were all pushing the requirement for the RCC at the various Command briefings. The file required for the purchase of the RCC was ready in all respects. The costings, specifications, spares, medical kit, supplier and manufacturer had all been researched and itemised. If and when the monies became available, the Diving Section would be ready:

> 2. Although the chamber has been deleted from the 1983 estimates I feel that if the Naval Service is to provide an adequate Diving Unit a recompression chamber is essential. Accordingly it is proposed to re-submit a case for the 1984 estimates.[8]

However, behind the scenes, working away in the naval stores, was Joe Forde. Mr Forde was the contracts officer for the Department of Defence (DoD) (Finance Branch) attached to the naval base overseeing the spending of monies as appropriated by the DoD. Joe was very bright, very thorough, and very well liked. He enjoyed sailing and fishing, and more importantly for the Naval Service and, in turn, for the Diving Section, he was also a keen amateur diver. Joe was very astute in his handling of naval monies, and his awareness of how the various systems worked and his unique position within the DoD allowed him to become aware of monies that might not be spent under a certain Army Corps subhead before the end of the financial year. That year was 1983. After a couple of unsuccessful attempts to secure the necessary money through the naval estimates of 1981, 1982 and even 1983, the opportunity arose again. An army ordnance subhead used for the procurement of certain munitions had not expended its allotted estimate monies. This was flagged to Joe Forde, and with the help of his colleagues in the DoD, this money was reallocated to the Naval Service estimates. The race against time had begun for the NS, and in particular the Diving Section. But the homework was done, the *I*s had been dotted and the *T*s long been crossed, so as Gerry O'Donoghue said in interview,

> We had the paperwork done … Danno mostly started it, he designed the damn thing … we basically designed this very large Kosangas cylinder with so many backups … it was a file on a desk going nowhere forever …[9]

Dan O'Neill also recalled:

> … I was never getting any money for anything; I was putting in for twenty
> thousand worth of gear and getting two thousand. So I put in for a chamber
> and I wrote up the specification for it … and GOD came back from doing
> his course [MCDO], and himself and Joe Deasy got talking and they got
> onto Joe [Forde] … the spec was there, the price was there, and would Joe
> buy the chamber … that expenditure was the guts of one hundred thousand
> punts … but that money finally came on the wing of money not being spent
> by somebody else in the DF [Defence Forces] … and we got the money 'cos
> I had the spec ready, that was the only reason … 'twas Joe got onto me, he
> must have been talking to Gerry and Peadar 'cos I had given up at that stage
> … so when he got the money he spent it … just think about it. Up to then I
> was getting two grand a year, and next minute there's a one-hundred-grand
> piece of equipment sitting there looking at us …[10]

Joe Forde rang Gerry O'Donoghue one day and asked him 'Can you spend
£80,000 punts?' The lieutenant was down in Joe Forde's office in less than an hour,
and handed Joe the file. The file was resubmitted, the finance sanctioned, the
supplier appointed and the manufacturer contracted. The recompression chamber
that was several years in the coming would arrive before the end of 1983. Gerry
said this of Joe Forde:

> Joe Forde actively liked the divers and he actively took up our case. He got
> us the chamber, the chamber is purely him. You know Danny and myself
> designed it, but Joe got us the money for it, and that was a turning point.[11]

On 6 December 1983 the then diving officer in charge of the Diving Section, S/
Lt Chris Reynolds (ship's diving officer), opened up a naval-stores LA19 requisition book, and proceeded to fill in the necessary columns to formally requisition
from stores, one 'De-compression chamber plus ancillary equipment as per order
E3092'. The arrival into the Naval Base and into the Diving Section of the recompression chamber was the culmination of nineteen years' hard effort, initially by Lt
Joe Deasy and followed by Lt Cdr Peadar McElhinney, Lt Cdr Dan O'Neill, Lt
Cdr Frank Lynch and latterly by Lt Gerry O'Donoghue. Ironically, their work was
only just beginning. From that day forth, the RCC – while its primary function

was to treat diving illnesses that might be incurred solely by naval divers – greatly enhanced the NS diving capability, particularly in matters of training new divers, and deep-diving work-ups. Importantly, it made the Naval Service compliant with BR 2806, particularly in training and in potential deep-diving operations where the presence of an RCC would be a critical requirement. January 1984 saw the RCC being properly installed for operation in the Diving Store. Though not the ideal location, it was a start.

In one sense the arrival of the RCC into the base must be seen in the context of the times. It was December 1983; the country, the Department of Defence and the Naval Service had little by way of spare cash. Everything was tight, everything had to be accounted for, everything had to be case-made, and everything was a struggle. It was often a case of what you had you held. The Diving Store had for years occupied a little office at the back of what were then the naval depot training offices for recruit training, an area that was and still is affectionately known as 'underneath the arch'. It was the size of a small box room, which in one sense perfectly suited the amount of kit that was being held there. It had by early 1980 installed itself in what was then the Seamanship Training Bay. In creating a picture of the area, as you came off the square towards the training offices and billets, you had to pass underneath the archway. Directly in front of you about 8 metres away was a set of very large sliding double doors, approximately 12-foot high by 10-foot wide, and when opened allowed access into what was called the 'drill shed'. These doors were roughly mid-point of the drill shed on the archway side. Back in 1980 this was a large shed-like structure, approximately 50-metres long by 15-metres wide. It had an apex roof and of course, as befitted the times, it was roofed in asbestos corrugated sheeting. To gain access to the Diving Store from the drill shed, there was a set of smaller double doors which opened into the Diving Store. This opening was a lot smaller than the front opening double doors that actually lead into the drill shed. The deck of the drill shed was timber planking that had endured the years of hobnailed boots and parades on rainy days. The divers were about to heap some more abuse onto those poor planks.

The day the chamber arrived

The recompression chamber arrived on the back of a flatbed articulated lorry, and, as suited the occasion, there was no fanfare upon its arrival. There were no problems with the off-loading as there was ample space for the dockyard crane to operate while on the square. With the delivery lorry having departed, the problem now posed was how to get the 2-tonne RCC complete with its rigid, hard-plastic wheels to the Diving Store. The front two wheels were on castors, so they could turn very much like a shopping trolley and behaved in exactly the same way. The boss had clearly foreseen this exact situation, for next to arrive on the scene was the base tractor. Hooked up, the tractor slowly manoeuvred the chamber in the direction of the large sliding doors, along with the help of any available hands guiding the 2-tonne trolley with a mind of its own in that direction. However, the next obstacle was not foreseen: the tractor wouldn't go through the doors for the opening was a bit too small. Undaunted, a Land Rover arrived to take up the duty, so all hooked up again – the 4-inch sill at the doors made up with chocks of wood – the Land Rover entered the drill shed and slowly towed the RCC up over the sill and into the drill shed. The RCC made into the drill shed, and while turning towards the diving-store doors, the RCC wheels, instead of running at right angles to the planking, started to run parallel with it. The RCC travelled only about a foot before it broke through the planking, and came to a halt. Things would have turned nasty if any more damage was done, and while the school commandant mightn't have been too happy about it, the base warrant officer Johnny Durkin would be so pissed off. The thoughts of the latter brought forward the solution: a thin-gauge metal sheeting was brought up from the BFW yard and placed down along the path of the RCC, Egyptian-style, towards the rather small-looking opening to the Diving Store. As the RCC was slowly driven towards the doors, the opening was not only getting closer but also seemed to be getting smaller. The boss was beginning to get an anxious look on his face.

The Land Rover had to stop towing, and the RCC was manhandled and manoeuvred into position directly in front of the doors and pointing in. The Land Rover took up a towing position at the other end to offer resistance to the RCC as it was being pushed into the Diving Store (due to a ramp-like step leading onto the store, as the store was at a lower level than the drill shed). The RCC was lined up and slowly shoved into the Diving Store. It got down finally, and was jockeyed into position using pallet trucks. The RCC was home – well, at least for a few years – but this sort of carry-on couldn't be good for anybody and certainly not the RCC or for the deck in the drill shed. It wouldn't be the last time that that exercise would be conducted.

An RCC on the move

Over the next few years two separate but in their own way linked issues would constantly be associated with the RCC. One was the actual siting of the RCC, and the other was the treating of civilian divers in the naval RCC. The first issue was not a huge deal, but it was a matter that raised its head from an early stage. In fact, the first letter regarding this siting was drafted on 24 April 1984. The then diving officer, Chris Reynolds, wrote to the officer commanding the naval depot on that date, regarding the siting of the RCC:

> 2. Present location: The recompression chamber, high pressure (HP) compressor and storage cylinders are housed in the Diving Store. The L.P. compressor and spare storage 'Pigs' are presently on the square.[12]

The DO went on to outline possible solutions for the long-term housing of the RCC, and suggested the annexing of the old sail-training bay at the back of the Diving Store. The officer commanding the naval depot, Commander Joe Deasy, replied on 10 August via his executive officer:

> 1. I have decided that the building opposite the cinema will be the recompression chamber room [old storeroom belonging to theatre group]. S/Lt Reynolds will have to make out a works requisition to breach an opening …
> 2. This does not pre-empt or preclude any long-term proposals re the oil-wharf areas.[13]

The DO replied to OCND on 23 October after having spoken to the relevant OC Corps of Engineers, Naval Base, Comdt Gaffney, who stated that the work would not commence until 1985, and that he (S/Lt Reynolds) was requesting that some of the ancillary equipment that was still on the square at this time be housed under a temporary structure for the winter period. The commander wasn't having any of it, and replied on 26 October:

> 1. Your Para 3 (attached) – NEGAT
> 2. Arrange to put the chamber in the Diving Store as heretofore.
> 3. Arrange for a platform or excavation for the Pig outside the diving – and within reach of the crane from roadway.

He also attached a PS to the letter: 'PS … Put steel plate runner under wheels while transiting drill shed.'[14] I wonder where that comment came from!

So the RCC made its home in the Diving Store. Now, it must be remembered that the store was exactly that. Everything that the Diving Section had was contained within the store, including its Gemini craft, which instead of being left out on the slipway would be brought up the hill to the side door, turned on its side, and slid and pulled through the side door inside for storage. The point here is that everything was contained in the store, including the recompression chamber.

Outside the Diving Store, as per the commander's directions, mounted on a concrete platform was sited the LP compressor. Placed at the back end of the store close to the recently installed Bauer HP compressor were the two 'quads'. Each quad was a bank of nine large *J* bottles, each capable of being charged to 210 bar pressure, though the compressor was capable of charging up to 330 bar. From here the HP air in the quads would pass through a large, dome-shaped valve called a dome loader, inside of which the HP air would be reduced down to LP air. As previously stated by Lt O'Donoghue, there were many ways of charging the RCC, which was the beauty about it – if one system didn't suit or didn't work, there would always be a backup. He often said that if all else failed and all your systems went down for whatever reason, 'Just give them half a dozen single sets and tell them to open them one at a time.' Funnily enough, in all the exercises, training and actual treatments undertaken over the years, this form of pressing down the chamber was never done. In 2009 the RCC was sent away for several months for a total overhaul of all its systems and for a fitting-out in a purpose-built container (described later in this chapter).

Recompression-chamber training commences

In 1984 the only person qualified in the Naval Service to supervise and operate the RCC was the MCDO. This issue, after all the years of waiting and letter writing, was not going to be let lie, and the first formal application to run an RCC supervisors' and operators course was filed by S/Lt Chris Reynolds, the base diving officer, for and on behalf of the MCDO, dated 4 April. The MCDO at the time was at sea as the executive officer on board the LÉ *Emer*, under the command of one of the original diving officers, Lt Cdr Frank Lynch:

> 1. Recent purchase of a recompression chamber has greatly enhanced ND

diving capability. It is at present installed and ready for operation in the Diving Store … There is therefore only one qualified RCC supervisor in the NS (Lt O'Donoghue).

2. Pending further MCDO and CD 1st class courses abroad, the following short term solution is proposed.

a. A two-week course should be carried out in RCC operation.[15]

The letter also went on to say how and when the course should be held, and a nominal roll of personnel was attached. It was suggested the course would run that summer on board the LÉ *Emer* while on patrol. The RCC, its ancillary equipment and all available diving personnel as requested deployed to the LÉ *Emer* to commence the first RCC supervisors course in earnest. It was to lead also to the longest recompression training exercise conducted by the Naval Service Diving Section to date, and a couple of other firsts to boot (see Chapter 8).

Following the long therapeutic exercise that had been conducted on board the LÉ *Emer* in July 1984, the RCC had proved its worth, even though it had only been in service for less than seven months. It now offered both divers and supervisors peace of mind that when conducting deep-diving operations, should an incident or emergency occur, the proper and necessary facility would be on site. It would allow for continuation training and deep-diving work-ups. It was a facility that was both an asset to the navy and, by extension, an asset to the state, and if being an asset to the state meant including the treating of civilian divers in the RCC, then Command was now committed whether it liked it or not. It's not too clear if, however, the Senior Command of the navy were overly excited about the last part, because, as the MCDO Gerry O'Donoghue pointed out to me during our interview, to get the RCC proposal over the line, he 'had to swear blind that no civilian would ever be treated in the naval recompression chamber'.[16] Gerry knew he was being more than loose with the truth, but the flag officer accepted his declaration and they moved on. The flag officer probably prayed that he'd be retired before that day would come (and possibly the MCDO as well), but it was only a matter of time:

> I knew we would have to do it, but I never wanted us to become a civilian recompression therapy facility … RCC for civvies purely as a back-up … it's only a secondary job.[17]

As luck would have it for the flag officer, Commodore Liam Maloney, he did retire before that day came. The first recompression therapy conducted in the naval RCC on a person other than a naval diver in exercise was conducted on 13 June 1987. The flag officer at that time was Commodore Liam Brett, and with a certain amount of irony that first patient happened to be an army captain.

First RCC therapeutic treatment case (and its consequences)

On Saturday 13 July 1987, while diving during a training camp for Defence Forces diving-club divers, a diver after a series of dives felt unwell. He informed his dive supervisor, and a couple of hours later the diver was undergoing a therapeutic treatment for a 'mild bend', as it was called then. He subsequently spent two hours twenty minutes in the chamber, and made a full recovery. There was nothing strange or spectacular in the treatment or the recovery of the diver, but what made this incident stand out was not that it was the first such treatment but that it finally opened the can of worms that was the treatment of personnel other than naval divers. In principal, it could be argued, this was contrary to the purpose for which it was bought. What made it even more interesting was that he was a member of the Defence Forces:

> We got lucky, the very first call we got to actually treat somebody who was an army officer who was diving down in Bere Island, as part of the army diving camp. Because it was an army officer [Defence Forces personnel], we were allowed to treat him and that changed the dynamic of the chamber. Now we actually started to treat people. One it raised the profile … and it also brought in the Army Medical Corps, who became much more interested in what we were doing.[18]

How right Gerry proved to be. As soon as this case had been successfully completed and the captain departed the naval base, the first letter referring to an actual SOP [standard operating procedure] for diving incidents and the possible requirement for the use of the RCC appeared. It was signed by the then captain of the naval base, Capt. Joe Deasy, on 29 July 1987, a little over six weeks from the date of the first treatment. It was essentially a guide for duty personnel, such as the SDO (senior duty officer) or the duty coxwain (twenty-four hours security NCO, manning the operations room). It attempted to formalise for those duty personnel how they should manage the requesting of the service of the naval RCC. This SOP was the start of the letter writing over at least a nine-year period. The recurring theme through most of the letters was this: what was the actual policy in dealing with both military and civilian divers and their treatment in the Naval Service RCC? No one, it seemed, could formulate one.

In 1994 the RCC finally moved from the Diving Store to a newly renovated storeroom beside what was called the cinema. This storeroom belonged to the Haulbowline Theatre group at the time. While the cinema was undergoing a refit, it was with the agreement of all parties that the storeroom be subdivided between the theatre group and the Diving Section so as to allow for the siting of the RCC. So, after the necessary renovation and interior works were carried out by the BFW, the RCC room was opened and business resumed. A report of a meeting with the Irish Marine Emergency Services (a forerunner of today's Irish Coast Guard) from the diving officer to the flag officer, dated 24 November 1994, stated in its conclusions:

> a. The Galway RCC is the only official Diving Casualty Reception Centre in Ireland. Although the chambers are nearly identical, the NS RCC, although a more modern chamber, does not provide:
> Hospital facilities.
> 24-hr medical on-call facility.
> In-chamber ventilatory and monitoring facility …
> b. The recompression chamber facilities in Ireland are therefore wholly inadequate, particularly along the south and south west coast where most of the diving activity is taking place.[19]

The *Lusitania* incident 1994

During the summer of 1994 a group of divers received permission to conduct a series of deep dives on the *Lusitania,* the historic wreck that lies 12 miles south of the Old Head of Kinsale. During one of the scheduled dives, two divers, Eugene Cahill – a civilian diver from Dublin – and Lt Chris Reynolds – who was diving in a private capacity while on annual leave from the Naval Service – had made the wreck in approximately 83 metres of seawater. Working according to the dive plan, both divers attached their excursion reels to the shot and proceeded out on their own in different directions. After several minutes on the bottom, Lt Reynolds noticed that his diving companion was having difficulties. He swan over to him and noticed that he was inverted, in a head-down attitude, and that a set had become unclipped, thereby causing Eugene Cahill to become inverted. Mr Cahill was in some distress while attempting to rectify his situation. The subsequent attempts to correct this by both divers were exacerbated by the stressed diver operating his suit inflation, and as both divers were ascending it became more difficult to correct. At approximately the 65-metre mark, the lieutenant couldn't control the diver anymore, and at this point the diver began his uncontrolled free ascent to the surface. Lieutenant Reynolds now had to face the prospect of conducting his own planned decompression stops while mid-water swimming, as they both had come free of the shot line. At the same time, Mr Cahill – having incredibly survived his free ascent to the surface – was in urgent critical need of medical and recompression treatment.

Mr Cahill was subsequently recovered by the Irish Marine Emergency Services SAR helo and transferred to the naval base recompression chamber:

1. At approx. 11:00 hrs on the 3 Aug 94 Naval Operations received a report from MRCC of a civilian diving casualty, which occurred during a dive on the wreck SS Lusitania. It was later established that the casualty was a Mr Eugene Cahill who had made an uncontrolled ascent from a depth of 83 metres, without carrying out the necessary decompression stops.

2. The Naval RCC was prepared and the casualty arrived at the Basin Landing Area at 13:30 hrs. He was immediately transferred to the RCC. After a full medical examination of the patient by the DF physician Dr. Mary Murphy, it was decided that the casualty should be recompressed as per the RN SOPs ... a team from the Regional Hospital was asked to assist, and two doctors, a nurse and ambulance staff arrived.[20]

The subsequent period of recompression – stopping at 18 metres to see if any improvement had taken place and with the patient breathing hyperbaric oxygen – showed no improvement in the patient's symptoms; in fact, things appeared to be getting more acute. At this point it was decided that it would be necessary to compress the patient further and to have him attended by a medical professional. Dr Kevin Dennehy volunteered to enter the RCC and to attend the diver; great credit is due to him for this. What should be noted here was that the doctor had never before been inside a chamber, nor had he ever treated anyone in such circumstances:

At this stage the casualty was in some distress and one of the doctors, a Dr
Kevin Dennehy, entered the RCC to attend on the patient.[21]

Meanwhile, Lt Reynolds was fighting his own battle for survival. The lieutenant had to complete his own required decompression stops before surfacing, but
as he had lost the shot line, he was free swimming mid-water while trying to
maintain the required depth setting. This is a difficult thing to do at the best of
times; however, the lieutenant was an experienced diver, and he controlled his own
stress. After some time he noticed what appeared to be a line in the water and
swam over to it. It was the shot line. Things would now get much easier for him.
Having completed the necessary stops, Lt Reynolds, on surfacing, made his way
to the naval base to assist in the treatment of Eugene Cahill.

The patient was then recompressed further to 50 metres, where he was
observed and treated by Dr Dennehy and the two naval diver attendants, CPO
Gerry Duffy and L/Sea Mick Daly. Eugene Cahill's incident was by no means
unique, but by surviving the free ascent and from such a depth, he certainly fell
into a very unique category. So much so that a Dr Maurice Cross, a consultant
specialist with the UK Diving Disease Research Centre, travelled over from the
UK at his own expense and to offer any advice that he could. Over the course of
the next thirty-nine hours, until 05:51 hrs on 5 August, the patient was treated
by the chamber supervising staff in accordance with RN therapeutic table 64, and
by the doctors in accordance with their own medical protocols:

> At 05:51 hrs on the 5 Aug 94 treatment was completed and the patient
> transferred by SHB [Southern Health Board] ambulance to the Regional
> Hospital, Cork.[22]

So, despite all the letters that had been written over the previous eight years
about the naval recompression chamber and whether or not it was or wasn't a
therapeutic facility, and whether it should or shouldn't treat civilians, and despite
the lack of any clear direction, the naval recompression chamber and its attending staff, when it was called upon in a true moment of urgency, effectively saved
Eugene Cahill's life. In a letter to Dr Mary Murphy, Dr Cross stated:

> I am deeply impressed with the way that you have managed to cope with an
> extremely difficult case of decompression illness in such a relatively simple

facility which was never designed for such cases … in my discussions with your naval colleagues, it is clear that the Cork facility was never intended to be a treatment facility except in the very rare event of a naval mishap.[23]

Dr Cross' letter was dated 24 August 1994; he obviously didn't hear what happened the day that Eugene Cahill vacated the naval RCC. As a direct result of the prolonged attendance to Mr Cahill during his treatment in the RCC, one of the attendants, L/S Mike Daly, a couple of hours later that very same day contacted CPO Gerry Duffy complaining of a pain in his left leg. There was only one possible diagnosis for that: mild decompression illness. Contact was made with Lt Cdr Gerry O'Donoghue, who had himself earlier that morning finished leading the naval diving team in the treatment of Eugene Cahill. Having first been examined by Dr Murphy, L/S Daly was treated in the RCC in accordance with RN table 61. After a period of two hours, L/S Daly responded well to the recommended treatment, and though he completed a full therapeutic session that day, he underwent a further session the following day in conjunction with Eugene Cahill, who himself was receiving follow-up treatments. On completion of this session, L/Sea Daly experienced no further signs or symptoms of his decompression illness:

> When it came to the stage where we were going on oxygen on the BIBs … I was out there [entry lock], and at one stage when I was on oxygen out there, I was apparently – somebody said it to me afterwards – I was asleep. So I obviously nodded off at some stage on the oxygen, which I have no recollection of myself, but someone said that to me afterwards … I should have been drawing from the BIBs … but I was aleep so I suspect that's where I got into trouble … because of the cramped conditions, I think I might have had a bit of stiffness, but 'twas nothing you wouldn't expect from being in the RCC for thirty-nine hours anyway … I went to bed and I woke up around twelve o'clock and it was like someone had a knife driven into my knee joint, and was wriggling it around, and it was just, you know, exactly like someone had driven something into your knee and were trying to expand it … the pain was excruciating … so we went over to the RCC and went back in again for another couple of hours, and back out and home. They put me back in the next day with Eugene and that was it, full relief after that treatment. As far as I can remember, it was his treatment but I

went back in with him and when I came back out of that I remember my leg, happy fucking days, my new leg …[24]

So, in the course of that two-day period, the RCC and its attending staff in essence defined itself. Though not exactly state of the art, nor indeed a true therapeutic treatment facility with all its attendant medical skills, it did when called upon exceed is own purpose. It would suit the Naval Service perfectly for many more years to come. Those two days saw the longest single therapeutic treatment of any person in the RCC, and in an ironic way that treatment directly caused the only Naval Service Diving Section 'bend' in its history to date, and the diver involved didn't even get wet. In the aftermath of the incidents, Lt Chris Reynolds wrote in his report:

> 7. Treating such patients not only provides an otherwise absent service to the community and excellent P.R., it also provides training and practise in the treatment of DCIs. L/Sea Daly was the first NS diver to suffer from a 'bend' and the fact that the NS could treat him promptly and successfully is a direct result of years of treating civilian patients. Indeed the types of injuries sustained by Mr Cahill could be sustained by any NS diver on a deep dive and only rapid recompression can save his life and prevent/limit long term neurological damage.[25]

In August 1995 the then officer commanding the naval base wrote to the flag officer:

> Para 3. In the interim however, it is felt that both the Naval Service and its personnel are at risk of litigation in the event of a fatality or serious injury occurring while a civilian patient is under their supervision. A policy must now be decided in order to reduce or eliminate this exposure.
> Para 4. A direction on policy this is requested.[26]

And in September 1995 a well-articulated letter written by the diving medical officer similarly pointed out that

> 1. The usage of the RCC for therapeutic recompression for civilian divers has increased greatly in recent years, to a point where it has become necessary to express grave concern about the practice in terms of access to the

facility, control and management of the casualty, availability of medical resources both human and physical and the question of liability in the event of an incorrect diagnosis, incorrect or failed treatment …

16. Recent experience highlights the need for critical analysis for organisation and delivery of recompression services for our coastline. This has to include analysis of the facilities required, staff required, staff availability, medical training, medical support and liability in the event of an accident, or failed or inappropriate treatment.

17. The increased frequency of diving accidents means that the provision of an ad hoc service on an informal basis is unsatisfactory and dangerous.[27]

On 25 June 1996 the diving medical officer, in a letter to OCNBAD, stated:

10. I feel it is time to properly formulate our approach to therapeutic recompression for non-service personnel as the demands for this service are ever increasing, and the risk for the service personnel involved in providing the service is also increasing.

11. The current situation is unsatisfactory.[28]

It was clear that the diving MO was worried not only about the actual treatment of divers presenting for treatment – that they should receive the required and necessary care – but clearly felt that the situation as it stood was placing service personnel – no matter how well trained they considered themselves to be – in a very invidious positions vis-à-vis liability for errors or, worse, negligence.

The third and next clearance diving officer (CDO) to hold the appointment of base diving officer, S/Lt Eddie Mulligan, in a reply to a verbal instruction for a review of the NS RCC procedures from OCNBAD, added his concerns in a letter of 25 July 1996 to OCNBAD:

Recommendations:

c. Formulation of NS Diving Accident and Therapeutic Treatment Policy:

(1) A board be convened consisting of a diving medical specialist, clearance diving officer and RCC supervisor to formulate the NS policy for treatment of Naval Service and ARW diving personnel requiring therapeutic recompression.

(2) This board should also examine the feasibility of providing emergency recompression or standard therapeutic treatments to civilians.[29]

The relevant authorities, Naval Service Command, the naval base medical officer, the Army Medical Corps, the legal officers and the diving officers were all involved. In essence, no one, it seemed, wanted to seize the initiative and actually gather up all the stakeholders and sit down and discuss the matters at hand. All were pushing the same door – there was no evidence or documentation available to indicate any contrary views or dissenting voices on any of the issues raised over the previous ten years, and yet there had not been one policy document written that stated the position of the naval and medical authorities on the use of the RCC primarily with civilian divers but also with naval/military divers.

In a letter drafted as a response to a directive from OCNBAD, dated 4 November 1997, for the first time a recommendation appeared that left little doubt as to what should happen with the chamber. S/Lt Mulligan stated that,

> As per the Diving Study Group's recommendations dated 15 March 95, I
> recommend the NS immediately suspend the use of the RCC for treatment
> of civilians until:
> A command policy is formulated and regulations amended.
> The RCC is upgraded to take H&S [health and safety] standards in to
> consideration.[30]

Report of Diving Study Group, 1995

On 4 November 1995 FOCNS issued a convening order to four naval officers directing them to assemble and convene a Diving Study Group. The four officers were Commander Gene Ryan, Lt Chris Reynolds, Lt Declan Fleming and Lt Gerry Rooney. Their task was to review diving both inside and outside of the Naval Service. Upon convening the board, the report said:

> Due to no clear policy on the roles for NS diving it became immediately
> apparent to the Board that prior to tackling the terms of reference it would
> be necessary to list and prioritise the roles of diving in the NS.[31]

This report is important in the context of things that did or didn't happen over the next several years within the Diving Section. It is important also in terms of the RCC, and in some ways the report was prescient in its view of the RCC and its use both within and especially outside the NS. On that list of roles as determined by the board was recompression chamber operations: 'A separate paragraph on the RCC is included in this report because the Board felt it requires special attention'. In giving its background to the RCC, the board mentioned the fact that the RCC had been used for therapeutic treatments on civilians and service divers (one only). It also started that 'it is expected that this role is likely to be required more frequently and for more complicated treatments in the coming years *until a proper hyperbaric facility is established in Cork Regional Hospital*' (my emphasis).[32]

Under the section titled 'Installations', the board mentioned the RCC room (its location mentioned earlier in this chapter), and what it believed should be its more relevant location. In section (2) (b) of Installations, it stated:

> (b) The RCC should be situated beside the base hospital. The logistics of this can be arranged by the OIC 6th Maint. Coy. But it is believed a new building may be required. X-ray and Vitalograph facilities should be available at the naval base. The NS should endeavour to supply full therapeutic facilities as a patient in as likely to be an NS diver as a civilian.[33]

In the section headed 'Recompression Chamber', the board recommended that

> … due to the present RCC conditions, the NS NO LONGER allow this facility be used for civilian emergencies until it is upgraded as detailed below. Notwithstanding this recommendation, the board feel that the NS can make a major contribution to the community at large by providing suitable RCC facilities.[34]

In the report, the board made eight recommendations in respect of the RCC, of which in the years to follow only the diving MO recommendation was acted upon:

> (2) Diving medical officer permanently located at the base hospital.
> (5) RCC moved to base hospital area and X-ray and Vitalograph facilities to be made available.[34]

S/Lt Mulligan, in response to another directive from OCNBAD on 20 November 1997, drew up another set of SOPs for the use of the naval RCC – this was SOP 1/98. It was a comprehensive SOP, and as outlined in the covering letter dated 18 December 1997, it dealt with the matter of liability for the minister of defence and with the referral costs to be borne by the Department of Health. Again, S/Lt Mulligan stated the situation as regarding civilian use of the RCC, and that the issue surrounding the upgrading of the RCC had commenced in part:

> 3. It is recommended that all civilian therapeutic treatments be suspended until SOP 1/98 is approved and sanctioned.
>
> 4. A programme to commence upgrading the RCC to recommended H&S [health and safety] standards, where feasible has commenced …[36]

By 1998 the base diving officer had changed, and Lt John Leech assumed command of the Diving Section. Lt Leech, in a letter dated 5 February 1998 to OCNBAD, essentially reiterated all that had gone before him. While adding nothing new to the continuing story, he did suggest for the first time that naval divers would be sent on diver-paramedics courses to upskill them in diver medicine:

> 9. My recommendation is to send suitably qualified personnel on the 'divers paramedic course (2 weeks) in the UK … and immediately thereafter run an RCC supervisors course (2 weeks). The NS will then have a pool of suitable qualified personnel capable of dealing with casualties which are likely to appear later this summer.[37]

On 23 March 1998 the diving medical officer sent another letter in response to discussions with Command. The letter contained all the same concerns and reservations about the treatment of civilians, lack of medical facilities – both support and follow up – and indemnity for all concerned. He also mentioned the 'qualifications of personnel to carry out such training', which was rather unusual given that all the RCC supervisors and chamber operators were qualified by the relevant MCDOs and, by extension, the Naval Service. In concluding his letter, the diving MO made the following points:

> 16. The question of legal indemnity has been raised many times in the past but is yet to be solved.
>
> 17. I feel that the whole question of therapeutic recompression not just within the Cork area but in the national arena must be tackled in definitive plans developed and implemented … I stress again the great reservations

I hold with regards to the current position and again I would agree with Lt Mulligan's recommendation of a board to decide on policy in this area. However, policy within the Naval Service cannot be treated in isolation from *the national policy to deal with diving emergencies* (my emphasis).[38]

Up to this point, the ongoing struggle to have a policy drawn up and agreed and implanted by all the relevant parties had failed to gather anything like momentum within the naval base, of which he was a part of. The diving MO had, it would appear, now added another new dimension, that of a 'national policy to deal with diving emergencies'.

On 6 September 1999 the minister of defence received a letter from a professor in the Department of Zoology and Animal Ecology of University College, Cork (UCC). In the letter he outlined that UCC had intended to conduct scientific research by diving in Lough Hyne, west Cork, and that he had been in contact with the naval base and the base diving officer, who essentially told him that his request could not be acceded to. He enquired of the minister

> Whether it would be possible for Haulbowline to be formally prepared to treat any bends casualties that arise from scientific diving at Lough Hyne (west Cork).[39]

Subsequently, the minister requested information in relation to the RCC and its background from the relevant naval authorities. A reply was prepared and sent to the flag officer for onward transmission to the Executive Branch, Department of Defence by OCNBAD. In his reply dated 24 September 1999, Capt. F. Lynch for OCNBAD, while detailing the pertinent information for the flag officer, stated in his conclusion:

> The Naval Service Diving Unit, and its associated recompression chamber, CANNOT, as it is presently constituted, provide therapeutic recompression (hyperbaric) treatment to civilians.[40]

Could it have been any clearer! Obviously not, for it still rumbled on. Part of the problem was that people were failing to differentiate between the recompression chamber as used by the Naval Service Diving Section for its training and deep-diving operations and a recompression hyperbaric facility with all the facilities that goes with it – medical staff, medical support, post-incident and/or follow-up recovery. The Naval Service Diving Section's RCC room never purported to be such a facility; it was purely a naval diving-support apparatus. Naval divers didn't care as long as it was serviceable and available for use on site when required. It should have been sorted out many years previously by Command; it consistently failed to grasp the nettle and in doing so ensured that it would rumble on for several more years to come. It simply should have been a matter of naval Command directing that the naval RCC is not available for civilian use, and let the various departments and ministers tell them otherwise.

In a letter from the Department of Defence Executive Branch, dated 17 November 1999, requesting further information on the 'Hyperbaric Recompression Facilities at the Naval Base', it is noted that

> from a technical point of view, the Naval Service RCC does not presently meet Health and Safety requirements for Therapeutic recompression but this will be rectified by modifications already in hand. Perhaps you would expand on what the difficulties are in this respect and the modifications that are required.
>
> You might also clarify whether, from a Health and Safety point of view, the current situation has a bearing on the use of the chamber for Naval Service personnel.[41]

The reply followed on 14 August 2000, when the recently qualified clearance diving officer, S/Lt Darragh Kirwan CDO, put pen to paper and sent a letter back to the flag officer. His reply was well written and direct; in it he stated with great clarity the issue surrounding the RCC and whether or not it complied with health-and-safety regulations:

> Para 3. The NS Manual of Diving and the BR 2806 are the regulations used by the NS when carrying out diving operations. The BR 2806 is the UK Military Diving Manual and is the Military Diving Accepted Code of Practice recognised by the Health and Safety Executive in the UK.
> Para 4. At present the NS Recompression Chamber meets all HSE and H&S regulations for diving operations. Therefore the RCC can be used as per the NS Manual of Diving and BR 2806 for all dive training, dives deeper than 42m and dives requiring decompression stops.[42]

In his conclusion, he stated a possible solution to the crisis:

> Para 7 … A possible solution would be the siting of an RCC in the grounds
> of the Regional Hospital, possibly manned by NS Diving personnel.[43]

So the flag officer in reply to D/COS Sp., dated 18 Sept 2000, apart from restating information already supplied several times over, mentions for the first time the possibility of establishing a study group on the matter involving the Naval Service, the Southern Health Board and UCC, though what exactly UCC had to do with anything in relation to establishing or formalising a therapeutic facility is unknown. All this did was introduce another unwanted element into what was already a long-running saga, though as time would tell it didn't gain any ground:

> Para 4 … as a first step, in view of the representations made to the Minister,
> I propose that a study group consisting of Naval Service, Southern Health
> Board and UCC representatives should be established with a view to
> addressing the various aspects of providing therapeutic and non-therapeutic
> recompression …

> Para 5: It is requested that my views be conveyed to the Executive Branch
> Department of Defence, who have requested an update on the current
> situation.[44]

On 27 September 2001 the OC Naval Operations Command issued a draft 'Policy on civilian use in recompression chamber'. It primarily stated that the 'NS Recompression Chamber (RCC) is for NS use'.[45] It also outlined where civilian requests for treatment should be directed: the Coast Guard, Galway Hospital, the local A&E department and Altnagelvin hospital in Derry. Further, it also outlined how requests for use arising from a state agency, Defence Forces personnel or a 'civilian close by and in a life threatening situation'[46] should be directed to contact the naval base. On the morning of 27 September 2001 a handwritten note dated August 2001 indicated that 'The Southern Health displayed no interest in the points raised in par. 7 at a meeting in OCNOC office in Aug '01.'[47]

On 22 April 2002 Lt D. Kirwan CDO, in a reply to the Irish Coast Guard for information in relation to the RCC and its availability, wrote: 'As it stands the RCC in the Naval Base is restricted to use by and for military divers.'[48] On 3 July

2002 the flag officer sent an updated letter (refer letter dated 27 September 2001) to the naval security personnel operating the Naval Operations room around the clock, and to whom the first call would come in. The actual paragraph is important in that it notes for the first time that the chamber is not a therapeutic facility, and, importantly, that from a naval perspective it is solely a 'working chamber':

> The NS Recompression Chamber (RCC) is for NS use. In the past it has been used to treat civilians, but this practice was stopped in 1996, as it is not a therapeutic facility and does not possess the necessary medical backup that can be offered in a hospital. *The RCC is solely a working chamber to facilitate Health and Safety regulations* [my emphasis].[49]

On 24 March 2003 the diving medical officer again wrote to the flag officer to state his concerns and worries in relation to the treatment of diving illnesses and the frequency of such calls. He concluded his letter:

> I therefore advise that in order that we discharge our duty of overall responsibility to our own divers and to maintain the hands-on experience of managing these problems that the service explores with other stakeholders the possibility of establishing a Level One treatment facility in the Cork Area.[50]

On 7 April 2003, by way of reply and in response to the DMO's letter of 24 March, FOCNS again wrote to D/COS Sp., highlighting the concerns that the DMO had about the increase in the frequency of civilian divers requiring treatment, and approving his participation in exploratory talks with the relevant stakeholders:

> Para 2. Lt Cdr O'Brien's concerns are justified. The nature of the work undertaken by the Naval Service Diving Section along with the frequency of civilian diving accidents merits the establishment of a level one facility. Para 4. Accordingly, I intend approving Lt Cdr O'Brien's participation with stakeholders in exploring such a facility. The establishment of a level one facility at Cork University Hospital (CUH) would be of considerable benefit to the Naval Service.[51]

Then things just stopped. For the next several years, any and all civilian cases ceased to be treated in the naval RCC. It was then that the irony of the entire situation became apparent. By closing the RCC to civilian use, the Naval Service Diving Section would consequently lose all the real-time, real-life experience that came with treating the civilian cases. Up to this point there had only ever been one case of a naval diver being treated for a 'bend'. Every other time the RCC was operated was either during training exercises or for surface decompression. So, in reality, the only way the Naval Service Diving Section was gaining its valuable experience in treating patients was with the very people it was trying to stop or divert from using the chamber. The valuable experience gained also by working in close cooperation with the diving medical officer and naval hospital staff would also stop. So pretty much from 2003 through to 2007, the Naval Recompression Chamber was stood down for the treatment of civilian divers who otherwise may have presented to the naval base.

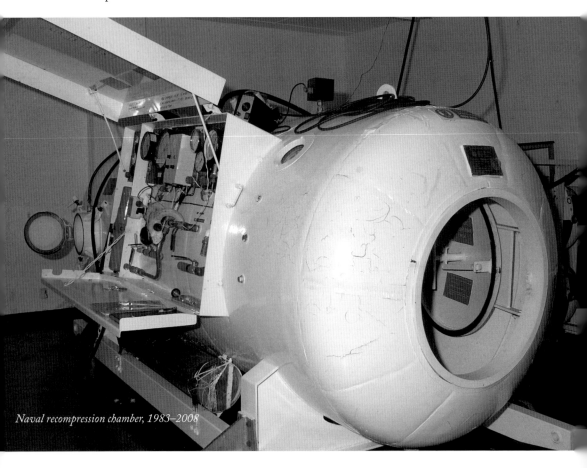

Naval recompression chamber, 1983–2008

However, the Naval Service Diving Section was busy in other ways with the RCC. It was decided to update and modernise the RCC and its systems, and also to finally containerise the RCC. This was a large undertaking by the Diving Section, and would, when concluded, involve a complete modernisation of the RCC and its systems. In early 2008 the RCC was dispatched to a UK-based company, Submarine Manufacturing Products Ltd, for the period of refurbishment; a temporary replacement system was hired in from an Irish-based company, Tusker Rock Divers Ltd.

Naval recompression chamber
1. Internal view: looking through the entry lock into the main chamber before refurbishment.
2. View into main chamber – note seats/bunks and internal aspect of medical lock on left-hand side towards back of RCC.
3. RCC Operation Panel pre-2008.
4. RCC undergoing its major refurbishment. Seen here in its container, while systems being installed mid-2008

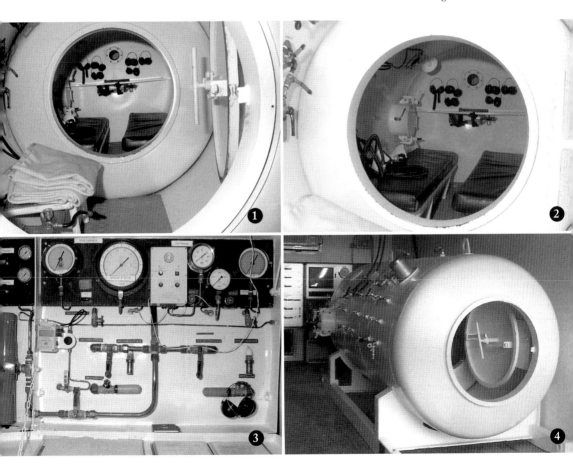

RCC major facelift and complete systems overhaul

- The containerisation of the RCC would see the chamber itself being housed in a bespoke, fitted 20 foot container, with the entry lock door facing outwards for entry but contained within the actual doors of the container.
- The old-style operating control panel previously placed on the side of the RCC was removed.
- A completely new set of operating control panels were fitted adjacent to the RCC, and integrated with the new internal CCTV camera suite.
- All pipework and fittings were replaced and new fitted systems installed to take into account the new operating systems for the supervisor and operators.
- A new CCTV real-time system was added, complete with a recording system.
- All main gas-supply and discharge systems were revamped.
- New hyperbaric fire extinguishers were fitted.
- A new oxygen-supply system was installed, complete with digital percentage monitors.
- New bleed valves were installed into both the main chamber and entry-lock exhaust lines for use when slow bleeds are required in conjunction with relevant treatment tables.
- New communications system and emergency telephone was installed.
- New hyperbaric lighting system was installed.
- De-humidifier and heating system was installed.

The fitting out of all the new systems, the addition of the new operating control panel, and the housing of the RCC inside the customised container made the job of operating and treating a patient infinitely more amenable for the chamber supervisor and operating staff. This total refurbishment of the RCC was the first since the chamber's arrival in 1983, so while the RCC lasted twenty-five years in its original format, there is no doubting that the RCC will last another twenty-five years in its new format, the irony being that in its early days the Diving Section spent plenty of time, effort and paperwork trying to secure the RCC into a dedicated building and to provide adequate resources and space for it, and now, after a major overhaul, upgrading and containerisation, the RCC is back outdoors again.

In 2008 Galway University Hospital closed the doors on its RCC when it

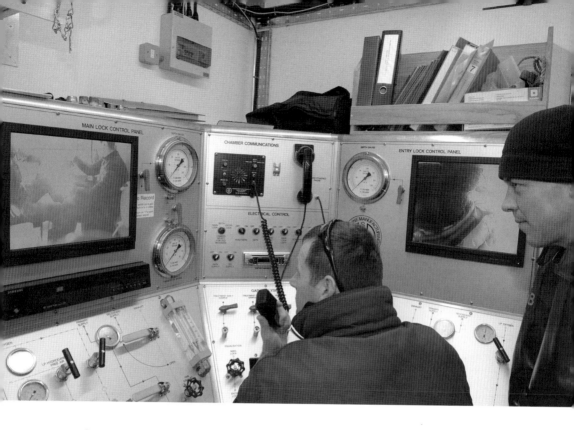

was decided to refurbish the naval RCC and its facility. The HSE contacted the Diving Section informally and discussed the possibility of the Naval Service RCC facility providing cover during the interim period. This discussion led to more formal talks between the diving officer, naval Command and the relevant government departments. Ultimately, it led to a memorandum of understanding between the Naval Service and the HSE in relation to the use of the naval RCC, the protocols involved, liability and the time period. The projected time was initially for a year – however, this was then pushed out to three years. It was a reversal of fortune somewhat, as the Diving Section would again be in a position to treat civilian divers, and, as important, to regain the skill and experience that comes with treating actual cases. It is also an ill wind that doesn't blow somebody some good, as the diving officers at the time, Lt Conor Kirwan, spotted an opportunity for some further training.

When speaking with Lt Cdr Conor Kirwan in 2014 about ROV training, it became clear that both the ROV training and the RCC were linked at one point in time in 2008. Conor said that while

The new operational control unit for RCC post-refurbishment 2009:
(left) Ciaran Woodward (RCC operator), (right) Paddy Delaney (dive supervisor)

initially rejecting the request from Galway, in discussions with his senior NCOs in the Diving Store he felt that a window of opportunity had arisen. If the request was acceded to, not only would it allow the diving staff to regain the lost first-hand experience of therapeutic treatments of civilian divers, it would more than likely open up access to monies for training purposes:

> … talking to the lads it became clear very quickly that the knowledge that the unit had in terms of treatment of people with DCIs [decompression illnesses] … that was something that was slowly being lost … so there was an opportunity to bring that back in. The requirement or request from the HSE was for one year, so there was a clear time line that it was only going to last for one year. Which obviously afterwards rolled out to three or four years, but what it also did was it gave us a unique opportunity to go back to the flag officer and say that yeah, we can deliver this capability but to do that we need to have access to a training budget – to qualify our divers as diver medical technicians who would be needed to be qualified to be able to deliver that service.[52]

In interview with Lt Cdr Darragh Kirwan in 2014, he recalled:

> The navy probably offered the more secure option from a point of view of making sure that it was always there [an RCC] and an operational option from a treatment point of view in what was a kind of defunct national policy or a non-existent national policy … we would have highlighted that this isn't a therapeutic facility, we don't have any of the requirements, we can't get a wheelchair in, we can't get a stretcher in. It is a diving-at-work chamber, now we can work around that, but there's obviously an element of litigation, there's legal issues that have to be ironed out.[53]

When interviewing Lt Cdr Tony O'Regan, I asked what his recollections were in relation to the RCC and its use during the period 2008 onwards:

> I remember briefing the HSE to say that ninety to ninety-five per cent of the diving incidents were occurring off the south and south-west coasts, and that they should relocate an RCC – lift and shift the whole lot into a new building in the Cork Regional … in the three years that we covered it,

there were, I think, eighteen cases. I think they spent more than a million or so on the refurbishment in Galway – its state of the art now.[54]

And so the Naval Service Diving Section continues to maintain its Naval Recompression Chamber facility on a daily basis throughout the year. Contrary to some beliefs, the Diving Section has maintained both fully trained and professionally qualified diving staff to operate the RCC since 1983. It was bought with the primary purpose of being available to treat naval divers and, by extension, Defence Forces personnel for diving illness that may occur when engaged in diving operations or training. However, given the people involved at the time, it would at best have been unrealistic to have expected that they did not know that it was only a matter of time before civilians would be treated in the naval RCC. They knew well but simply didn't say anything. Thus, its capability and functionality was designed around meeting those needs and meeting the relevant HSE requirements for a working RCC in support of naval diving operations. Over the past thirty-one years, it has treated some thirty-eight persons with diving disorders, ranging in the main from mild bends up to and including a full serious neurological disorder. Those presenting were from all walks of life, of both sexes and from several different countries, and all those treated left the RCC in a better condition than when they arrived.

The supervision and operation of the Naval Service RCC is a rarely acknowledged skill and service that the divers of the Naval Service Diving Section provide both to civilians and the state. It is a facet of the Diving Section that is rarely appreciated by anybody other than those who have received treatment in it over the years, and, indeed, speaking from personal experience as one of those Naval Service RCC supervisors, I can attest also to the lack of appreciation by even some of those that were treated. They treated people and will continue to treat people because they can. They are professional divers; they have supreme confidence in their own ability, in their group ability and in the Naval Service RCC.

The Naval Service Diving Section Recompression Chamber remains on short-notice standby at the naval base Diving Section ready to treat whomever, whenever. It is available to be deployed at short notice anywhere around the country by road or by sea. Whether it remains in the naval base or goes on its travels, it will continue to be manned by professional naval divers.

8

FIRST RECOMPRESSION CHAMBER SUPERVISORS COURSE AND THE LONGEST EXERCISE NEVER PLANNED, 25 JUNE–13 JULY 1984

The concept behind the running of ths course was to train up a group of diving officers and NCO divers (petty officer and above) in the use of the RCC and its ancillary systems so that the Diving Section would have a number of personnel fully trained in the functioning, operation and supervision of RCC operations ready and available should there be a requirement for them. There would be a series of lectures relating to signs and symptoms of decompression sickness, the related illnesses and disorders, and the recommended therapeutic treatment tables. Allied to all this, of course, was the practical side of the operation of the RCC: the setting up of all the equipment, the RCC, the necessary high-pressure and low-pressure air supplies, the emergency back-up systems, power, and all the logistical requirements that went with the operation of an RCC. All this was essentially very new to the Diving Section and, indeed, to most of the divers present, for although they had all trained in the UK, very few had any real hands-on experience of an RCC, its operation and its systems.

However, within the ranks of the naval divers was the senior NCO diver, CPO George Jefferies, who was one of the mainstays of the Diving Section. George was an NCO of great presence and ability. His knowledge of diving was only surpassed by his knowledge of seamanship. At this time, there was very little that CPO Jefferies didn't know about diving or diving spreads, as he had spent considerable time working with several offshore diving contractors during his personal-leave periods. This experience was incalculable both for the Naval Service and for those divers that would work and dive with George over the years. The course also required an element of real-time deep diving (not just simulated), often in excess of 35 metres, so that all personnel involved would gain the maximum benefit from deep diving, good timekeeping, good surface dive-team organisation, and, of course, in the theoretical and practical sides of surface recompression and RCC operations.

On 25 June 1984 the LÉ *Emer* prepared to depart the naval base at Haulbowline on completion of the loading and securing of equipment. The RCC and its ancillary equipment needed to be well secured, but also had to be placed in the right positions as they would be welded and stropped to the deck. Once all was secured and the executive officer, Lt Gerry O'Donoghue (MCDO/Boss), was satisfied that the ship was secure and in all aspects ready for sea, he informed his commanding officer, Lt Cdr Frank Lynch. The LÉ *Emer* under his command then sailed out of Cork Harbour, took a right turn after Roche's Point, and steamed overnight to Galway Bay.

Commodore Frank Lynch (retd)

The next two weeks would be a full-on diver-training exercise, with a weekly programme of diver training, deep dives, RCC simulated operations and practical exercises. Numerous dives would be required to act out as many simulated diver illnesses and diving incidents as possible, the principle being that the diving supervisor was also the Recompression Chamber supervisor (though not always). Not alone was the RCC to be used for therapeutic treatments in accordance with specific treatment tables as laid down in the *Diving Manual* BR2806, it was also to be used for surface decompression. Surface decompression essentially means that the diver would do any required decompression stops in the chamber on the surface (in this case, the deck of the ship) instead of in the water.

So it was a busy period of diving and exercising for all concerned – not only for the diving personnel but also for the ship's company, as the ship was required to anchor and move as the necessity for deeper or shallower water was required. The deep dives normally took place in the mornings, and generally followed the format of two divers being deployed down to the concrete 'shot weight' that was secured to the end of the shot line, which in turn was secured to the side of the ship. Depending on dive time, tides, visibility and the movement of the ship swinging at the anchorage, the divers would undo a swim line that was attached

to the shot and conduct a circular search around the shot. Both divers would be 'buddied up', that is, they would have a light line attached from one diver's right upper arm to his buddy's left upper arm, thus keeping both divers together. One of these divers would also have a deep-diving lifeline attached around his waist and marked accordingly. This lifeline would be the means for passing signals between the divers and the surface. There would of course be a stand-by diver, who would be dressed and on immediate notice for deployment in the event of any emergency.

The conduct of the dives would be determined by the dive supervisor in conjunction with the MCDO and on his instructions. For example, if the MCDO wanted the supervisor to deploy his divers to 35 metres for twenty minutes bottom time, and then conduct 'surface decompression', the diving supervisor would have to arrange, organise, plan and brief his dive accordingly. Exercises were planned and conducted, divers were leaving surface and 'making bottom' at 42 and 45 metres in less than a minute – in fact, each pair of divers was in competition with each other. And so the exercises went without incident until the final week of diving, when things took what could only be described as a curious turn.

The following events would see another simulated diving exercise leading in turn to the longest recompression-chamber 'training exercise' ever conducted by the Naval Service Diving Section to date (2014).

The longest RCC 'exercise' never planned

Early on the afternoon of Wednesday 11 July two divers were scheduled to conduct a dive to 30 metres as part of an exercise for the diving supervisor, Lt Joe Whelehan, who was under training. Having received their dive brief from the dive supervisor, they were casually pulled to one side by the Boss. Unbeknownst to the dive supervisor, the Boss gave the divers a further brief that would see one of them on completion of the dive present to the dive supervisor symptoms of a mild bend (simulated), such as a joint pain in his elbow. PO Gerry Duffy and PO Martin Buckley (the present author) dressed and prepared for the dive. When ready, and on command from the diving supervisor, the divers entered the water, swam to the divers' shot line, and conducted their in-water pre-dive checks on each other. When both divers and the supervisor were happy that all was in order, he gave the order for the divers to 'leave surface'. Thus began the supervisor's timing of the dive. (When conducting diving operations, particularly deep-diving operations, where the possibility of surface or in-water decompression is a real possibility, all timings and the accurate reporting of the timings are vital to good dive management and any subsequent treatments.) Both divers left surface and descended quickly to the bottom. Visibility was good, and as the bottom time was short, just fifteen minutes, they both stayed on the heavy shot line admiring the view.

The planned dive to 30 metres for fifteen minutes was passing quickly, and while expecting the signal to 'leave bottom' from the supervisor, the divers themselves left bottom early and ascended to the 21-metre mark and waited. The signal to leave bottom arrived as expected, but the divers didn't answer. Knowing that the supervisor would send the signal again, the divers waited and for a second time and again didn't answer. The third signal wasn't long in coming, and was more emphatic that the previous times, and this time the divers answered knowing that the supervisor would now be pushed for time, still assuming that his divers were at 30 metres. ('Bottom time' is the duration the diver spends in the water commencing when he leaves the surface to when he gives one pull to say he has left 'bottom', the most important signal for the diver to pass to the surface.) The delay by the divers in answering extended the planned bottom time, and the

Some of the 'students' on the RCC supervisors course (excluding the scallop – don't know how that got there) receiving a practical lecture in marine biology (l–r): Paddy Carolan, Shane Anderson, Mark Mellett, George Jefferies; Dan O'Neill (lying down)

supervisor was now having to be readjust his dive plan and was facing the possibility of having to give the divers decompression stops using the RCC. The divers ascended at a slower rate than required, thus furthering the supervisor's growing angst. Somewhere between the 21-metre mark and the surface, the divers got the fantastic idea that they would like some company. They signalled via their lifeline the signals for assistance, which they knew would come in the form of the stand-by diver, CPO Paddy Carolan. So while approaching the surface, somewhere close to the 9-metre mark the divers noticed a rather fast-approaching diver descending the divers' lifeline. Paddy had arrived, only to be greeted by two divers with no demand valves in their mouths, wearing big grins and giving him the big thumbs up. Paddy's eyes opened to the size of golf balls – the only thing that stopped his eyes from falling out of their sockets was his face mask.

Realising that his and everyone else's chain was being yanked, he duly offered up the vertical middle finger of his right hand, muttered something that sounded very much like 'flankers', and went back up to the surface. The divers followed him and broke surface very shortly after Paddy, and gave the thumbs up, indicating to the supervisor that they were well, no doubt much to his relief.

Meanwhile, back on the surface, while both divers were ascending the boarding ladder, Joe had already informed the diving crew that some surface decompression would be required and to stand by. The main chamber had already been pressed down to 18 metres 'chamber bottom set' on the gauge (the chamber had been pressurised with air to a predetermined depth set by the operator, normally 18 metres). Thus, the main chamber was at its pre-set depth, with the entry lock still at the surface, door open and awaiting the divers. The principle here is that should the divers require surface decompression for whatever reason, when they get out of the water they would transfer quickly into the entry lock, close the door and be pressed down to the main chamber's depth. This is a much faster procedure than pressing the main chamber due to the much smaller volume of the entry lock, especially if it has two divers in it.

So both divers surfaced and exited the water, and as they made their way to the deck they were informed to hurry up as they would be conducting some surface decompression. Joe enquired were both divers well, to which he was informed by Diver Duffy that his knee was aching a bit since he surfaced and that his hip was acting up a bit. Joe also wanted a quick account of the dive and what the problems were. The divers gave him as realistic an explanation as was possible about why they delayed leaving the bottom and why they required assistance on the way up, while at the same time trying to maintain the storyline. However, even the two divers could see that he wasn't falling for it. The Boss, who was standing beside Joe, looked even more sceptical (if that was possible), and both divers at this stage should have seen the signs. The Boss was already three steps ahead in his payback plan. Joe told the divers to get into the chamber and to expect a therapeutic table to deal with Gerry's poor impression of a mild bend symptom. Both divers entered the entry lock and commenced procedures to be pressed down 18 metres.

In the time it took the entry lock to be pressed down to 18 metres and the divers crossing into the main chamber, both divers were laughing so hard that tears were streaming down their faces. The supervisor requested an update on Gerry's 'illness'. If it was possible at that stage for either diver to have given a coherent, intelligent answer, everything might have been fine, but as both divers couldn't, matters worsened. Not only was Gerry's 'sore knee' bothering him, he was now also presenting with some girdle (hip area) pains just for good measure. This sealed the divers' fate. The 'pain' had not been relieved – in fact, Gerry's condition appeared to have worsened at 18 metres, and the supervisor was left with no option when faced with such symptoms but to press both divers down to 50 metres just to be sure. Gerry O'Donoghue liked to recall his version:

> Gerry [Duffy] was told to come up and give the symptoms for a mild bend to the supervisor, and of course do you think he could fucking obey the instruction for one second … no he feckin couldn't … so he came up and he was doing great and Joe [Whelehan] was saying 'Yeah, mild bend, mild bend', and then Duffy shoved in a serious bend symptom … and you could see the bubble over Joe's head, coz Joe's not stupid, and you could see the bubble go … 'Fuck no, Jesus' … and I said, 'What do you think, Joe – quick, quick', and he said 'No, that's a serious bend' … 'So what you going to do, Joe?' … so he said 'Forty-two hours' and I said, 'Fine, off you go' … so we slammed you in.[1]

The chamber operator was ready, and having received the necessary command from the supervisor, the operator opened the air-supply valve to the main chamber, thus commencing the pressing of the main chamber down to 50 metres, with the divers still laughing:

> Then I had to go back to Frank [Lt Cdr Frank Lynch, OC LÉ *Emer*] coz the ship had to sail [the ship had to sail that day as it was due to return off patrol on the Friday] … we can do our recompression underway, everybody's up, including all hands and the cooks … so I put it back to Frank, I said look, well, the good news is we're almost finished, the bad news is I have to do a serious bend decompression all the ways back to Cork … and Frank said, after a bit of thought, what happens if the ship sinks … I said, well in that case the doors will have opened up at 50 metres and they can get out and might in fact be the only two survivors![2]

The pressure at 50 metres in an RCC is noticeable in a number of ways. The air is hot from the pressurisation process, though it cools down somewhat after a short while. The air density is five times that of the outside air, so it makes breathing a little bit more of an effort, particularly when exhaling. Talking is also spectacular as the compressed air inside the chamber causes the ears to receive the voice signals differently, and can make the most mundane of accents incredibly funny. This is what both divers faced when arriving at 50 metres. Both divers reported 'well' to the supervisor. What should have happened within the first few minutes of settling at 50 metres was that the divers should have realised that by now that both the Boss and Joe were really having a sense-of-humour failure. But ours wasn't really helped by the fact that we were now both 'narked' (suffering from nitrogen narcosis) to some degree. So while those outside the chamber were being rather boring, we inside still thought the look on Paddy's face was hilarious. We missed the opportunity to commence our return to the surface by a much shorter therapeutic table by having Gerry's symptoms resolve themselves. However, as we were playing out our parts perfectly, the Boss simply

The naval recompression chamber on the after deck of the LÉ Emer, awaiting its less than spectacular occupants

said 'fuck yas, you langers' or words to that effect. The next two hours were spent at 50 metres; we were definitely going to miss the barbecue that night. Given that we had previously dived to 30 metres and then subsequently dived, albeit in the RCC, to 50 metres, we had now seriously compromised ourselves for recompression. We had become our own patients and had to be treated as such. We would be treated in accordance with the Royal Navy's Manual of Diving BR. 2806, Table 55, Long Air Table. Gerry O'Donoghue recalls that

> … my point was that if the ship sank we'd have bigger problems than you
> two langers in the chamber. Now it probably wasn't the smartest thing I
> ever did, but, hey, you do what you have to do.[3]

Both divers settled in, for there was no going anywhere for the next forty-two hours and fifty-five minutes; our estimated time of exit was sometime early on Friday morning as the ship would be approaching Cork Harbour. Over the course of the two days, there would be a great many firsts for the Diving Section and for the RCC. Even though the RCC had only been in service a short period of time, no one was really ready for this type of exercise. So what was learned from it? We learned that it was possible to have baths in it, which the designer (Dan O'Neill) probably never envisaged. This piece of lateral thinking was managed by filling the entry lock with fresh cold water up to a couple of inches just below the hatch combings. Towels would be provided along with soap. When ready, the hatch was closed and the entry lock pressed down to the same depth as the main chamber. Once the pressure had equalised across, the main chamber door could be opened. It was only a matter of determining who was going to have his bath first, as it was very welcome and was a great relaxation therapy. You manoeuvred your way through the hatch, and just sat down in the water, your back to the hatch resting your head on the towel, and both legs dangling back into the main chamber. It was heaven in a steel tube. Washing the other guy's back was a necessary evil as personal cleanliness was essential given the high humidity within the chamber, so the back washing was a bit different. When finished, the diver would re-enter the main chamber, close the hatch, and the operator would then bring the entry lock back to the surface. When the entry lock would be passing through 9 metres or so, the operator would then open the three-quarter-inch valve situated underneath the entry lock, and vent all the water out of the entry lock, It was a very fast and very efficient way of getting rid of the water – just don't be standing in front of it. Then, when on the surface, a quick clean out and refill ready for the next guy. On a couple of occasions, particularly when one of the surface crew would come down to keep us company, it was only a matter of time before one of us would pee in the bath water before he had to return back to the surface. It couldn't have been nice for him, but, again, we thought it funny.

Going to the toilet wasn't any great issue either. Having a pee was easy – we just pee'd into the bucket provided for our comfort. However, having a poo was a little bit more awkward, if not a little bit more sheepish for the particular individual. We tried to time this event with a 'flush through' of the RCC, for obvious reasons. (A 'flush through' occurs when the chamber operator would open the air-inlet valve in the entry lock and open the air-exhaust valve in the main chamber to flush out the stale air and replace with fresh air, while maintaining the depth of the chamber. It's also quite noisy.) But needs must, and we used the bucket again, with all the necessary trimmings. At pressure, the sense of smell is also somewhat curtailed, so going to the toilet didn't necessarily mean a whole lot to us at depth. However, when the bucket had to be sent to the surface for emptying of its precious contents, the smell that greeted the operators at the surface was often not for the faint-hearted. 'Mature' was how one diver described it. We learnt, too, that lobsters don't take too kindly to being put into medical locks and being recompressed, leastwise not the one that George Jeffs and the surface crew sent down to myself and Gerry. We just thought that surface was sending down a cuppa to us, but when we opened the medical-lock door, there was a decidedly unhappy lobster looking at us. We wasted no time in closing the medical-lock door and refusing their offer.

We learnt that you can have a relatively comfortable sleep as well, as long as one could sleep between the 'flush throughs'. This seemed to happen rather more frequently when the operator saw that you might be having a nap. This required a bit of skill and concentration on the operator's part, as he was required to maintain the operating depth of the chamber while 'flushing through', and ear defenders on the occupants' part. Meals were generally lukewarm or cold depending on our depth, as they had to come down in the entry lock or the medical lock – either way they had to be pressurised, so it was like chill-blasting the food with compressed air. We were required to be awake and alert when moving from stop to stop – it was a treatment requirement, but it always felt like the operator's way of having a bit of the *craic* with us.

The passage down to Cork began early on the Thursday morning so as to enable the OC to plan a comfortable journey back. The transit back was pleasant, as the surface conditions were good, with no need for an extra bucket in the chamber, luckily enough. Time passed, and as we were getting nearer the surface the 'stops' were getting longer and longer. No particular problem with this, but it did become interminable when we hit the 6 and 3-metre mark. Anyway, as the ship was approaching the outer limits of Cork Harbour at 07:30 hrs on Friday 13 July 1984, the last couple of inches of air pressure vacated the RCC and the chamber was on the surface by gauge. The protocol now required that the divers remain in the RCC for one minute, and on exiting the chamber report 'well' to the supervisor. On exiting the chamber, both divers, blinking in the morning sun, reported 'well' to the supervisor and shook hands all round. The Boss was very pleased with everybody, shook our hands and called us wankers. The entire exercise was recorded in the author's diving logbook thus:

> Simulated serious bend diagnosis – Chamber bottom 50mtrs – Therapeutic decompression carried out as per Royal Navy B.R. 2806 Table 55 – Recompression Therapy – No ill effects felt during exercise carried out in 65'-75' heat – Max depth 165 feet –Duration 42 hrs 55 mins. [4]

So concluded the longest RCC exercise conducted to date (December 2014) by the Naval Service Diving Section. The ship berthed and secured alongside the naval base that morning, and the RCC and ancillary equipment was offloaded and returned to the Diving Store. The next time such a long and enduring therapeutic treatment table would be required would be ten years later, when on 3 August 1994 a diver involved in diving on the *Lusitania* wreck in 80 metres off Kinsale Head had an incident at depth and free ascended to the surface. This treatment was only a couple of hours shorter.

It should also be mentioned that Lt Cdr Dan O'Neill, Lt Shane Anderson, S/Lt Mark Mellett and S/Lt Chris Reynolds all passed the course. As for the rest of us, well, we just unloaded the chamber and put away the gear!

9

JUMPING FROM HELICOPTERS, DUBLIN, 24 AUGUST 1998 (WELL, THAT COULD HAVE GONE BETTER!)

The earth makes a sound as of sighs and the last drops fall from the emptied cloudless sky.
A small boy, stretching out his hands and looking up at the blue sky, asked his mother
how such a thing was possible. 'Fuck off,' she said.

Samuel Beckett

On the afternoon of Sunday 24 August 1998, at approx. 14:05 hrs, a Sikorsky S61 search-and-rescue (SAR) helicopter operated by the Irish Marine Emergency Service and loaded with nine members of the Naval Service Diving Section commenced a high-speed run along the River Liffey heading towards the East Link Bridge. The divers – under the command of the diving officer Lt John Leech and preparing to take part in an SAR display as part of the Tall Ships festival – were no doubt enjoying the spectacle from the large cabin of the Sikorsky. At the end of its run, it transitioned into a torque turn and returned along its track, over the East Link Bridge in the direction of the Matt Talbot Bridge, approximately a mile upriver to the west. The display involved the deployment of the divers in sequence as the helicopter transited the Liffey back in the direction of the Matt Talbot Bridge. The deployment height for the divers was to have been approximately 10–15 feet, and a deployment forward speed for the helicopter of not more than 10 knots, or a little over 11 miles per hour. What ensued was not in the preflight briefing or, indeed, in the minds of the divers about to be deployed, and would subsequently be investigated by the Air Accident Investigation Unit (AAIU) and the Naval Service. The incident itself involved the largest number of naval divers ever injured in any operation or event, and ironically involved no actual diving. Some were injured seriously enough to see them unable to dive for several months. The display wasn't part of the scheduled list of events that were to be run that Sunday to entertain the crowd of what must have been several tens of thousands lined up along both sides of the Liffey.

The AAIU report (rep. no. 1999/008) describes the incident in very great detail, as would be expected. It describes the background and history of the flight, and goes on to describe the injuries sustained, the experience of the Naval Service Diving Section personnel involved, the flight crew's experience, and even the jumping technique of the personnel involved. In the section entitled 'Demonstration pressures', the report states:

> It was also a somewhat rare opportunity for the Naval Service Diving Section to perform in front of such a large audience. Again there also would have been considerable pressure to provide a spectacular display'.[1]

It would have been argued by those same personnel involved that there was no pressure on them, implied or otherwise, to perform spectacularly, but spectacular it proved to be. In the section entitled 'Military regulations limitations for dropping personnel', the report outlines the parameters for the deployment of divers or swimmers from helicopters of the Royal Navy, the US Coast Guard, the Canadian Defence Forces and the Irish Naval Service (in line with the Royal Navy). The report notes that the maximum forward speed limit is 5 knots (6 mph) and that the height limitation is 20 feet. It also goes on to mention:

> In discussion following the accident, some of the above organisations expressed concern with the practice of holding equipment, such as fins, during personnel drops from helicopters. It was their concern that this practice can lead to injuries and loss of equipment. The possibility of leg injuries resulting from the wearing of fins in high jumps is understood. For this reason, these organisations adopted the procedure of low altitude jumps, with the jumpers wearing their fins. For the purpose of this display the naval divers carried their fins under their arms.[2]

According to the section entitled 'Naval Service Diving Section experience',

> All nine members of the Naval Service Diving Section had completed

the standard Naval Service divers course. This course included jumping into the water from stationary ships or bridges, at heights of up to 40 feet.

All but one of the members of the Diving Section had previously jumped from helicopters, but on average only 2 or 3 times. Previous jumps from helicopters were done at the hover or with very low forward speed, of approximately 3 to 5 knots. The procedure used previously was to hover the aircraft at a height of 20–30 feet, drop a Diving Section member, then move forward to clear the swimmer in the water, re-establish the hover, and then drop the next Diving Section member.

All the Naval Service Diving Section were trained Naval Service divers, but for helicopter jumping exercises they are referred to as swimmers, as they are equipped for swimming, with drysuits, hoods, knives, goggles and fins, and were not wearing air bottles, weights or other diving equipment.[3]

In the section entitled 'Conclusions', the report states:

The display team (l–r): Mick 'George' Daly, Nigel McCormack, Paddy Delaney, Gordy Cummins, Louis Linnane, Trevor Murphy, Damian McCormack, Jim Cleary (missing is J.F.M. Leech)

The injuries to the members of the Naval Service Diving Section were
caused by the excessive forward speed of the aircraft.
The following factors contributed to the accident:
The helicopter jumping techniques used by the Naval Service.[4]

However, two prior sections of the report do not support the conclusion, and they
make interesting if not damning reading, at least for the flight crew. In the section
entitled 'Analysis', the report states:

Data obtained from the aircraft's flight recorder show that the swimmers
jumped from the aircraft when it was travelling at a forward speed varying
between 26 and 31kts, at a height varying between 22 and 31 feet. This data
is shown in Annex A. The FDR (Flight Data Recorder) evidence is supported by photographs and video taken by members of the Garda Síochána
and members of the public.

The injuries to the Diving Section members were consistent with high
forward speed entry into the water, in that the injuries and bruising were
concentrated on the left side of their bodies, which in turn is consistent with
exiting the aircraft on the right side facing directly out of the doorway.[5]

In the section directly following that, entitled 'The decision to dispatch', the report
states in the first paragraph:

As noted above, the Naval Service Diving Section personnel were not in
a position to determine for themselves if they were in a suitable jumping
envelope, with regards to speed and height of the aircraft.[6]

I interviewed one of the naval divers involved, Louis Linnane. Louis described
the flight, the deployment from the helicopter and the gathering of the injured
parties onto a first-aid pontoon:

There was one doctor and he was very, very good, and there were a lot of
Red Cross and Order of Malta personnel, all very capable people. But
Nigel at this stage was unconscious, frothing at the mouth … it was like an
epileptic fit, with froth coming out of his mouth … the doctor came over
and had a look at Nigel … I have to say, the doctor, whoever he was, he was

on the ball. He was sharp out; he had a good train of thought. Straight away he had Nigel's suit J-knifed off him [a J-knife, shaped like a large *J* and with two very sharp blades at the hook end of the *J*, is used by emergency crews for cutting shrouds, safety belts, etc]. Nigel was frothing from the mouth, like I say, the doc got me and Paddy to hold him down, actually had to kneel on his shoulders, and what he did was he decompressed his chest. He put a large syringe into his chest … as soon as the needle went in the pressure came off, you could see the colour coming back into his lips … and you could see the colour coming back into his face, which was great.[7]

Louis went on to describe George's ignominy at being hoisted back up into the very helicopter that he so had elegantly departed from a few minutes earlier. Luckily for George, in this case he could probably plead severe concussion as his defence. Louis also was injured, though it wasn't apparent at the time:

George was number two I think, he tells a very funny story. You have to appreciate we were coming back up along the Liffey from the Point Depot towards O'Connell Street direction. George exited the aircraft; the first thing he knew that something was wrong was that he was eye level with the sign that was on the Point. That was the large billboard that was easily 30–40 feet up in the air. He always says it was *The Phantom of the Opera*, and George says he was eye level looking at the 'Phantom' and he knew that things were wrong with that … which was funny, he jumped out of the helicopter only to be airlifted back into it a few minutes later. He ended up going to Tallaght hospital … the rest of us ended up on the first-aid pontoon on the Liffey. They had a system going, a triage system, whoever was the worst of us ended up going into the ambulances … I started noticing that I was in a fair bit of pain as well. I was crunched over and was finding it hard to stand up straight … I knew also that as soon as I had gotten to the Mater that my suit would be J-knifed off of me.

Now, you know Gordy [Cummins] – he's a big fucking guy, strong as a horse. I was doubled over at this stage. I had internal bleeding, my stomach was starting to swell and I couldn't sit up straight … and I got Gordy, grabbed him, pulled him close and said 'Gordy, get this fucking suit off me before I get into that fucking A&E' – all I was concerned about was my suit – 'Get it fucking off me, Gordy.' So he eventually got me head and the arms out of the suit, and in fairness to the Mater, as soon as we got there they had a full team waiting for our arrival, and as they were lifting me onto the trolley, Gordy was literally wrestling the rest of the suit off me as we were going in … that was my biggest concern at the time, but in fairness to Gordy he got the suit off me, which was a huge relief to me.[8]

Louis – always a funny man – continued:

The next thing, when we went in, the whole A&E was cleared for us … it was nearly overkill, but it was brilliant that they provided us with this service at such short notice. So they had the five or six of us in beds all looking at each other – it was really strange. It was the first time that we had all managed to have eye contact with each other, we just started laughing … 'What the fuck happened here?' … we were all broke up, now none of us bad, but enough to shake us up, it was part surreal and a little bit funny at the same time![9]

It would only happen in the navy. Louis described how, after a couple of days lying in hospital hooked up to monitors and drips of all sorts, a group of naval staff officers arrived in to say hello and check their health. Not wanting to overstay their welcome, they left Louis with the parting words that they would have him back to sea as soon as he was healthy again: 'Awww shit,' said I to meself, and that was that, they all traipsed off then![10]

I also got to speak with Mick Daly, known also as 'George'. George spoke about that day, and like Louis saw its funnier parts, particularly with the benefit of hindsight. I asked George for his recollections, memories and comments, but first I asked George about his injuries. He simply stated:

Left eye black and blue, split open. Got six or seven plaster stitches. Bruising down left side of body. Shoulder strapped up. Physio and kisses.

I remember on the way to the airport we were briefed by John Leech. He told us exactly what he wanted, between 5 and 10 knots and 20 feet up to a maximum ceiling of 30 feet, and that was what he was going to tell the pilot – I have no reason to believe anything other than that …

I can't remember the sequence but I think I was number two out. I remember going to the door – just as I was going out the door, I remember looking at the sign *Phantom of the Opera* on the roof of the Point Depot, and going 'Ohhhh shit' as I was jumping out, then it was lights out after that for me!

Then, to add insult to injury, being injured by the helicopter and then being winched back up again by the exact same crew … they weren't that keen on lifting us up at all … I was definitely concussed because I don't have any recollection of anything after the jump. I was inside the hospital before I had any recollection of anything. I don't remember any X-rays or anything, so I must have been well concussed. My injuries were all my ribs, all bruising down my left side. 'Twas all badly bruised around my ribs … I still feel the effects of it, down my left side.

I remember the lads chatting about it later, and they were saying that the crowd thought it was fantastic. The Garda boat and divers were there, and they came over and started to help out, but then they obviously got the Garda machine in gear and there were Garda outriders going in all directions, left right and centre. The lads were telling me later, there were ambulances going in all directions and they were closing off junctions – all sorts of things … and they were telling me, when Blaa [Paddy Delaney] jumped, he fell backwards and he bounced when he hit the water, he was like the Dambusters, the bouncing bombs. When he came around, he was like 'Ohhhh my sweet Jesus', and he could hear the crowd clapping and cheering, they thought it was fantastic, they thought it was part of the display!

Two things I remember: we had to get all our work gear together and put it into the minibus – all our work clothes and stuff as we had changed into our diving suits. Now, two things come to mind: one was that while John [Leech] was inside doing the brief, we did a group photograph by the helicopter. John came out – now we also put the camera into the minibus with our gear, and then it fucked off. John was like a fecking Antichrist 'cos we took the photo without him and now there's no photographic evidence of him ever having been there [see picture] … and then he was like a complete and utter bastard altogether when he realised that he still had his clothes with him and the minibus was after going. He was like 'How the fuck am I going to get my clothes back there!' … we were all taking the piss: 'I'll take the trousers' 'you take the shirt', and we were all laughing about it afterwards. Imagine what they would have thought in the hospitals when they were ripping the suits off us and the clothes falling out.[11]

In finishing up the interview, George added a few other observations:

> We were joking about it afterwards and about Louis' near-miss with the Matt Talbot Bridge – the lads reckoned another second later and Louis would have been getting the southbound DART to Dalkey – stuck to the front of it, like a bug! … In hindsight, it was a bit kinda daft really, you would have assumed that it would have been a straightforward manoeuvre! … sure 'twas like a big oul visit to the fair for us, Martin, you know the way we were, sure we'd do fucking anything, Martin … you know the way … yeah, that sounds like a great idea, sure let's do it for the *craic*.[12]

Further to the interview and several hours later, I received a phone call from George, with another little anecdote about his stay in hospital that I thought spoke volumes about navy divers and how they focus on the important stuff in a navy diver's life:

> When I finally came to me senses in the hospital and started to think reasonably straight, I got this fucking chill down my back … my suit! – my made-to-measure fucking suit! They told me what had happened and that they had had to cut it off me. I tell you, Martin, it was like a fucking death in the family, I just could have fucking cried … goes to show you what my biggest concern was, says more about the navy's budget for suits too.[13]

Before closing this chapter, special mention must be made of the Garda Water Unit, which was on duty that day patrolling the river and whose swift corrective actions undoubtedly saved a couple of the guys from suffering far more serious consequences while lying disabled in the river. Particular mention must be made of Garda Dave Mulhall. Mention must also be made of both the Garda Traffic Corps and the emergency services for their immediate response to the incident. Never in the history of the Naval Service Diving Section did a nine-man team of divers depart a dive site so quickly and with so much unwanted attention and fanfare!

THE CHIEF, HIS DESK AND
AN UNDERWATER CAMERA
(A VERY SHORT STORY)

Every diving chief's office desk is sacred to him. It's his right of passage, it comes with promotion. To interfere with the diving chief's desk could be considered a hanging offence. This particular day, the chief was off duty, so his desk had been commandeered by the PO and the L/S.

The underwater stills camera, a 35mm Nikonos V, was being stripped down and cleaned. The chief's desk was cleared and a clean sheet spread over it. So the camera was stripped and cleaned, and just needed to be reassembled, but that would have to wait till the following day.

The following morning, the chief, the PO and the L/S open the Diving Store and proceed to open up the office. The chief enters the office first. The PO and the L/S follow. The chief spots what he considers to be a desecration of his desk. The chief hasn't quite come to terms with the sight in front of him. His desk has been violated. There is something on it and he can't quite make out what it is or, more importantly, what it's doing there in the first place. It could be that he's in shock. He looks faint. With the chief not quite putting together the right words to ask the right questions, the conversation ends up going something like this:

Chief (pointing towards the table) What the fuck is THAT!
PO   That's a camera, Chief.
Chief (looking at the PO) Arsehole.
He turns to the L/S for a more understanding and informative answer.
       Yeah, I bleeding know that … but what's it fucking for?'
L/S   For taking pictures, Chief.
Chief (looking at the L/S) Another fucking arsehole.
Rest of the morning: silence … heaven!

10

AND FOR THE NEXT FIFTY YEARS …
POSSIBLY

This is not the end, this is not even the beginning of the end, but it is perhaps, the end of the beginning.

Winston Churchill

So, as this book draws to an end, it's safe to say that it's not anywhere near the end of the story. In trying to find the right way or ways to finish up what can only be described as a brief account of the some of the history of the Naval Service Diving Section, I returned to the interviews I had with Dan O'Neill and retired Flag Officer Commodore Frank Lynch (FOCNS, 2002–10). I listened again to what they had to say, particularly about the early years. Danno:

> … the way I always saw it, when George [Jefferies] and Eamon [Butler] came back, that was really probably the start of the growth of the diving unit as such. Now Joe [Deasy] was there, but Joe did his course as part of TAS [torpedo and anti-submarine] diving. Now credit Joe – he worked hard to achieve his 'dream' of a naval diving unit, and he did genuinely promote it, so he should get lots of credit for that. He put in for courses, he spoke to the British embassy people, and he got the courses assigned for Peadar [McElhinney] and the four boys next … but Joe, in fairness to Joe, when he came back he set about getting the first suits, the Siebe Gorman DVs [demand valves] and sets … Joe promoted the idea of the Diving Section: 'The navy must have divers, it's essential, it's all about SAR, ship's hull inspections, etc." Joe was a huge advocate, that is to his eternal credit … but at that time there was nobody ashore either. Peadar was at sea, Joe was

at sea. They were literally hot bunking it at sea, they were doing four [hours] on, four off, there were none of them ashore … there was no structure, but it was really when George and Eamon came back that they formed the basis of the diving unit.[1]

Frank Lynch drew a particularly stark picture of the manpower issues at that time in the service:

It was shocking, it was quite shocking. Around the time I was commissioned, the navy was down to around 350 men, and then we joined the EEC. I was the only cadet taken on that year [1968] – in fact, I was the only cadet for about seven years, and Rory Costello transferred over from his army class to join me. There were about 350 then in the navy, and between then [1971] and 1977 – that was only a period of about six years – the navy jumped up to about 750 men approximately, but in 1977 the number of people that actually left the navy was something like 350 men, and so the numbers stayed the same in the navy – that is, nearly fifty per cent left the navy. There was a fifty-per-cent turnover in personnel. Everyone was so inexperienced, you were only waiting for the next mistake or accident to happen, and so it was in this environment that you were trying to introduce a new thing like diving.[2]

During the interview I had asked Frank was there ever a deliberate policy by naval command in relation to the Diving Section. The short answer was 'No', which wasn't a great surprise, so I asked Frank how, in the absence of a deliberate policy, did the Diving Section move forward as a unit/section. Frank elaborated on this:

Operational success drove the success of the Diving Section – one thing begot the other. The operational success of the Diving Section and its effectiveness drove its own success … If you think about it, if you think about the totally barren environment back in the early Seventies, and the very fact that it grew, I mean, the people that were involved, the people that drove it through the years, the people that died, there has to be a considerable feather in their caps. It was a smaller version [Diving Section] but it was certainly on a par with the performance of the ships.

The divers to a large extent provided their own momentum. The divers were pushing hard to develop the unit as best they could, and to make it with the best equipment to allow them to do their job. There wasn't a White Paper or there wasn't a policy as such … it was a combination of its own proven operational success.

The people that were in there had to be exceptional people to get in as there was such a huge failure rate, so there were good-quality people actually bringing it along all the way … it produced very exceptional people, I think you know.[3]

In conclusion, Frank mentioned a couple of things that may not have been common knowledge, even to the Diving Section officers in charge:

Certainly, over the time when I was there, we took on what the White Paper had said. The command team as a whole had no doubt that the diving had to get money. So when the estimate [budget] process came in every year, there was a kinda … from the view point of others, the divers got away with murder in the equipment they were getting, but that was the viewpoint of the other departments who were also trying to get money for other things … and even when things began to shorten in, there was a complete acceptance that the resources just had to go to the divers, that it was a very important area … I don't know who coined the phrase 'the Ninth Ship', but that describes the Diving Section very eloquently indeed.[4]

When talking to Mark Mellett for this book, he described the context in which he coined the term 'the Ninth Ship', which has stuck to the Diving Section for the past few years. Mark was captain of the naval base at the time (OCNBAD):

I described the diving unit as the 'Ninth Ship' because it gave a service delivery equal to that of any ship in the service … for such a small unit it gave such service and it was always in the hotspot of operations, whether it was a body recovery, car in the river, even if you look at it in the context of serious incidents in terms of recovery of sunken trawlers, the recovery in terms of the tragedy of the diver off Hook Head where we were getting beaten up by the press and certain politicians in the Dáil. But the diving officer at the time – Darragh – held the line. Some guy went against the advice and died, and then we had to recover his body as well in what was already a very difficult operation … So from my perspective, the utility of the Diving Section as a strategic resource for the service was always from my perspective 'the Ninth Ship'. So therefore we had to resource it as best we could.

As for the future and where the Diving Section may see a future role, the ROV side of things in terms of commercial off-the-shelf is fine, but I think we really have to move into the area of AUVs [autonomous under-water vehicles] … in terms of ports and approaches security, I think that that type of technology support [to physical diving operations] is essential.[5]

Similarly, when discussing the future of naval diving with Lt Cdr Tony O'Regan, and about its possible future roles, equipment and training, Tony commented:

… as you are aware, the NSDS as a whole has always had a dual-headed system: operational outputs and training. Our future as a whole is about delivering NS and a DF capability, focusing on training personnel with up-to-date equipment and remaining concurrent with the commercial industry. Continued training with subsurface technology such as ROVs, side-scan sonars and hand-held sonars to assist the divers' search capability must remain a continuous plan for future-proofing capabilities, but should also include AUVs. Through long-term goals and correct purchases, we aim to improve on what we can deliver.

Next year will see the introduction of military mixed-gas re-breathers. This will be a major leap forward for us and the NS in terms of capability, and will represent a substantial change in the DF role of naval diving. However, with this new capability comes added responsibility to training, standards and safety procedures. These additional roles will need to be balanced with the continued focus on operational requirements and training outputs. Mixed-gas diving is a major investment that will place the INS on a par with its fellow European navies, opening doors to knowledge and training facilities within pooling and sharing.[6]

Tony mentioned that the way forward for the Naval Service Diving Section as regards equipment and its capability would be through the use of what are commonly called re-breathers. There are many types of re-breathers on the market, many produced and used by civilians, and are by no means cheap. Whether these particular types of re-breathers are suitable for a naval-diving team is subject to debate. The use of military-type re-breathers raises the stakes even higher. There is a huge cost implication with this type of equipment, not only in the actual price per unit but also in demand for resources. It demands and requires further enhanced logistical support, technical support, manpower, proper facilities and dedicated training time for personnel. The average cost of a military re-breather is anywhere between €30,000 to €80,000 per unit, depending on manufacturer, design and capability of the unit. These units can be large and weigh about 40 kilos in air, but are designed for the water so lose a lot of their weight when submerged. This type of diving is as simple as it is dangerous. It requires training. If this equipment comes into service, a new era of training and fitness needs to evolve. This is not a type of diving or a type of equipment that can be treated lightly. If mistreated or untrained for, it can, will and has killed. It will need constant deep-diving training and constant diving with the equipment; it will be a huge asset to the Diving Section, the Naval Service and to the state.

Lt Cdr Conor Kirwan, when asked about possible future roles, training and equipment for the Diving Section, expressed his own thoughts on the subject:

> I was involved for the last two years, specifically with the EDA [European Defence Agency] in a pooling and sharing initiative specifically in diving. What that did – and also what we have done in terms of the International Dive Schools' Association – is it brings military diving-school comman-dants together. So you suddenly found yourself sitting at a table as the navy OIC Diving and also head of the Naval diving school, sitting down with the head of the French diving school, the head of the German diving school … and you have got three different tiers in military diver or navy diver specifically … navy diver: you have three different types of diver across Europe. You have got your ship's diver, you've got your salvage diver and you've got your clearance diver. They're your three different types of diver, and there are three different types of courses that are catered for … it became very clear that for EOD diving – which is a military role and a core military role – that the only way or route for the Diving Section to go down is clearance diving … The equipment that we use is just a vehicle to get down to the seabed to carry out a tasking. But the tasking is where the technical ability comes in … from a salvage point of view, be it cutting or

welding or working under the water, and from an EOD point of view it's working with ordnance, so therefore we have to be training to that level all the time.[7]

In relation to the use of re-breathers – training with them and diving to depth with them – Conor had this to say:

> The problem with diving at the moment [within the Naval Service] is we have a core group of personnel, eight or nine individuals who are chasing themselves in terms of training … we can't support [re-breathers] with those numbers. We have been caught to a certain extent and for the last number of years, in that we have been getting numbers through the diving courses which are small … we can't reduce the standard of the diving course because the nature of the job we do from a military point of view is that it demands that we maintain the highest standards.[8]

Historically, the numbers of qualified divers of all ranks and qualifications within the Naval Service has rarely exceeded forty to forty-five. This figure rises and falls with the years, but in general a good average figure certainly would be forty. The problem arises when trying to fill the vacancies that may exist within the section; generally, these slots need to be filled by ratings and not NCOs, where there are fewer possible vacancies. In an attempt to achieve a system whereby the Diving Section would over a short period of time – possibly two to four year or so – gain bigger numbers of personnel – particularly junior ratings and within the Seamens' Branch, though not exclusively – Conor offered a possible solution. By having more Executive Branch/Seamens' Branch divers in the service (more than divers from the other departments within the navy), it would allow Command the flexibility to seriously consider filling the existing establishment figure of twenty-seven divers for the Diving Section, which in turn would allow the Diving Section to turn its attention to seriously addressing the re-breather deep-diving capability. Historically, the greatest number of divers have come from the Seamens' Branch, or Executive Branch as it is called now, and similarly for the officers the greater numbers also have come from the Executive Branch. The establishment of the Diving Section and the appointments (manpower) therein are weighted again historically in favour of personnel from the Executive Branch. Thus, it affords the greatest chance of a seaman diver being posted to the Diving Section rather than a colleague from another branch. Any attempt to improve the manpower situation would have to be considered with this in mind:

> … there is a two-tier system in diving, where you have your CDOs and seamen divers, and you have your 'everybody else'. If you look at things historically over time, what you have is everybody else – and this is very much a generalisation – would be ship's diver standard, while all the specialised training, experience and competency that comes from training and experience, and is generally all seamen and CDOs by definition. But also seamens, because it makes sense because of CS4 [military document outlining the numbers of personnel allowed in a particular corps, section or unit of the Defence Forces: the number allowed cannot be exceeded] – they are the only ones who are going to come back into the unit … my take is, we just bite the bullet. We put in now that, yes, there is a two-tier system and the people inside the Diving Section are seamen and mechs from a maintenance point of view in that they maintain the equipment inside, but …if we were to fill the establishment with those twenty-seven seamen and that's where the focus goes on the ordinary seaman, then we would have the capability to go to re-breathers.[9]

When speaking about manpower shortages, particularly those involving low diver numbers in the Diving Section, I always loved recalling a particular little anecdote from many years ago. When I was the chief in the Diving Section at the time, I had cause to go to then shore operations commander, Commander Noel Goulding. Noel was a seasoned veteran of the navy whose bark was certainly worse than his bite. Anyway, this particular day I was in his office to get some monthly-returns paperwork signed by him. He was behind his desk and, looking up to see who it was, he greeted me with his usual 'Hey langer, how's it going?' 'All good, sir,' says I. 'How're things down below in the store – anything strange or startling happening down there?' 'Feck all, sir, really, 'cept the usual manpower crisis, shortage of divers, you know yourself.' With that, he put down his pen, leaned back in his chair and put his hands behind his head. He then took off his glasses and looked at me: 'Jaysus, Chief,' he says, 'it's remarkable, I don't understand why there's a shortage at all: every fecking time my daughter goes out for a night in Cork, she tells me every langer she meets is either a navy diver or wants to be a navy diver!' There was no answer to that.

The newly qualified CDO, S/Lt Shane Mulcahy, commented when asked the same questions about where he saw the future of naval diving and about the equipment:

> … if we were going to focus on 'military' naval diving … looking at developing an EOD diver level, then that's something I would focus on, looking at developing that side of our training. At the end of the day, naval divers will never be specialists in any one area; we will always have to be jacks of all trades and masters of none … but for the moment that's where the focus has to be on all of our training.[10]

What about re-breathers?

> It is the logical, though not necessarily the next step, but it is the logical evolution of military diving. Mixed-gas diving, and especially re-breathers in that regards, is something we definitely have to be looking at in terms of where we need to be going in the future if we are going to be a legitimate EOD capability force.[11]

Gerry O'Donoghue had this to say when asked for his thoughts on the future direction of the Naval Service Diving Section:

> … the problem is there are two ways of looking at it. In any business there has to be a reason for doing things – you can't keep inventing roles that actually don't exist … we could train up saturation teams, a mixed-gas team in six weeks, we literally could. So if we suddenly said what shit do we need, 75 metres, TriMix, we could do that in six weeks because of the quality of the divers we have. So let's have the file ready, let's have the orders ready, everything done and let's send two guys on a TriMix course. But let's not do stuff that's going to fall into disuse because we don't have use for it. I'm speaking now as a naval 'manager' as opposed to a 'diver' … you need to be careful not to let the 'toys' take over from the operations.[12]

In my interview with Gene Ryan, retired commander and former commander of Fleet Operations in the Naval Service, I asked him a question which has in some sense dogged me since I began this project. My question was this: did he think there should have been more medals or awards handed out over the years either to divers or the Diving Section as a unit?

> Without doubt, without doubt, absolutely. I think, I know, we are very bad
> at that in the navy ... there have been diving jobs done where medals should
> have been awarded ... I mean, if you were to do a risk percentage on a job,
> what's the percentage of this guy not coming back. What is the percentage
> of this diver not coming back from the dive? Some of the jobs that you guys
> did, the percentages were beyond fifty per cent without doubt, and for me
> that is tantamount to a Distinguished Service Medal [DSM]. Think about
> it, chiefs of staff get the DSM ... really, I find that very odd ... divers that
> go into the water with more than a fifty per cent chance of not coming back,
> that's distinguished service ... its within their power to commend a unit ...
> but we are bad at it, we are very bad at it. I think there's an Irishism, we are
> terrible as a nation like this. We have a begrudgery in this country towards
> each other, and I think we are happy begrudging each other something.
> When you see the diving unit since its inception in the 1960s, right up to
> the Gerry O'Donoghues of this world being the first MCDO, all that sort
> of thing ... we should, as a navy, be giving more commendations and medals
> to people who do dangerous or distinguished service work.[13]

Gene then had more of a suggestion than a question of his own. He reminded me of the stresses and strains that divers must have been under and experienced over the years, and he offered this to me:

> Another issue ... is the personal effect all this diving has on divers and their
> families... because some of the stuff – Jesus wept – I mean I saw some of
> the bodies and I wasn't diving at all, but you guys had to take them out of
> the water in their decomposed state, put them in the bottom of the Searider
> or Gemini or whatever, and then put them into a body bag with their eyes,
> ears and noses gone – all that sort of stuff. Particularly if you had young
> children in that state, and the smell ... so I had great admiration for the
> divers, but I'm sure before we went and got ourselves counselling services,
> I'm sure that there are divers particularly in the early days that must have
> had a harrowing time, I'm sure they still do ... it's always there with you.[14]

There can be no doubting that for the Naval Service Diving Section, the future lies in the area of technology, not only in the actual diving equipment but also in the area of sub-surface search equipment. It is clear in the comments from all areas of diving and Command that the way forward is now in re-breathers. This will be fantastic for the section, but great care must be exercised. Re-breathers, amongst other things, will now allow the diver greater freedom and latitude of mobility at depth. Even though he will of course be bound by the regulations and the conduct of the operation, he will nonetheless have greater latitude. Training and dive standards will have to be raised even further. This will not present any problems for the divers and for the officer in charge; however, Command will have to play its part in this area, too, especially in the area of manpower. As has been said previously, this type of diving cannot and must not be taken lightly, especially when operating the sets at depth, past the 50 to 60-metre depth ranges. Simply stated, mixed-gas re-breathers are lovely, but in the end they are just another means of killing oneself.

Sub-surface search equipment such as AUVs (autonomous underwater vehicles) and Work Class ROVs are not a million miles away either. These are very real requirements not only for the Naval Service but also for the state. The waters around our shores are not particularly shallow, and given that the service is entrusted by the state to maintain its maritime security and integrity, then the service should have the means to effect that. AUVs and Work Class ROVs are not a means to an end, but they are necessary tools in that area. The ability to search for and recover items from below the 100-metre mark is becoming the norm. Currently (2015), two aircraft have crashed into the oceans, one off Western Australia (Malaysian Airlines MH370) – currently being searched for – and the other in Indonesia (Air Asia QZ8501), which has been found. Sub-surface search technology has played and is playing a very large part in the search and recovery of these aircraft, due in no small part to the large areas involved and the depths of water. It happened off our coast once before, and given the growth in airline traffic through our airspace, it would be prudent to be prepared for the worst.

CONCLUSION

Only those who will risk going too far can possibly find out how far one can go.

T.S. Eliot

The Naval Service Diving Section has been fifty years a growing. It remains to be seen how the Diving Section will develop and evolve in the future, but the one thing I do know for certain is that it will be well led, served and nurtured by the finest officers, NCOs and ratings the navy has to offer. In its fifty years of operation, the Diving Section has never lost a diver while on operations. In the countless hours of dive time and the thousands of dives completed, the Diving Section has only ever had one 'bend', and that occurred while treating a patient in an RCC.

The naval divers of today have a duty of care. They are the custodians of the history of the Naval Service Diving Section both within and outside of the Naval Service. They are the custodians of a history that has been forged over the past fifty years by every diver that has come before them – a history that was forged through hard work, determination, perseverance and endurance, and a history that has extracted from every diver blood, sweat, tears, laughter and for some even life itself.

> From this day to the ending of the world,
> But we in it shall be remembered.
> We few, we happy few, we band of brothers;
> For he to-day that sheds his blood with me
> Shall be my brother …
>
> *William Shakespeare,* Henry V

APPENDIX 1

NAVAL DIVING SECTION EOD OPERATIONS, 1987–2014

Year	Location	Details
1987	Helvick Head, Wexford	Disposal of sea mine
1987	Sherkin Island, west Cork	Disposal of sea mine
1987	Baltimore, west Cork	Disposal of WW2 mk 17 contact mine
1991	Dunmore East, Wexford	Disposal of 2 WW2 mk 17 contact mines
1991	Glandore, west Cork	Disposal of mk 17 contact mine
1991	Kinsale Hbr, west Cork	Disposal of mk 17 contact mine
1992	Glandore, west Cork	Disposal of mk 17 contact mine
1992	Schull, west Cork	Disposal of sea mine
1992	Glandore, west Cork	Disposal of sea mine
1992	Cork Hbr, Cork	Disposal of sea mine
1993	Irish Sea	Sinking of MSC *Irwell* by disposal
1995	Baltimore, west Cork	Disposal of WW2 sea mine
1995	Off Cork Hbr, Cork	Disposal of mk 7 British depth charge
1996	Union Hall, west Cork	Disposal of 37mm ammunition from German navy U-boat
1997	Kinsale, west Cork	Disposal of sea mine
1997	Kinsale, west Cork	Disposal of sea mine
1997	Glenbeigh, Co Kerry	Disposal of sea mine
1997	Kinsale, west Cork	Disposal of sea mine
1997	Lambay Island, Dublin	Disposal of explosive ordnance
1998	Trenabo Cove, west Cork	Disposal of unidentified sea mine
1998	Baltimore, west Cork	Disposal of WW2 hedgehog bomb
1998	Fenit Harbour Kerry	Disposal of navigation hazard, wreck removal
1999	Cork Harbour, Cork	Disposal of WW2 German navy torpedo head
1999	Galley Head, west Cork	Disposal of unidentified object
2000	Dunmore East, Wexford	Disposal of WW2 mk 17 buoyant mine
2002	Cork Harbour, Cork	Disposal of naval artillery shell
2005	Helvick Head, Wexford	Locate WW2 mine and disposal
2005	Baltimore, west Cork	Locate WW2 mine and disposal
2007	Courtmacsherry, west Cork	Locate WW2 mine and disposal
2008	Broadhaven Bay, Mayo	Shell disposal
2012–	South coast	UC 42 (German navy U-boat, WW1 mine-layer, V mines)

APPENDIX 2

NAVAL SERVICE DIVING SECTION JOINT TASK FORCE/ C&E OPERATIONS

Vessel Name	Location	Year
Front Guider	Money Point, County Clare	1996
MV Tia	Castletown Bere, W. Cork	1996
Aegir	Galway Docks	1997
MV Kyushu Star	Money Point, County Clare	1997
MV Xanadu	Ringaskiddy, County Cork	1997
MV Dinan	Ringaskiddy, County Cork	1997
MV Caro	Ringaskiddy, County Cork	1999
Moor Laker	Ringaskiddy, County Cork	2000
Sofia	Ringaskiddy, County Cork	2000
MV Pittsburg	Foynes, County Clare	2005
MV Pride	Foynes, County Clare	2005
MV Buzzard Bay	Foynes, County Clare	2005
MV Green Chile	Foynes, County Clare	2006
Specified location/suspicious buoys	Dublin Bay	2010
An May	Money Point, County Clare	2013
Maersk Norwich	Ringaskiddy, County Cork	2014

APPENDIX 3

NAVAL SERVICE DIVING SECTION, RECOMPRESSION CHAMBER THERAPEUTIC CASES TREATED, 1983–2014

Name		*Date*	*Remarks*
1.	Phil Lane	13/6/1987	
2.	Dave Woosnam	5/8/1987	
3.	Rory Jackson	25/8/1987	
4.	Joe Minogue	28/6/1988	
5.	Dave Morey	3/7/1988	
6.	Clive Lloyd	23/6/1990	
7.	John Chamberlain	2/10/1990	
8.	Shannon McNeill	10–11/9/1993	
9.	Keith Reading	10–11/9/1993	
10.	Eugene Cahill	3–5/8/1994	Longest treatment to date
11.	Michael Daly	5/8/1994	First naval diver
12.	Graham Messenger	6/8/1994	
13.	Robert Meadows	25/8/1994	
14.	Edwin Owen	2/6/1995	
15.	Francis O'Sullivan	20/6/1995	
16.	Audrey Gleeson	26/6/1995	First female
17.	Jamie Powell	21/8/1995	
18.	John Sheridan	30/8/1995	
19.	Michael O'Riordan	8/8/1997	
20.	Giles Brunet	18/8/1997	
21.	Ian Everatt	29/9/1997	
22.	Philip Le-Milot	3/10/1997	
23.	Nick O'Brien	2/6/2008	
24.	Pat McGrath	10/5/2009	
25.	Dave Furlong	10/5/2009	
26.	Bill O'Brien	17/6/2009	
27.	Patrick Egan	28/6/2009	
28.	Brendan Flanagan	17/8/2009	
29.	Niall Tivy	2/6/2010	
30.	Bernadette Collins	4/7/2010	
31.	Firas Jundi	2/8/2010	
32.	Seamus Pender	5/9/2010	
33.	Paul Coleman	11/9/2010	
34.	Paul Coleman	17/9/2010	Return treatment
35.	Michael Ryan	26/9/2010	
36.	Michael Ryan	29/9/2010	Return treatment
37.	Ger Ward	30/1/2011	
38.	Darragh Rossiter	26/6/2011	
39.	AN Other	2012	

APPENDIX 4

NOMINAL ROLL OF NAVAL SERVICE DIVERS, 1964–2014
(O) = officer

Trained by the Royal Navy in HMS *Drake* & HMS *Vernon*

1964
1   Joseph Deasy (O)

1969
2   Frank Lynch (O)

1970
3   Peadar McElhinney (O)
4   George Jefferies
5   Eamon Butler
6   Paddy Lynch RIP

1972
7   Anthony Sheridan
8   Johnny O'Neill

1973
9   Paddy Carolan
10 Noel Garrett
11 Tommy Johnson RIP
12 Denis Sheridan

1974
13 Dan O'Neill (O)

1975
14 Liam Donaldson (O)
15 Gerry O'Donoghue (O)

1976
16 John Walsh
17 Martin Carroll

18 Tony Behan

1977
19 Mark Mellett (O)
20 Brendan O'Halloran (O)

1978
21 Gerry Duffy
22 Muiris Mahon
23 Reggie Lloyd
24 Frank Moody

1979
25 Philip Gray
26 Chris McMahon
27 Dermot O'Sullivan

1980
28 Chris Reynolds (O)
29 Shane Anderson (O)
30 Ollie McMurrow
31 Decky Kelly
32 Billy Lahive
33 Martin Diggins

1981
34 Tom Meehan (O)
35 Ron Long (O)
36 Paul Logan (O)
37 Martin Buckley
38 John Lynch
39 Paulus Forde

Trained by the Naval Service Diving Section

1982: 1st Course
40 Ciaran Monks
41 Damien Power
42 Brendan Cotter
43 Jimmy O'Keeffe

1983: 2nd Course
44 Mick Boyle (O)
45 Joe Whelehan (O)
46 Jimmy Bartley
47 John McCarthy
48 Owen Murphy
49 Alan McDonald

1984: 3rd Course
50 John FM Leech (O)
51 Bob Frazier
52 Alan Kenna
53 John McGrath
54 Tony Moore

1985: 4th Course
55 Mattie Byrne
56 Martin Hensey
57 Martin Doyle

1986: 5th Course
58 Bob McCarthy (O)
59 Mick Goode
60 Derek McCabe
61 Paddy O'Grady
62 Wesley Cooke
63 Tony Lyons

1988: 6th Course
64 Tom Kennedy
65 Ciaran Woodward
66 Brian Fitzgerald (O)
67 Davy Byrne
68 Derek Kane

1989: 7th Course
69 Mick Daly
70 Paul Shanahan
71 John Kearney
72 Declan Fleming (O)

1990: 8th Course
73 Frank Cunningham
74 Noel Dunne
75 Alan Smith
76 Noel Hickey
77 Steve Mulcahy
78 Brian Byrne (brother of Davy Byrne, 6th diving course)

1992: 9th Course
79 Niall Browne
80 Duncan Byrne
81 John Robinson
82 Pat Gillick
83 Malcolm McCormack
84 John Harrington RIP.
85 Adrian Hickey
86 Aidan Lennon
87 Brian Scanlon
88 Mike McCarthy
89 John Dowling (O)
90 John O'Brien

1993: 10th Course
91 Pat McDonagh
92 Kevin Fergusson
93 Paddy O'Donnell
94 Eddie Mulligan

11th course was cancelled, with all students failing to complete the course

1995: 12th Course
95   Barry McCormack
96   Louis Linnane
97   Chris Peters
98   Conor McManus
99   Keith Barrett
100 Enda Broderick
101 Nigel McCormack

1996: 13th Course
102 Paul McCarthy
103 Jim Cleary
104 Paul O'Neill
105 Gerry Braine
106 Damien McCormack

continued over

1997: 14th Course

107 Paddy Delaney
108 Gordon Cummins
109 Darragh Kirwan (O)
110 Trevor Murphy
111 Johnny McGroarty
112 Joey Morrison
113 Joey Manning

1998: 15th Course

114 Anthony O'Regan
115 Dave O'Brien
116 John O'Regan

2000: 16th Course

117 Ron Boyle (O)
118 Colm Cotter

2001–02: 17th Course

119 Courtney Gibbons
120 John Glennon

2002: 19th Course

121 Alan Cuddihy
122 Brian Murray
123 Dermot Halpin RIP

2004: 20th Course

124 Johnny Fenton
125 Cian O'Mearáin (O)
126 Conor Kirwan (O)
127 Mick O'Brien
128 Mick Hickey
129 Eddie Kennedy
130 Liam Kavanagh

2006: 21st Course

131 Alex Casey
132 Shane O'Shea
133 Ian Kavanagh
134 Colin Reay
135 Barry Cronin
136 Dave Shanahan
137 Martin Tarrant (O)

2007: 22nd Course

138 Ron Carey (O)
139 Donal O'Sullivan
140 Seamus Claffey

2008: 23rd Course

141 Anthony Bones
142 Dave O'Brien
143 Chris Sheridan
144 Tom Lonergan

2009: 24th Course

145 James Walsh
146 Martin O'Sullivan
147 Barry McCabe
148 Matthew Martin
149 Ben Murphy
150 Dave O'Leary
151 Kieran Carr (O)

2011: 25th Course

152 Shane Mulcahy (O)
153 Steve Payne
154 Derrick Browne
155 Jonney McBrearty
156 Brian O'Sullivan (O)

2012: 26th Course

157 Alan Lynch
158 D. Humphries

2013: 27th Course

159 Chris Morgan
160 Stephen Whitty
161 Gary Price
162 Keith Dempsey

2014: 28th Course

163 Gareth Smith
164 Ryan Carroll
165 Diarmuid Hallahan
166 Stephen Stack (O)

Total number of divers trained:	**166**
Total number trained in UK:	**39**
Total number of NCO/ratings:	**136**
Total number of officers trained:	**30**

as of December 2014

APPENDIX 5

LAYPERSON'S GUIDE TO SOME OF THE EQUIPMENT MENTIONED IN THE TEXT

Sub-surface Search Equipment Suite, 1999

Side-scan sonar

The Klein System 2000. This is the first of two active side-scan sonar systems that are operated by the Naval Service Diving Section. The Klein System 2000 consists of a towfish, the surface control panel unit (CPU) and the power/telemetry umbilical required to power the towfish

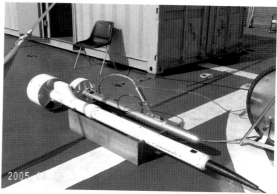

via the CPU and to allow the various processing signals to pass between both pieces of equipment.

Side-scan towfish

This is the subsurface part of the system. It is a 4-foot long cylinder (towfish). The cylinder itself is made from steel, with the first 12 inches of the towfish being solid steel to protect the sonar transducers and associated electronic package that is housed in the rest of the towfish from head-on impact. There are two transducers housed on either side of the towfish. These transducers are about 18 inches in length and are placed within the walls of the towfish so that they are facing out and downwards. The transducers convert the electrical energy from the transmitter into mechanical energy, vibration; this vibration is then transferred into the surrounding water as an oscillation pressure (on the surface, audible high-speed clicking is heard). And like surface radar scans, when this energy strikes the seabed or object, some it is returned back towards the towfish. This return signal is then essentially turned back into electrical energy by the same transducer, which in turn is detected by the receiver element of the transducer, and from there the signal is received in the CPU for processing into a digital picture on the screen.

The transmission/receiving and processing of the signals is near instantaneous. An unfortunate consequence of the siting of the transducers in the towfish is that as they do not look exactly downwards, the system is prevented from seeing or scanning directly underneath the towfish – thus, there is a potential blind spot. This is offset by either using the existing software in the CPU to merge the picture as seen on the CPU screen, or, when conducting a search, by ensuring that the search legs have a built-in overlap of at least twenty-five per cent. At the after end of the towfish is the tailfin, which is required to maintain the towfish on a straight and level depth when deployed.

Control panel unit

This unit is the brains of the sonar search suite. This is where everything about the sonar is controlled. All search parameters for the towfish are controlled from here. It has numerous functions and capabilities, but the more important would is the viewing screen that displays the picture produced by the sonar. It includes a greyscale-printer unit that allows the operators to trace on paper the search as it being conducted, and it also allows the search to be digitally recorded for playback at a later time.

Umbilical

A multicore cable that carries the power and signal streams to and from the towfish. It is housed on a portable reel, with the length of the umbilical approximately 200 metres. The umbilical itself is quite strong, with a breaking strain in direct pull of 1000 kgs, and sharp bends and nips should be avoided. It is connected to the towfish via SubCon connectors. These types of connectors allow the male pin ends connect into the female connector ends on the towfish, and when mated form a watertight connection between the male and female ends that allows the information to flow uninterrupted back and forth through the cable.

Operation of system

In simple terms, the towfish maintains a depth setting by two means. Firstly, the amount of cable that's paid out behind the towing vessel; secondly, the speed of the towing vessel. Theoretically, the towfish needs to be in clean water, which is water that is free from noise, so it needs to out of the towing-ship's wake and deep enough so that it gets a really good image of the seabed. The towfish transducers can be configured using the CPU to operate in a multitude of settings, displays, frequencies and ranges. This is normally determined by the object being searched for: its depth, its height off the seabed, and the nature of the seabed in the search area. The operating depth of the towfish is important as it cuts down the dead space (blind spot) directly underneath the towfish; this is produced because the sonar transducers are fixed into the sonar towfish assembly to look down and out to the sides but not directly downwards. So the image begins about the five and seven-o'clock positions, not the six-o'clock position. Also, the faster the towing vessel goes, the greater the chance the emitting signals from the towfish outwards will miss the towfish when it echoes back to it (depending on the distance or range that has been set).

Geometrics G880 Magnetometer

The G880 Geometrics Magnetometer is an item of equipment designed to detect magnetic anomalies within a pre-set range (set by the operator). It is a sophisticated and complex piece of equipment in its own right; however, the vast majority of the complex work is carried out by the software housed in both the electronics package that is housed on the mag towfish and on the systems laptop. Unfortunately, this system was never fully utilised by the Diving Section as it was a effectively a high-end Ferrari when what we really needed and should have got was a four-by-four. There are three components in the system used by the Naval Diving Section.

Magnetometer (towfish/mag)

The Magnetometer is similar in shape to the side-scan-sonar towfish, but is greater in diameter and longer, weighs about 15 kgs, and comes in two halves, each half connected to the other by an internal electronics cable. The towfish when being assembled is slotted together, and both halves are fixed by a series of grub screws around the diameter. The umbilical is then attached to the head of the towfish by first connecting both the towfish and umbilical via two cables mated together by male and female SubCon connectors, and then the umbilical end is slotted into the towfish and screwed together.

Umbilical cable

A multicore cable that carries the power and signal streams to and from the mag. It is housed on a portable reel and the length of the umbilical is approximately 200 metres long. The umbilical itself is quite strong, with a breaking strain in direct pull of 1000 kgs, and sharp bends and nips should be avoided. The mag end is, as mentioned, attached to the head of the magnetometer itself, while the deck end is connected to the systems laptop as used by the operator. The telemetry signals as transmitted and received are passed via a slip-ring assembly that's in-built into the umbilical reel.

Operator systems laptop

A laptop obviously with all the necessary software programmed to allow the mag towfish to display its data and for that data to be displayed in such a format as can be read and understood by the surface operator. The normal display available for general viewing was the coarse and fine-needle trace displays. For all intents and purposes, the displays looked very much like those of a display, where the trace needles get excited should they pass through or over a magnetic anomaly.

Sub-surface Search Equipment, 2001

Remote operated vehicle (ROV)

The last days of December 2000 and early January 2001 saw the arrival of the Diving Section's first remote operated vehicle (ROV). This ROV belongs to the Sub-Atlantic Cherokee inspection class of ROVs.

The complete ROV system includes the surface control unit and the deck winch with 300 metres of umbilical. The arrival of the ROV and its systems added a whole new level of professionalism, expertise and competency within the Diving Section, and similarly on a strategic level added a new level of operational capability for the Naval Service, the Defence Forces and the state. The system when it initially arrived into the section was in individual units; there was therefore an immediate requirement for the system to be containerised. This obviously provided answers to several key issues such as storage, movability, security and operational usage. The subsequent container was purpose designed by the Diving Section and technicians to cater for all aspects of the operational requirements for the ROV.

ROV and on-board systems

- Height 32 inches, length 56 inches, width 34 inches.
- Weight in air: 240 kgs/529 lbs.
- Frame: polypropylene, with a large syntactic foam buoyant lid covering and protecting the ROV's 2 electronics pods beneath it. It is positively buoyant until any necessary ballast weights are added, depending on user configuration and requirement.
- Power supply to the ROV: 440 VAC 3 phase and neutral, 50/60Hz 10kVa.
- A five-function manipulator arm sited on the right-hand side of the ROV at the front. It has a slew through a radius of 100 degrees, and because of the amount of functionality was quite manoeuvrable. The jaws at the end of the manipulator are sensitive enough that they are capable of picking up an egg without breaking it, or have sufficient strength to close and grip onto something and stay closed (it can be compared to a human arm from the shoulder to the fingers, but with rigid fingers).
- Four electric motors/thrusters, two single propeller thrusters at the rear of the ROV to provide forward and stern propulsion, one twin propeller lateral thruster providing right and left propulsion, and one twin propeller vertical

thruster providing up and down thrust.

- Equipped with two cameras – colour and black and white – housed in front of the ROV in its housing. This housing is motorised and when controlled from the surface the cameras are capable of 180-degree tilt up and down function, and 200 degrees pan left and right function.
- 3 x 500 watt halogen lamps, dimmer controlled from the surface.
- Fitted with a Sub-Atlantic Sector Scanning Sonar. Capable of scanning out to 1,000 metres, and though capable of 360-degree scanning arc, due to the siting of the sonar head within the framework and syntactic buoyancy foam of the ROV, this arc is reduced to approximately 200 degrees.

Surface control unit (SCU)

This unit controls all the necessary functionality of the on-board ROV systems. It is from this unit that the ROV pilot/technician controls the movements and operational capability of the ROV. It is man portable, and is contained within its own housing; however, it is sited and worked from within the dedicated ROV container. The SCU operates and controls the following:

- Controls and displays the sector scanning sonar system.
- Houses the VHS video unit for recording of diving operations.
- Controls and houses the two camera monitors.
- Controls and displays the power supply both to the system and critically to the ROV. The power requirements are 440 VAC and 220/240 VAC.
- Houses the earth-fault monitoring system, which shuts down the system if it detects an earth fault anywhere.
- Houses the emergency stop button.
- Houses the remote hand-held ROV controls console. This console allows the pilot or technician to operate the ROV controls outside and away from the SCU.

Remote hand-held ROV control console

This unit is plugged into the SCU and offers the pilot/technician the flexibility to operate the ROV away from or outside of the ROV container, though it is limited by the length of the console cabling. This console allows the pilot/technician to operate the following ROV systems and functionality:

- Zoom lens function on the colour camera.
- Power-to-thrust ratio on all thrusters.
- directional functionality of the ROV propulsion thrusters.
- Auto/depth hold or height-hold function of the ROV.

Manipulator controller console

This console is similar in function to the remote hand-held ROV console. It controls all five functions of the manipulator arm (imagine a human arm from the shoulder to the fingers). It controls:
- Slewing left/right function of the manipulator.
- Up/down function of the upper arm.
- Up/down function of the lower arm.
- Rotational function of the wrist.
- Open/close grip/jaw function.

Umbilical and deck winch

The umbilical consists of downlink/uplink channels, each link carrying eight analogue, twelve-bit, sixteen digital-switch channels. The umbilical is negatively buoyant and is housed on a self-stowing winch. The telemetry is fed through a slip-ring assembly on the winch with a feed umbilical coming from the slip-ring junction box back to the surface control unit.

Naval Recompression Chamber (RCC), 1983–2008

The Naval Diving Section's RCC can be envisioned as an oblong cylindrical steel cylinder approximately 10 feet long and 4 feet in diameter and lying on its side. The cylinder at one end has a dome-effect end, and a hinged steel door or hatch at the other end that opens inwards. Then visualise the cylinder being divided into two parts internally, one section longer than the other. The longer section, or main chamber, is approximately 7 feet in length, while the shorter section, or entry lock, is approximately 3 feet in length. The main chamber is separated from the entry lock by means on an internal steel hatch, approximately 20 inches in diameter, hinged on the main chamber side – thus, it opens inwards into the main chamber and to the right. The entry lock is similarly fitted with a hatch that is hinged internally – thus, it opens inwards and to the right. So to enter into the main chamber of the RCC, one must first enter through the entry lock. This lock is accessed through the hatch (as described above), and directly in front is the internal hatchway that leads directly into the main chamber. All this is within arm's length as it is a small space.

The hatchway into the main chamber itself is round. A combing runs around the circumference of the hatch – thus, when the main chamber hatch is closed, it gives the main chamber of the RCC a completely sealed unit when in operation. This internal hatch seals from the inside to out. The main chamber is where all therapeutic treatments are carried out. Similarly, the entry-lock hatch when closed seals the entry lock off to the outside, or what the navy terms the 'surface'. Both the entry-lock and main-chamber hatches create a seal by being pushed onto rubber O seals set into the combing surrounding the respective hatches. As air pressure is applied internally into either lock, the build-up of pressure in the lock pushes the hatches outwards and onto the seals. The RCC is set onto a skid-like cradle that in turn is affixed by four 10-inch solid-plastic castor-like wheels to allow for some manoeuvrability.

Both the entry and the main chambers are pretty much mirror images of each other except in size and in a couple of smaller details. The theory is that each lock, though joined together, is separate and independent of the other. The means of pressurising the RCC is by compressed air. Each lock has air-supply valves going in, and air-venting valves coming out, with the necessary pressure gauges fitted to show the pressure. Also fitted are depth gauges that allow the supervisor or operator to know what depth the chambers are at. On each of the two chambers is fitted a 'coarse' depth gauge, while on the main chamber only is fitted a therapeutic 'fine' depth gauge. This gauge is more crucial to therapeutic treatment as it is more accurate in its depth reading than the coarse gauge. Valves on the outside are in general mirrored on the inside, as it is possible under extreme circumstances to operate the chamber from within, though not recommended.

Lighting for the RCC is through two hard, clear, plastic tubes approximately 5 inches long and which are threaded through the roof of each chamber, over which is placed a Canty light – essentially, a projector lamp placed inside a black box that fits over the hard plastic tube. When the lamp is turned on, the lamp shines down onto the top of the plastic tube, which then transmits the light through itself and into the chamber. Built into the walls of both chambers are viewing ports 5 inches in diameter – one on the entry lock and two on the main chamber.

Fitted externally is a battery-operated communications box that permits voice comms into both chambers via a hard-wired system to fitted speakers. Underneath each chamber is fitted a ¾-inch quarter-turn valve.

Internally, the main chamber is fitted out with two benches that double as either seats or beds. These seats run along either side of the main chambers, while the entry lock is fitted only with a small seat. Fitted also into the main chamber towards the front is a 'medical lock' – a small lock similar in operation to both the main and entry-lock chambers; however, it is only used for passing in and out small items from the main chamber, such as tea/coffee. The air supply to the RCC is either via a low-pressure compressor air supply or via a high-pressure quad supply, though in general it is best to supply the RCC with low pressure. Finally, and most importantly, the RCC is fitted with an internally fitted oxygen-supply system called BIBS (built-in breathing system). The BIBS supplies medical oxygen through two sets of oral nasal masks to two persons either in the main chamber or in the entry lock.

RCC, 2009–14

The RCC was sent to SMP Ltd in the UK for a complete midlife refit and refurbishment in 2009. On its return, the RCC was housed in a customised 20-foot container designed to accommodate it and the necessary operating systems. The major changes and refurbishments that had taken place now made operating the chamber more efficient for both operators and supervisors, and brought the RCC into line with current regulations pertaining to the operation of an RCC in the workplace. The RCC is now practically unrecognisable from its former self, and now affords operators and supervisors a degree of comfort and privacy not experienced before. The principal changes are:

- New supervisor/operator control panel unit fitted. Major gauges, valves and communications within arm's reach.
- Internal CCTV with recording facility fitted to both chambers.
- Revamp of all HP and LP air and oxygen-supply lines.
- Oxygen supply and flow meters installed.
- Slow-bleed valves installed.
- New communications system fitted.
- Heaters and air conditioning units fitted inside the container.

NOTES & REFERENCES

Preface

1   Interview with Mark Mellett, RADM, 10 March 2014.
2   Interview with Frank Lynch (Cmdre; retd), 29 November 2013.
3   Interview with Joe Deasy (Cmdre; retd), 20 August 2013.
4   Interview with Gerry O'Donoghue (Lt Cdr; retd), 18 August 2013.

Introduction

5   Pádhraic Ó Confhaola, 'The Naval Forces of the Irish State, 1922–1977' (PhD thesis, NUI Maynooth, 2009), p. 28.
6   Ibid., p. 35.
7   Ibid., p. 40.
8   Ibid., p. 44.
9   Ibid., p. 45.
10   Ibid., p. 102.

Chapter 1

11   Interview with Eugene Ryan (Cdr; retd), 17 October 2013.
12   Interview with Joe Deasy (Cmdre; retd), 20 August 2013.
13   Ibid.
14   Ibid.
15   Interview with Frank Lynch (Cmdre; retd), 29 November 2013.
16   Interview with Peadar McElhinney (Capt..; retd), 12 August 2013.
17   Interview with George Jefferies, 19 September 2013.
18   Ibid.
19   Ibid.
20   Interview with Johnny O'Neill, 28 August 2013.
21   Interview with Anthony Sheridan, 25 November 2013.
22   Interview with Johnny O'Neill, 28 August 2013.
23   Interview with Anthony Sheridan, 25 November 2013.
24   Interview with Paddy Carolan, 26 September 2013.
25   Interview with George Jefferies, 19 September 2013.
26   Ibid.
27   Interview with Danny O'Neill (Cdr; retd), 6 August 2013.
28   Interview with Liam Donaldson (Lt Cdr; retd), 14 February 2014.
29   Ibid.
30   Interview with Gerry O'Donoghue (Lt Cdr; retd), 18 August 2013.
31   Interview with Martin Carroll, 14 August 2013.
32   Interview with John Walsh, 15 August 2013.
33   Ibid.
34   Interview with Mark Mellett, RADM, 10 March 2014.
35   Interview with Gerry Duffy, 9 October 2013.
36   Interview with Mossy Mahon, 6 January 2014.
37   Gerry O'Donoghue (Lt Cdr; retd), email to Martin Buckley, 28 October 2014.
38   Interview with Chris McMahon, 23 December 2013.
39   Interview with Phil Gray, 30 October 2013.
40   Interview with John F.M. Leech (Lt Cdr; retd), 7 May 2014.
41   Interview with Chris Reynolds (Lt Cdr; retd), 11 February 2014.
42   Ibid.

43   Interview with Shane Anderson (Lt Cdr; retd), 11 June 2014.

44   Ibid.

45   Interview with Tom Meehan (Lt Cdr; retd), 13 June 2014.

46   Interview with Ron Long (Lt; retd), professor NUIG, 27 May 2014.

47   Comdt Paul Logan, e-mail to Martin Buckley, 15 June 2014.

48   Author's recollection, 2014.

49   Interview with Gerry O'Donoghue (Lt Cdr; retd), 18 August 2013.

Chapter 2

50   Lt Gerry O'Donoghue, 'Ships divers course, 1982', letter to FOCNS, 1 November 1982, *Naval Service Diving Section Files, 1982.*

51   Lt Gerry O'Donoghue, 'Recompression chamber, diving course, 1982', letter to FOCNS, 3 November 1982, *Naval Service Diving Section Files, 1982.*

52   Interview with Damien Power, 2 December 2013.

53   Ibid.

54   Ibid.

55   Ibid.

56   Lt Gerry O'Donoghue, '1st NS ships divers course', letter to FOCNS 24 January 1983, *Naval Service Diving Section Files, 1983.*

57   Capt. W.J. Brett, CONB, '1st NS ships divers course', letter to FOCNS, 25 January 1983, *Naval Service Diving Section Files, 1983.*

58   Cmdre L.S. Maloney, FOCNS, '1st NS ships divers course', letter to CONB, 2 February 1983, *Naval Service Diving Section Files, 1983.*

59   Lt Gerry O'Donoghue, 'Ships divers course, 1983', letter to FOCNS, 22 April 1983, *Naval Service Diving Section Files, 1983.*

60   John McCarthy, email to Martin Buckley, 2 February 2014.

61   Interview with Jim Bartley, 21 February 2014.

62   Ibid.

63   Lt Gerry O'Donoghue, '2nd naval ships divers course', letter to FOCNS, 15 July 1983, *Naval Service Diving Section Files, 1983.*

64   Interview with Gerry O'Donoghue (Lt Cdr; retd), 18 August 2013.

65   Interview with ARW NCO (retd), 10 February 2014.

66   Ibid.

67   Ibid.

68   Interview with senior ARW student (retd), 8 January 2015.

69   Interview with ARW NCO (retd), 10 February 2014.

70   Interview with ex-ARW NCO, 23 September 2014.

71   Ibid.

72   Ibid.

73   Interview with ARW NCO (retd), 10 February 2014.

74   Lt Gerry O'Donoghue, '3rd naval service ships divers course, 1985', letter to COND, 4 April 1985, *Naval Service Diving Section Files, 1985.*

75   Interview with John F.M. Leech (Lt Cdr; retd), 30 October 2013.

76   Ibid.

77   Ibid.

78   Lt Gerry O'Donoghue, '3rd naval service ships divers course, 1985', letter to COND, 1 November 1982, *Naval Service Diving Section Files, 1985.*

79   Interview with Damien Power, 2 December 2013.

80   Ibid.

81   Ibid.

82   Ibid.

83   Interview with RADM Mark Mellett, Department of Defence, 10 March 2014.
84   Gerry O'Donoghue (Lt Cdr; retd), email to Martin Buckley, 28 October 2014.
85   Lt Gerry O'Donoghue, 'OLMCDO course, 1985', letter to CONBAD, 7 March 1985, *Naval Service Diving Section Files, 1985.*
86   Cmdre L.S. Maloney, FOCNS, 'International long mine warfare and clearance diving officers course', letter to CONBAD, 13 June 1985, *Naval Service Diving Section Files, 1985.*
87   S/Lt Chris Reynolds, 'Course report, ILMCDO course 1985', letter to FOCNS, 30 April 1985, *Naval Service Files 1985.*
88   Ibid.
89   Ibid.
90   Interview with Gerry O'Donoghue (Lt Cdr; retd), 18 August 2013.
91   Interview with Eddie Mulligan (Lt; retd), 17 November 2013.
92   Ibid.
93   Ibid.
94   Ibid.
95   Interview with Lt Cdr Darragh Kirwan, 19 March 2014.
96   Ibid.
97   Ibid.
98   Interview with Lt Cdr Tony O'Regan, 4 April 2014.
99   Ibid.
100   Ibid.
101   Ibid.
102   Interview with Lt Cdr Conor Kirwan, 13 March 2014.
103   Ibid.
104   Interview with Lt Shane Mulcahy, 24 April 2014.
105   Interview with S/Lt Stephen Stack, 7 May 2014.
106   Ibid.
107   Reply to email, Lt Cdr O'Regan, 22 January 2015.

Chapter 3
108   Capt. Joseph Deasy, OCNBAD, 'Order for the assembly of a court of inquiry', letter to board members, date unknown, *Naval Service Diving Section Files, 1989.*
109   Interview with Chris Reynolds, 11 February 2014.
110   Interview with Declan Fleming, 10 September 2014.
111   Interview with senior ARW student (retd), 8 January 2015.

Chapter 4
112   'Claudia haul was five tons', *Irish Times,* 1 October *1984*
113   'S.-E. coast search by navy divers', *Irish Times,* 2 April 1973.
114   Ibid.
115   Interview with Peadar McElhinney (Capt.; retd), 12 August 2013.
116   'Navy divers end search off Helvick', *Irish Times,* 6 April 1973.
117   Interview with Peadar McElhinney (Capt.; retd), 12 August 2013.
118   Ibid.
119   Interview with Johnny O'Neill, 28 August 2013.
120   Interview with George Jefferies, 19 September 2013.
121   Ibid.
122   Interview with Paddy Carolan, 26 September 2013.
123   Interview with Tommy Lavery, 22 December 2013.
124   Lt Dan O'Neill, 'Search for missing person, Loch Inagh, County Galway, request of Gardaí',

letter to COH,[Commanding Officer, Haulbowline], 28 October 1976, *Naval Service Diving Section Files, 1976.*

125   Interview with George Jefferies, 19 September 2013.

126   Ibid.

127   Lt Dan O'Neill, 'Search for missing person, Loch Inagh, County Galway, request of Gardaí', letter to COH,[Commanding Officer, Haulbowline], 28 October 1976, *Naval Service Diving Section Files, 1976.*

128   Lt Frank Lynch, 'Report on search for missing persons of Rathlin O'Birne', letter to COH [Commanding Officer, Haulbowline], 17 December 1976, Naval Service Diving Section Files, 1976.

129   Interview with Paddy Carolan, 26 September 2013.

130   Lt Frank Lynch, 'Report on search for missing persons off Rathlin O'Birne', letter to COH [Commanding Officer, Haulbowline], 17 December 1976, *Naval Service Diving Section Files, 1976.*

131   Interview with John Walsh, 15 August 2013.

132   Interview with Gerry Duffy, 9 October 2013.

133   Interview with Gerry O'Donoghue (Lt Cdr; retd), 18 August 2013.

134   Ibid.

135   Ibid.

136   Ibid.

137   Ibid.

138   Interview with Chris Reynolds (Lt Cdr; retd), 23 October 2013.

139   Extract from author's diving logbook, 22 June 2014.

140   Ibid.

141   Lt Shane Anderson, 'Report, diving operation, Gt Blasket Island, August 87', letter to OCN-BAD 26 August 1987, *Naval Service Diving Section Files, 1987.*

142   Extract from author's diving logbook, 22 June 2014.

143   Author's recollection, 2014.

144   Ibid.

145   Ibid

146   Extract from author's diving logbook, 22 June 2014.

147   Lt Declan Fleming, 'Report on diving operation, Lough Derravaragh', letter to OCNBAD, 29 January 1992, *Naval Service Diving Section Files, 1992.*

148   Author's recollection, 2014.

149   Interview with Tom Lavery, 22 December 2013.

150   Lt Declan Fleming, 'SitRep, diving operation, Lough Derravaragh', SitRep to FOCNS/OC-NBAD, 11 January 1992, *Naval Service Diving Section Files, 1992.*

151   'Bronze spearhead from Lough Derraghvarragh, Co Westmeath', press release, date unknown, 1992.

152   '"Carrickatine" report unable to establish cause of disappearance', *Irish Times*, 10 November 1998.

153   Lt Cdr Tom Touhy, 'Report on search for missing F/V SO-878 "Carrickatine"', letter to FO-CNS 8 December 1995, *Naval Service Diving Section Files, 1995.*

154   Ibid.

155   Lt Eddie Mulligan, 'Report on Diving Operation 10/96, F/V "Jenalisa"', letter to FOCNS, 30 March 1996, *Naval Service Diving Section Files, 1996.*

156   Ibid.

157   Ibid.

158   Author's recollection, 2014.

159   Interview with Niall Brown, 23 December 2013.

160   Lt Declan Fleming, 'Report on diving operation 40/96, Moneypoint, 14th to 20 August

1996', letter to OCNBAD, 3 October 1996, *Naval Service Diving Section Files, 1996.*

161   John Kavanagh, FOCNS, 'Examination of wreck off Donegal Coast', letter to Diving Officer, Lt E. Mulligan, 26 November 1997, *Naval Service Diving Section Files, 1997.*

162   Roddy O'Sullivan, 'Wreck found off Donegal may not be the "Carrickatine"', *Irish Times,* 4 Sep*tember 1997.*

163   Lt J.F.M. Leech, 'Report on diving operation 14/98, Mr Hugh Coveney TD', letter to OCN-BAD, 20 March 1998, *Naval Service Diving Section Files, 1998.*

164   'Search for crew of Spanish fishing vessel to continue', *Irish Times,* 4 October 2000.

165   Interview with Lt Cdr Darragh Kirwan, 19 March 2014.

166   'Trawler smashed', *Connacht Tribune,* 5 January 2001.

167   Interview with Lt Cdr Darragh Kirwan, 27 March 2014.

168   'DNA tests on bodies', *Connacht Tribune,* 7 Sep*tember 2001.*

169   'Father, son and grandson feared drowned', *Irish Times,* 16 February *2002.*

170   Author's recollection, 2014.

171   Cdr Pat McNulty, 'Kilkeel County Down, presentation to LÉ Eithne', letter to OCNOC, 31 October 2002, *Naval Service Diving Section Files, 2002.*

172   Interview with Lt Cdr Darragh Kirwan, 27 March 2014.

173   Author's recollection, 2014.

174   'Divers say bodies may be at site of boat wreckage', *Irish Times,* 9 Apr *2002.*

175   Interview with Lt Cdr Darragh Kirwan, 19 March 2014.

176   Ibid.

177   Lt Darragh Kirwan, 'Report on diving operation no. 37/03', letter to OCNOC, 7 August 2003, *Naval Service Diving Section Files, 2003.*

178   Interview with Lt Cdr Darragh Kirwan, 19 March 2014.

179   Lt Darragh Kirwan, 'Report on diving operation no. 37/03', letter to OCNOC, 7 August 2003, *Naval Service Diving Section Files, 2003.*

180   Ibid.

181   Lt Cdr Interview with Darragh Kirwan, 27 August 2014.

182   Lt Darragh Kirwan, 'Report on diving operation no. 59/05', letter to FOCNS, 15 December 2005, *Naval Service Diving Section Files, 2005.*

183   Ibid.

184   Athor's recollection, 2014.

185   Lt Darragh Kirwan, 'Report on diving operation no. 59/05', letter to FOCNS, 15 December 2005, *Naval Service Diving Section Files, 2005.*

186   'Dark days for Irish Fishermen', *Irish Times,* 4 Apri*l 2006.*

187   Lt Darragh Kirwan, 'Report on diving operation no. 31/06', letter to FOCNS, 27 May 2006, *Naval Service Diving Section Files, 2006.*

188   Ibid.

189   Lt Darragh Kirwan, 'Report on diving operation no. 01/07 search of Irish registered fishing vessel *Pere Charles*', letter to OCNOC, 12 February 2007, *Naval Service Diving Section Files, 2007.*

190   Ibid.

191   Interview with Lt Cdr Conor Kirwan, 13 March 2014.

192   Ibid.

193   Ibid.

194   Interview with RADM Mark Mellett, D/CoS Support, 10 March 2014.

Chapter 5

195   CONS, copy of 'Signal', signal actioning COH (to despatch diving team), 15 January 1979, *Naval Service Diving Section Files, 1979.*

196   Lt Dan O'Neill, 'Report, diving operations at Whiddy Island, Bantry, 16.1.1979 to

31.1.1979', letter to COH, 7 February 1979, *Naval Service Diving Section Files, 1979.*

197 Dan O'Neill, 'Report, Diving Operations at Whiddy Island, Bantry, 16.1.1979 to 31.1.1979', letter to COH,7 February 1979, *Naval Service Diving Section Files, 1979.*

198 Lt Dan O'Neill, 'Report, diving operations at Whiddy Island, Bantry, 16.1.1979 to 31.1.1979', letter to COH, 7 February 1979, *Naval Service Diving Section Files, 1979.*

199 Interview with Dan O'Neill (Cdr; retd), 6 August 2013.

200 Interview with John Walsh, 15 August 2013.

201 Interview with George Jefferies, 30 September 2013.

202 Interview with Martin Carroll, 14 August 2013.

203 Interview with Gerry Duffy, 9 October 2013.

204 Interview with Tommy Lavery, 22 December 2013.

205 Lt Dan O'Neill, 'Report, diving operations at Whiddy Island, Bantry, 16.1.1979 to 31.1.1979', letter to COH, 7 February 1979, *Naval Service Diving Section Files, 1979.*

206 Gerry O'Donoghue (Lt Cdr; retd), email to Martin Buckley, 28 October 2014.

Chapter 6

207 Interview with Mossy Mahon, 6 January 2014.

208 Ibid.

209 Ibid.

210 Ibid.

211 Ibid.

212 Interview with Gerry Duffy, 16 June 2014.

Chapter 7

213 Lt Joseph Deasy, 'Diving incident', letter to OCBC, 30 August 1967, *Naval Service Diving Section Files.*

214 Interview with Dan O'Neill (Cdr; retd), 6 August 2013.

215 Lt Dan O'Neill, 'Report, diving operation at Whiddy Island, Bantry', letter to COH,7 February 1979, *Naval Service Diving Section Files, 1979.*

216 Ibid.

217 Lt Gerry O'Donoghue, MCDO, 'Recompression chamber, manning', letter to FOCNS, 20 August 1982, *Naval Service Diving Section Files, 1982.*

218 Lt Gerry O'Donoghue, MCDO, 'Recompression chamber, diving course, 1982', letter to FOCNS, 3 November 1982, *Naval Service Diving Section Files, 1982.*

219 Ibid.

220 W.J. Brett , Capt., 'Recompression chamber', letter to FOCNS, 25 August 1982, *Naval Service Diving Section Files, 1982.*

221 Interview with Gerry O'Donoghue (Lt Cdr; retd), 18 August 2013.

222 Interview with Danny O'Neill (Cdr; retd), 6 August 2013.

223 Interview with Gerry O'Donoghue (Lt Cdr; retd), 18 August 2013.

224 S/Lt Chris Reynolds, 'Final location of recompression chamber', letter to CONBAD, 24 April 1984, *Naval Service Diving Section Files, 1984.*

225 Cdr Joseph Deasy, 'Diving equipment, housing', memo to diving officer, 10 August 1984, *Naval Service Diving Section Files, 1984.*

226 Cdr Joseph Deasy, 'Diving equipment, housing', memo to diving officer, 26 October 1984, *Naval Service Diving Section Files, 1984.*

227 S/Lt Chris Reynolds, 'Supervision of recompression chamber diving', letter to FOCNS, 11 Apr 1984, *Naval Service Diving Section Files, 1984.*

228 Interview with Gerry O'Donoghue, 18 August 2013.

229 Ibid.

230 Interview with Chris Reynolds, 23 October 2013.

231   Lt Chris Reynolds, (MCDO), 'RCC meeting with IMES, 22 November 94', letter to OCND, 24 November 1994, *Naval Service Diving Section Files, 1994.*

232   Lt Cdr Gerry O'Donoghue (MCDO), 'Therapeutic recompression, Mr Eugene Cahill, 3/4/5 August 94', letter to FOCNS, August 1994, *Naval Service Diving Section Files, 1994.*

233   Ibid.

234   Ibid.

235   Dr Maurice Cross, 'Fax/memo from Maurice Cross', letter to Dr Mary Murphy, 24 July 1994, *Naval Service Diving Section Files, 1994.*

236   Interview with Mick Daly, 2 April 2014.

237   Lt Chris Reynolds, 'RCC treatments, 05/06 August 94', letter to OCND, 16 August 1994, *Naval Service Diving Section Files, 1994.*

238   P.J. McElhinney, Capt., 'Therapeutic recompression facility, Naval Base Haulbowline', letter to FOCNS, 23 August 1995, *Naval Service Diving Section Files, 1995.*

239   William O'Brien, Comdt, 'Usage of RCC for civilian divers casualties', letter to Cdr E. Ryan, 15 September 1995, *Naval Service Diving Section Files, 1995.*

240   William O'Brien, Comdt, 'Use of naval RCC for therapeutic recompression', letter to Capt. P.J. McElhinney, 26 June 1996, *Naval Service Diving Section Files, 1996.*

241   Edward Mulligan, S/Lt CDO, 'Therapeutic recompression', letter to OCNBAD, 25 July 1996, *Naval Service Diving Section Files, 1996.*

242   Lt Edward Mulligan, CDO, 'NS recompression chamber', letter to OCNBAD, 4 November 1997, *Naval Service Diving Section Files, 1997.*

243   Cdr Gene Ryan, 'Report of the Diving Study Group', report to FOCNS, 16 March 1995, *Naval Service Diving Section Files, 1995.*

244   Ibid.

245   Ibid.

246   Ibid.

247   Ibid.

248   Lt Eddie Mulligan, 'Therapeutic recompression', letter to OCNBAD, 18 December 1997, *Naval Service Diving Section Files, 1997.*

249   Lt John F.M. Leech, 'Therapeutic recompression', letter to OCNBAD, 5 February 1998, *Naval Service Diving Section Files, 1998.*

250   W. O'Brien, Comdt, 'Re. therapeutic recompression', letter to Cdr Costello, 23 March 1998, *Naval Service Diving Section Files, 1998.*

251   Prof. John Davenport, 'Hyperbaric treatment facilities at Haulbowline Naval Base', letter to Minister of Defence, Michael Smith TD, 1 September 1999, *Naval Service Diving Section Files, 1999.*

252   Capt. Frank Lynch, 'Hyperbaric recompression facilities at naval base', letter to FOCNS, 24 September 1999, *Naval Service Diving Section Files, 1999.*

253   M. O'S., Executive Branch, Department of Defence, 'Re. hyperbaric recompression facilities at the naval base', letter to FOCNS, 17 November 1999, *Naval Service Diving Section Files, 1999.*

254   S/Lt Darragh Kirwan, 'Therapeutic recompression facilities in the naval base', letter to FOCNS, 14 August 2000, *Naval Service Diving Section Files, 2000.*

255   Ibid.

256   J.J. Kavanagh (FOCNS), 'Therapeutic recompression facilities, naval base', letter to D/COS. Sp., 18 September 2000, *Naval Service Diving Section Files, 2000.*

257   Capt. Frank Lynch, 'Policy on Civilian Use of Recompression Chamber', letter to NOC Staff 27 September 2001, *Naval Service Diving Section Files, 2001.*

258   Ibid.

259   Capt. Frank Lynch, 'Policy on civilian use of recompression chamber', letter to NOC Staff, 27 September 2001, *Naval Service Diving Section Files, 2001.*

260   S/Lt Darragh Kirwan, 'Reply to PQ on recompression chamber (RCC) availability', letter to Irish Coast Guard, 22 April 2002, *Naval Service Diving Section Files, 2002*.

261   Capt. Frank Lynch, 'Policy on Civilian Use of Recompression Chamber', letter to NOC & Ops Staff, 3 July 2002, *Naval Service Diving Section Files, 2002*.

262   Lt Cdr W. O'Brien, 'Recompression facilities, diving accidents', letter to FOCNS, 24 March 2003, *Naval Service Diving Section Files, 2003*.

263   Capt. Frank Lynch, 'Recompression facilities, diving accidents', letter to D/COS Ops, 7 Apr 2003, *Naval Service Diving Section Files, 2003*.

264   Interview with Lt Cdr Conor Kirwan, 13 March 2014.

265   Interview with Lt Cdr Darragh Kirwan, 27 March 2014.

266   Interview with Lt Cdr Tony O'Regan, 4 April 2014.

Chapter 8

267   Interview with Gerry O'Donoghue (Lt Cdr; retd), 18 August 2013.

268   Ibid.

269   Ibid.

270   Extract from author's diving logbook, 2014.

Chapter 9

271   Department of Transport, Tourism and Sport (2014), AAIU, report no. 1999–008, http://www.aaiu.ie/reports/aaiu-investigation-reports (accessed 23 Apr. 2014).

272   Ibid.

273   Ibid.

274   Ibid.

275   Ibid.

276   Ibid.

277   Interview with Louis Linnane, 24 April 2014.

278   Ibid.

279   Ibid.

280   Ibid.

281   Interview with Mick Daly, 2 Apr 2014.

282   Ibid.

283   Ibid.

Chapter 10

284   Interview with Danny O'Neill (Cdr; retd), 6 August 2013.

285   Interview with Frank Lynch (FOCNS Retd.) 29 November 2013.

286   Ibid.

287   Ibid.

288   Interview with Mark Mellett, RADM D/COS Support, Dept. of Defence, 10 March 2014.

289   Interview with Lt Cdr Tony O'Regan, 4 Apr 2014.

290   Interview with Lt Cdr Conor Kirwan, 13 March 2014.

291   Ibid.

292   Ibid.

293   Interview with S/Lt Shane Mulcahy, 27 Apr 2014.

294   Ibid.

295   Interview with Gerry O'Donoghue (Lt Cdr; retd) 18 August 2013.

296   Interview with Gene Ryan (Cdr; retd), 17 October 2013.

297   Ibid.

BIBLIOGRAPHY

Primary Sources

Recorded interviews

ARW NCO
Anderson, Shane
Bartley, Jimmy
Buckley, Martin
Brown, Niall
Byrne, David
Carolan, Paddy
Carroll, Martin
Daly, Mick
Deasy, Joseph
Donaldson, Liam
Duffy, Gerry
Forde, Joe
Fleming, Declan
Gray, Philip
Kirwan, Conor
Kirwan, Darragh
Lavery, Tommy
Leech, John FM
Linnane, Louis
Long, Ron
Lynch, Frank
Mulcahy, Shane
Power, Damian
O'Donoghue Gerry
O'Neill, Dan
O'Neill, Johnny
O'Regan, Tony
Mahon, Mossy
McMahon, Chris
McElhinney, Peadar
Meehan, Tom
Mellett, Mark
Mulligan, Eddie
Jefferies, George
Reynolds, Chris
Ryan, Gene
Sheridan, Anthony
Smith, Alan
Stack, Stephen
Walsh, John

Documents

AAI, Air Accident Investigation Branch, Department of Transport, Tourism and Sport (2014), AAIU, report no. 1999–008, www.aaiu.ie/reports/aaiu-investigation-reports (accessed 23 April 2014)
Naval Service Diving Section Files, Naval Base, Haulbowline

Letters/memos/faxes

O'Brien, William, base MO
Davenport, Professor John
Cross, Dr Maurice
O'Sullivan, M., Executive Branch, Department of Defence

Other sources

Wikipedia

Newspapers and periodicals

An Cosantóir
Irish Times
Irish Independent
Connaght Tribune

Secondary Sources

Anglo-Irish Treaty, 1921 (National Archives of Ireland, DE 2/301/1)
Fanning, Ronan (ed.), Documents on Irish Foreign Policy (Dublin, 2000)
McGinty, Tom, The Irish Navy (Kerry, 1995)
Ó Confhaola, Padhraic, *The Naval Forces of the Irish State, 1922–1977*, PhD thesis, NUI Maynooth, October 2009

INDEX